'KITTY O'SHEA'

The Story of Katharine Parnell

Mary Rose Callaghan

Mary Rose Callaghan was born in Dublin and educated at University College, Dublin. She is a teacher and a writer, the author of four novels: *Mothers, Confessions of a Prodigal Daughter, The Awkward Girl* and *Has Anyone Seen Heather?* She is married to Robert Hogan and divides her time between Dublin and Delaware in the United States.

'KITTY O'SHEA'

The Story of Katharine Parnell

Mary Rose Callaghan

Pandora

An Imprint of HarperCollins*Publishers*

Pandora
An Imprint of HarperCollins*Publishers*
77–85 Fulham Palace Road,
Hammersmith, London W6 8JB
1160 Battery Street,
San Francisco, California 94111–1213

First published by Pandora 1989
This edition 1994
1 3 5 7 9 10 8 6 4 2

A catalogue record for this book
is available from the British Library

ISBN 0 04 440882 X

Printed in Great Britain by
HarperCollinsManufacturing Glasgow

To Maureen Duggan

CONTENTS

ILLUSTRATIONS

FOREWORD

If lovers are valiant, then Katharine O'Shea Parnell was a valiant
woman. This is a love story, indeed a great love story and like other
great love stories it begins when the hero and heroine meet and ends
when one, he, dies. It is the account of two absorbed, perhaps self
absorbed characters, passionate lovers who considered the world well
lost. If indeed they considered the world at all:

> The storms and thunderings will never hurt us now,
> Queenie, my wife, for there is nothing in the wide world that
> can be greater than our love; there is nothing in all the world
> but you and I.

Her lover, Charles Stewart Parnell, was wrong of course. In herself,
Katharine provided a scapegoat of satisfying proportion and gender to
keep the screams of lust and corruption ringing for a very long time. She
was held responsible for quashing Home Rule for Ireland.

Katharine O'Shea took on, without any idea of the enormity and
ferocity of her antagonists, the Irish nation, the British establishment,
the Catholic Church, the Irish Parliamentary Party, her family, her
husband and her children. That she survived at all was extraordinary.

Gemma O'Connor

PREFACE AND ACKNOWLEDGMENTS

The material on Parnell and his times is immense, and many of the standard works have been referred to in the text. However, the following volumes have been of particular use in this study and would probably be of most use and interest to the general reader.

Of primary importance is Katharine Parnell's own book, *Charles Stewart Parnell: His Love Story and Political Life*. This book was written in her later years, long removed from the events which were central in her life. Although it is particularly valuable for the inclusion of Parnell's many letters to her, the charge has been made that the manuscript has been doctored, probably by her son Gerard, to present his father, Captain O'Shea, in a more favourable light. That may well be, but major portions of the work are the only source for crucial matters and moments of Katie's life, and seem to me utterly authentic.

Her memoir does not, however, answer all the questions and even glosses over some of the most significant. Its chief critic was Henry Harrison who, as a young MP and devoted follower of Parnell, spent much time with Katie straightening out her affairs after his leader's death. His volume *Parnell Vindicated: The Lifting of the Veil* is a persuasive account by a man who was on the scene shortly after the major events.

Of value for its information about Katie's family is *A Century of Letters* compiled by Katie's niece, Minna Evangeline Bradhurst. The one other study devoted to Katie herself is Joyce Marlow's excellent *The Uncrowned Queen of Ireland*.

Of the many volumes on Parnell, primacy of place must be given to F. S. L. Lyons's long, factual and well-researched, if somewhat phlegmatic volume, *Charles Stewart Parnell*. Of the other Parnell lives, St John Ervine's *Parnell* is probably the most readable, although too much a literary production and too skimpy on facts. Jules Abels's *The Parnell Tragedy* is better documented, if not entirely persuasive in its most speculative aspects. A sound short life is Paul Bew's *C. S. Parnell*. A superbly researched account of Parnell's own family background is R. F. Foster's *Charles Stewart Parnell: The Man and His Family*.

Among the notable accounts by people who actually knew Parnell are T. M. Healy's *Letters and Leaders of My Day*; R. Barry O'Brien's *The Life of Charles Stewart Parnell, 1846–1891*; William O'Brien's *The Parnell of Real Life*; T. P. O'Connor's *The Parnell Movement, Charles Stewart Parnell: A Memory* and *Memoirs of an Old Parliamentarian*; and John Howard Parnell's *Charles Stewart Parnell: A Memoir*. John Howard was Parnell's older brother, and Parnell's sister, Emily Dickinson, published another memoir, *A Patriot's Mistake*, but this is a much less reliable book.

Among specific studies of the politics of the day, Conor Cruise O'Brien's *Parnell and His Party, 1880–1891* is extremely reliable and intelligent.

Finally, I must note the enthusiasm and sagacity of my editor, Gemma O'Connor, who initiated this project. I would also like to thank my husband, Robert Hogan, who has been of invaluable help to me; Helen O'Neill of Monkstown and Kay Doherty of Belfast who traced down copies of novels by Lady Emma Wood and Anna Steele; Paula Howard of the Dublin Central Library, Pearse Street; Central Library, RTE; The National Library; The British Museum; Fintan Vallely of Rathmines; Kevin Loughney of Dublin; and Kathy Parks of Delaware.

PROLOGUE

A woman brought sin into the world. For a woman who was no
better than she should be, Helen, the runaway wife of Menelaus,
ten years the Greeks made war on Troy. A faithless wife first
brought the strangers to our shore here, MacMurrough's wife and
her leman O'Rourke, prince of Breffni. A woman too brought
Parnell low.

James Joyce, Ulysses

The woman always lost, and Joyce's pontifical Mr Deasy could have
considerably extended the list to include hundreds more notable
women whose fates ranged from the unhappy to the tragic. But it was
not merely the extraordinary women, the Antigones and Joans, who
attacked their society and who lost. It was equally the passive,
compliant accepting woman – the Cordelias and Ophelias, the Juno
Boyles and the Linda Lomans who lost also.

Woman did not make her role in western society. It was thrust upon
her, but it was not really a role of complete subservience, as many
feminists allege. Its effect may have sometimes been subservience, but it
was also often a romantic idealisation that placed her upon an
impossibly lofty pedestal. Hence the Roman matron like Coriolanus's
mother Volumnia, who was meant to embody the quintessential virtues
of the state. Hence also that impossible repository of virtue and beauty,
the heroine of medieval Courtly Love. Hence too Dante's Beatrice, and
all the Lauras and Stellas the Renaissance sonneteers rhapsodised
about.

When a fiction is imposed upon reality, a grim conflict predictably
ensues. The events of history and the great masterpieces of literature
have frequently illustrated such conflicts; and in history, if not always in
literature, the reality usually seemed to win out. Thus women often fell,
and sometimes jumped off their pedestals; and literature quickly totted
up the moral debits and credits of the act; you were either an impossibly
bad woman or an impossibly good one.

The Victorian age, perhaps more than most others, accepted this
formula. It was an age which immensely elevated the idea of family
life. 'This is the true nature of home,' wrote Ruskin in *Sesame and*

Lilies, '. . . it is the place of Peace, the shelter, not only from all injury, but from all terror, doubt, and division . . . it is a sacred place, a vestal temple, a temple of the hearth watched over by Household Gods. . . .' 'It was a place apart,' added the modern critic Walter E. Houghton in *The Victorian Frame of Mind*, 'a walled garden, in which certain virtues too easily crushed by modern life could be preserved. . . .' It was, in other words, the very foundation of society, and from it flowed all the virtues which illuminated and supported that society.

The presiding deity of this temple in the walled garden was Woman, the Wife, the Mother, the idealised repository of virtue and goodness. She was, to give her the title of Coventry Patmore's much-read poem, 'The Angel in the House'. Or she was even, as the poet of the age, Tennyson, described her:

> No Angel, but a dearer being, all dipt
> In angel instincts, breathing Paradise,
> Interpreter between the gods and men,
> Who looked all native to her place, and yet
> On tiptoe seem'd to touch upon a sphere
> Too gross to tread, and all male minds perforce
> Sway'd to her from their native orbits as they moved,
> And girdled her with music. Happy he
> With such a mother! faith in womankind
> Beats with his blood, and trust in all things high
> Comes easy to him, and tho' he trip and fall
> He shall not blind his soul with clay.

In this idealised fiction of the Poet Laureate, a nod is given to reality in the line about the man tripping and falling. And trip and fall he did. An 1850 article on 'Prostitution' in the *Westminster Review* cites 50,000 prostitutes known to the 'police in England and Scotland, and 8,000 merely in London. Quite obviously the idyllic life around the temple in the walled garden was something of a fiction. However, the goddess in the Victorian temple, although wife and mother, was also something of a Vestal Virgin; and in reality the Vestal Virgin often lost out to the Girl with the Swansdown Seat.

This was easy enough to explain away by the Double Standard. But, of course, this dual morality for men and women was itself based on the fiction that men had a baser, lower nature than women. Women might, indeed, inspire and redeem men and bring out all that was finest and best in their nature – but the men did need to be inspired and redeemed.

But what of the woman, like Katharine Parnell, who fell?

This woman was the exception. And after her fall she was an outcast and a pariah, and there were no extenuating circumstances. She was irremediably, irredeemably beyond the pale.

In literature, a perfect example of this attitude was Lady Isabel of

East Lynne. East Lynne was Mrs Henry Wood's widely read novel of 1861, which was immediately dramatised and became one of the most frequently produced plays of the nineteenth century. Lady Isabel's case was prototypical and consummately embodied the public's attitude. She was the saintly, the innocent, the perfect example of the Victorian wife and mother. Yet she became convinced, through one of those stacked-deck plot convolutions that the Victorian writers were so addicted to, that her husband was unfaithful. Crushed by this, she allows herself to be swept away by her sympathetic admirer, Sir Francis Levison. He, of course, is the suave cad who seduces and abandons her, and her destiny ever after is one of suffering heaped upon suffering. She suffers incredible poverty. She even returns, made unrecognisable by her suffering, to become the governess to her own child in the home of her now remarried husband. Her child then dies in her arms and she cries, 'Dead – dead – and he never called me mother!'

The lesson was amply clear to readers and to audiences: the fallen woman might finally find a home in heaven, but there would be none for her in this world.

This stern doctrine was embodied in hundreds of middle-brow and low-brow plays and novels, and even Charles Dickens accepted it in such fables as that of Steerforth and Little Emily in his masterly *David Copperfield*. It was a simple, unassailable and universal message for Victorian society, but its simplicity was broadened to something of a philosophic social relevance by that other great spokesman of the age, Tennyson. In *The Idylls of the King* it is Guinevere's liaison with Lancelot that brings the society toppling down, and infidelity is shown to be the crucial, central and unforgiveable social crime.

But the fables of literature reflect the fictions of its society, and in the Victorian age the fictions of Lady Isabel and Queen Guinevere were sometimes played out in real life.

In 1836, the Prime Minister of Great Britain was cited as co-respondent in a divorce case. The Prime Minister was Lord Melbourne; his accuser was George Norton, the younger brother of Lord Grantly and a very minor public official; and the woman in the case was Caroline Norton, a granddaughter of Richard Brinsley Sheridan, a reigning beauty of the day, and a fluent writer who had had a play produced at Covent Garden, whose volumes of verse were earning her the title of 'the female Byron', whose novels sold well, and who was subsequently a forceful political pamphleteer for women's rights.

George Norton was a dense, sluggish and brutal lout, who did not scruple to use violence against his wife. Caroline was not merely a beauty, but also an able, fascinating and witty person. Melbourne was old enough to be her father; and, although he spent many delightful hours with her, the delight was never sexual.

At any rate, in the divorce court Norton's unfounded accusations were torn to shreds, and Melbourne was completely absolved and imperturbably continued his brilliant career. But, although Melbourne went on to become the revered mentor of the young Queen Victoria, his supposed mistress, Caroline, lived ever after under the lowering cloud of public suspicion and disapproval. Indeed, this suspect, this 'fast' woman, even became the heroine of George Meredith's *Diana of the Crossways* which exploited her notoriety forty years after the reasons had been established as groundless. The big question, in Caroline's case, was whether she had sold cabinet secrets to the press. It was an accusation she could never live down. Even Melbourne's modern biographer, David Cecil, cannot resist quoting with approval Melbourne's statement to Queen Victoria, 'All the Sheridans are a little vulgar.'

It is an interesting footnote to history that Katharine Parnell was to know George Meredith, who frequently read to her aunt. However, as she tells us in her memoir that she did not think much of his novels, and as the book was published five years after she met Parnell, it could not really have influenced her behaviour. It is merely coincidence that there were to be certain parallels in the two women's lives. Like Caroline Norton, Katharine was to be unhappily married – although Willie O'Shea, bad as he was, was not in the same league as George Norton. She was also to become friendly with a Prime Minister, and to live under the same public suspicion and disapproval. Indeed, many Irish people at the time considered she was a spy in the pay of the Liberals who used her to bring down Parnell. This, however, is a calumny. The accusation probably sprang from Henry Harrison's charge that the divorce was stage-managed by Chamberlain as a political device. But as F. S. L. Lyons wrote, 'No solid evidence, it is necessary to insist in the face of Harrison's eloquent pertinacity, has ever emerged to demonstrate the existence of such a conspiracy.'

Like most upper-class English women, then and now, Katharine knew little about Ireland or its politics. She was dragged into that arena, at first, in an innocent enough effort to advance her husband's career. Ironically, although she is today known by his name, if she had died as Willie O'Shea's wife she would never have been the subject of a biography. She entered history the day she met Charles Stewart Parnell. For the next ten years she was used by him as a conduit of communication to Gladstone, who knew quite well that they were having an affair and who was only interested in her because of this. During this time, she developed an astute political canniness and manipulated events in an effort to keep the status quo between Willie and Parnell. However, she was essentially private and wished only to live a domestic life. Home Rule failed and Parnell fell. But in all of the public vilification that followed the divorce case, Katharine remained quite indomitable and unashamed. Because of her courage and because her drama was acted out on a public stage, it will always be a significant chapter in the annals of women's liberation. She was remarkable in her loyalty – to Willie long after he deserved it and then to Parnell. For years she was the loved companion of her aged aunt. When this aunt wanted to leave her some extra money, Katharine's brothers and sisters tried to have the old woman declared insane and committed to an asylum. Katharine was influential enough to scotch this hideously callous plan. Until Parnell died she was a fighter. In his struggle for the leadership of the party, she utterly supported him, although such action was completely against her own self-interest. She wanted what he wanted: Home Rule for Ireland. The tragedy was that it cost his life. And Katharine lost everything when she lost Parnell. Although unlucky in her men, she was best as a wife. But if feminism is to serve any purpose, it should extol the forgotten virtues of loyalty and courage. It was not only the Joans who were remarkable and who lost. It was also the Katharines, and the Juno Boyles. The final irony, of course, is that *any* remarkable woman, unless she was extremely lucky, was inevitably on a terrific collision course with society.

When the woman jumped off, or even seemed to jump off the pedestal, she always lost, and never more so than in the Victorian age.

But the age was changing.

Today, although Ireland is still a divided nation, the passions of a hundred years ago are mainly forgotten. When I was writing this book some people gave me blank looks if I talked about Katharine Parnell. Only when I called her 'Kitty O'Shea' did they register any recognition, and even then many had only heard of the popular Dublin pub named after her. Because of her name, most people mistakenly thought she was Irish. Hardly anyone knew that she most probably never even set foot in the country which was to play such a part in her life. Nor did they realise that she actually married Charles Stewart Parnell.

He called her 'Queenie' and 'Wifie'. Her family and friends called her 'Katie'. Nobody ever called her 'Kitty' except the newspapers. In Victorian times it was a name with *demi-monde*, feline and coquettish associations and does not appear to have been popular until the reports of the divorce scandal. According to the *Oxford English Dictionary*, 'kitty' referred to 'a young girl or woman', occasionally 'a light woman'. And in his *Dictionary of Slang*, Eric Partridge says that this meaning was used well into the twentieth century. He also says that 'kitty', like 'pussy', was a common name for female pudenda. It was not a flattering sobriquet, and one that Katharine and her husband detested. Yet it is as 'Kitty O'Shea' that she has been remembered by the world. And the imputation still is that she was a designing trollop, a married woman who ensnared the 'Uncrowned King of Ireland' and was thus instrumental in destroying his career, perhaps in hastening his death, and probably even in prolonging a nation's struggle for freedom for a quarter of a century.

The facts, however, are not so simple. They rarely are, and an historian often finds that something as seemingly simple as the mere establishment of a fact is in reality the most impossible task that he or she has. Many of the facts in the life of Katharine Parnell and of her famous husband are a matter of indisputable public record. But some are not, and these hazy, often tenuous matters pose basic questions about the motives and characters of the chief actors in this quintessentially dramatic story.

In some interpretations of the evidence, Katie and Parnell are totally ennobled; in others they are utterly vilified. Neither view is entirely true and the only way to a semblance of the truth in the matter is to hold to the one basic fact which no one has ever denied – that they were overwhelmingly in love. However they acted – insofar as we can tell – stems from that one irrefragable fact.

In literature, love is an ideal, and lovers act ideally. In life, love may be an ideal, but lovers often act pragmatically. And from that notion, literature would blame the pragmatist – and history often does. The thesis of this account is that it should not.

This biography has at its core, then, the love of a married woman for a famous man, Charles Stewart Parnell. It is part of a life, not the whole story. Consequently, some topics which would bulk largely in the life of Parnell, such as the Irish Land League or the first Home Rule Bill of 1886, are little touched upon, for they do not significantly involve her and his life together in either its public or its private consequences. Neither was it possible to unearth much information about Katharine after the death of Parnell. Instead, this is a study of how Victorian morals and mores conflicted with Victorian actuality. In this instance, the story did have intense repercussions far beyond its private drama; and its social point is still enormously pertinent.

As a story, the drama of 'Kitty O'Shea' resembles Granville Barker's brilliant and neglected play *Waste*, in which a politician is destroyed by a scandal. The chief difference is possibly that the real-life story is more a tragedy than a simple drama. And probably another difference is that the basic real-life story seems so central to human experience that its tragedy has with time tended to be transmuted into legend. This account primarily attempts to relate the facts, inasmuch as they can be known or plausibly surmised. But, if the story retains the relevance and power that I believe it does, its retelling could not conscientiously ignore either its tragic or its legendary implications. The public exposure of their love affair was to have a profound effect on the political life of Parnell's country, Ireland, and Katharine's, England, for a generation. Even today, Katharine is popularly blamed for the failure of the Irish Home Rule movement.

This is a myth.

According to F. S. L. Lyons, Parnell's fullest biographer and one of the most learned historians of the period, there were 'Himalayan problems' to be surmounted in the gaining of Home Rule for Ireland, problems that were totally unconnected with the divorce scandal of 1890. There was the split in the Liberal Party, the opposition of the Tories, and the inflexibility of Ulster Protestantism, not to mention the final difficulty of getting a bill through the House of Lords.

The irony is that even if Parnell had lived, Home Rule would most probably not have been granted any earlier and the scenario for Ireland would have been the same. Nevertheless, the legend is that Katharine brought the whole edifice toppling down. Legend likes a scapegoat, and history has drummed home the lesson that the woman always loses.

But history is changing.

CHAPTER 1

THE WOODS

We are all shaped, perhaps blindly, by the issues of our time and our parents' time, and it is impossible to understand anyone without knowing something about the time in which they lived. Katharine Parnell was born into a quickly changing world. In 1845, the year of her birth, Queen Victoria had been on the throne of England for eight years, and Benjamin Disraeli, a future Prime Minister, published a novel called *Sybil or the Two Nations* in which we can read:

> 'Well, society may be in its infancy,' said Egremont, slightly smiling; 'but, say what you like, our Queen reigns over the greatest nation that ever existed.'
> 'Which nation?' asked the stranger, 'for she reigns over two.'
> The stranger paused; Egremont was silent, but looked inquiringly.
> 'Yes,' resumed the younger stranger after a moment's interval. 'Two nations; between whom there is no intercourse and no sympathy; who are as ignorant of each other's habits, thoughts and feelings, as if they were dwellers in different zones, or inabitants of different planets; who are formed by a different breeding, are fed by a different food, are ordered by different manners and not governed by the same laws.'
> 'You speak of—' said Egremont, hesitatingly.
> 'THE RICH AND THE POOR.'

The problem was that too much had happened too quickly. From being a rural economy, England had been jolted into becoming a modern industrial empire. New inventions created factories which needed workers, and people flocked from the land to the new northern cities where the majority of them lived in terrible poverty and squalor. People were always on the verge of starvation, and so they were forced to send their children of five to work as much as fourteen hours a day in coal mines where they were beaten to stay awake. Women and boys dragged trucks of coal on their hands and knees through damp, narrow tunnels. It was not until 1847 that a factory act established a ten-hour day and a fifty-eight-hour week for all women and young persons. To make things worse, there had been bad harvests in the 1830s and 1840s which drastically raised the price of corn. Employment on the new railways was erratic, and slack periods threw thousands into the workhouse. The years of Katie's childhood came to be known as the 'hungry forties'.

The new wealth created by the manufacturing middle class did however have some beneficial effects, and one was the growth of railways. In the first decades of the century, people had depended on the horse to get from one city to another; but by 1837 it was possible to reach Manchester via Birmingham from London by rail, and by 1850 over 6,500 miles of track were open. The electric telegraph was invented, improving communication for the rich; and the new penny postal service made it possible for the poor to keep in touch with their families.

There were other reforms and changes which affected all strata of society. The flogging of women, for instance, was abolished in 1820, and slavery in 1833. The Poor Law was humanely amended in 1834, and the first Health Act came on the books in 1848. The Oxford Movement was shaking the traditional bastions of the Anglican Church, but the most important change of all had been the reform of Parliament in 1832.

This had been brought about by a Whig government which extended the franchise to all tenant farmers in the county shires, and to all householders in the town boroughs who owned property to the rateable valuation of £10. Up to this time, the Mother of Parliaments had not been too fussy about where or how she recruited her children. The shires had enjoyed a fairly wide suffrage because male owners of property to the value of 40 shillings a year were allowed to vote, but the situation in the towns was chaotic. From ancient times, the town had been allowed to return two members to Parliament, but this custom took no account of the new towns in the north. Cornwall, for instance, returned forty-four members for town and county in 1832, while cities like Birmingham, Manchester, Leeds and Sheffield returned none. But the worst abuses were the pocket boroughs, towns metaphorically in the pocket of some big landlord, and the rotten boroughs which were actually bought and sold.

The new Act, as well as considerably extending the franchise, got rid of these abuses. Women, of course, were not mentioned, and indeed were not even allowed to vote until after the First World War. Nor was there yet a secret ballot. That reform did not come until 1872, and so the landlord still controlled his tenant's vote. Nevertheless, the Act of 1832 was a revolutionary step, even though, like many significant changes in history, it had to be extorted from the Whig government.

Katharine belonged to a family of Whigs. Her father, uncle, grandfather and great-uncle were politically active. Two of them had been MPs, and her uncle, William Page Wood, was to become Lord Chancellor of England in Gladstone's first ministry. The Whigs were the forerunners of the Liberals who were to feature so importantly in Katie's life. According to the historian Anthony Wood, 'the term Whig implies the natural opponent of the Tory.' Although nothing like the Left and Right of today, the Whigs were at least nominally liberal and progressive, while the Tories were conservative and slow to change. The first Whigs had been aristocratic rebels who would not tolerate a popish prince and who had invited William of Orange to be King in 1688. Broadly they stood for democracy, although by our standards a rigidly limited one, and for the reduction of the power of the crown. They had been in power for most of the eighteenth century, but had fallen into a state of chaos during the first half of the nineteenth.

Still, it was difficult in the days of Katie's childhood to draw firm dividing lines between the two main parties. The Tories broadly represented the old landlord aristocracy and stood for all the old patriarchal values, the Anglican Church and protection in trade. However, although nominally democratic, the Whigs were nearly as conservative as the Tories, and both parties had been badly frightened by the excesses of the French Revolution.

As the wealth of the country shifted from the aristocracy, another party grew up to represent the new manufacturing middle classes. They were the Radicals, and Utilitarianism was their doctrine. This was a belief in the greatest good for the greatest number, but they were also committed to *laissez-faire* economics and the limitation of government controls. The two policies were more than somewhat contradictory, but eventually, towards the end of the century, they were subsumed into the coalition of the Whigs and Radicals which formed the great Liberal Party.

Although the victory at Waterloo in 1815 ensured peace in England for the next hundred years, there followed in its aftermath a period of great social unrest. During the Napoleonic Wars, the price of corn had been artificially high and, relying on this situation continuing, landlords mortgaged their estates for improvements. It was a mistake, because after the war ended in 1815 the price of corn fell, thereby bankrupting hordes of farmers. In consequence the landed interest who still dominated the House of Commons passed the Corn Laws which forbade the importation of foreign corn until the price rose above 80 shillings a quarter – a lot of money at the time. The price of bread, then, was kept artificially high and, as it was the main diet of the working classes, the burden was heaviest on them.

In 1846, when Katie was only a year old, the Corn Laws were repealed. Ironically, it took a Tory, Sir Robert Peel, to bring this about, as the Whigs had been too much in a state of chaos and too closely connected with the old landed interest to dare to repeal them. Peel, however, had been elected in 1841 and gradually in his budgets had been moving towards Free Trade. Then, in 1845, the Irish potato crop was struck by blight. As England's harvest weather was bad, it quickly became clear that it would be impossible to feed the millions of starving Irish from England alone. Foreign corn, then, was allowed to be imported to provide the poor with cheaper bread. The old landed interest no longer entirely dominated the country, but it was not only the new manufacturing middle class that was becoming influential. The voices of the hungry, landless poor were also beginning to be heard, and nowhere were they raised more stridently and violently than in Ireland.

Katharine Wood was never, even when times were hard, in danger of real poverty, but this social change was to have a central effect upon her life.

Probably the most notable of her ancestors was her paternal grandfather, Sir Matthew Wood. He was descended from an old West Country family, the Woods of Tiverton, although his branch of the family had settled in Gloucestershire. He had been knighted by Queen Victoria in his old age and was a famous Whig MP, and twice Lord Mayor of London. He is remembered partly for championing the oppressed in the social upheavals after the defeat of Napoleon, but mainly for having befriended Princess Caroline, 'the injured Queen of England'.

The episode is not without its drollness.

When mad old George III finally died in 1820, his wasteful and philandering son, the Prince Regent, became George IV. He had legally married Caroline of Brunswick, but the marriage was a disaster, and Caroline had gone to live on the Mediterranean while he dallied openly with several other women, setting his usual profligate and rakish example to society. Now, however, Caroline returned to England to claim her rights as Queen. George was furious and instructed the Tory government of the day to start divorce proceedings against her. The King had always been unpopular, and now the people were outraged at Caroline's treatment, and she became their favourite. Suddenly the cabinet found itself on a collision course with the country. The Whigs, then in opposition, befriended Caroline; and Matthew Wood put his London house at her disposal and rode with her in a coach to the coronation of her husband at Westminster Abbey. When she knocked on the door, the doorkeeper asked, 'Who knocks?'

'The Queen,' she replied.

But he would not let her in, for she did not have the proper admission ticket. And, luckily for the government, she was to die a few months later.

Sir Matthew's eldest son, John Page Wood, who was to be Katie's father, was a student at Cambridge where he was studying for Holy Orders. While on holiday in Cornwall he had met and fallen in love with Miss Emma Michell, a 17-year-old beauty. The young people were determined to marry, but Matthew Wood sent his rich brother Benjamin to 'stop that nonsense'. Instead of stopping it, however, Benjamin promptly fell in love with Emma's older sister Maria, the

Aunt Ben who was to have such an influence on Katie's later life, and uncle as well as nephew returned from Cornwall engaged.

Like the Woods, the Michells were an old West Country family. Their name was derived from the ancient Cornish village of Michell and both were always pronounced Mitchell. They traced their origins back to the time of Queen Elizabeth when a Michell had been an MP for Truro. In 1700 another was Mayor of Truro, and generations later another was the grandmother of the poet Shelley. Emma's father, Sampson, had run away to sea as a young boy, and in 1783 entered the service of the King of Portugal, eventually becoming Admiral and Commander in Chief of the Portuguese navy. He married a young woman called Annie Shears in 1787 and, according to family legend, proposed romantically with the song 'O, Nannie, wilt thou gang with me'. They had five children. The eldest, Frederick, became a famous English admiral, Maria became Aunt Ben, Charles became the first surveyor general of the Cape of Good Hope, and Emma became Katie's mother. Their early childhood was spent happily in Lisbon, but when Napoleon's army invaded Portugal, the family fled, not even stopping to pack, to the safety of a British ship. They then settled in Truro while their father, Sampson, followed the Portuguese King into exile in Brazil where he unfortunately died in 1809.

John Page Wood and Emma Michell married in 1820. As an orphaned child, Emma had been poor, and her marriage did not bring about any immediate improvement in her financial state. Katharine tells us in her memoir written in old age, *Charles Stewart Parnell; His Love Story and Political Life*, that:

> the improvident young pair found it extremely difficult to live on the very small allowance that was considered sufficient for my father at college. They appear to have been very happy notwithstanding their difficulties, which were augmented a year later by the birth of a son; and while my father became 'coach' to young men of slower wit, my mother, who was extremely talented with her brush, cheerfully turned her beautiful miniature painting to account for the benefit of her young husband and son. She soon became an exhibitor of larger works in London, and the brothers Finden engraved several of her pictures.

Their young son, who was already reading prodigiously at the age of three, died when he was only four.

John Page Wood's first job was as chaplain to Queen Caroline, and when she died he attended to her last rites. On that occasion he was surrounded by the Wood family, among them his father Matthew and Emma who had been appointed her Lady's Maid. The unfortunate woman's last words were reported to have been, 'I think I am going to die but it doesn't matter.' She requested the Woods to engrave the words 'Caroline, the injured Queen of England' on a plate and affix it to her coffin. But they had to rush the body out of England to Brunswick for burial, and the plate was fixed on the wall of the church to which her body had first been brought.

Katie grew up surrounded by mementos of the Queen. The family treasured a jewelled snuff box and a ring that had been presented to Matthew Wood. There was also a quaintly spelled letter addressed to 'The Revd. John Wood, my Chapplain', in which the Queen enclosed 'the half years Sallery in this Papear', and there was also a half-finished sock that Caroline had been knitting for Emma's little boy John. Emma was always telling stories about Caroline and fond of reciting a popular rhyme of the day:

> Queen Caroline travels in an open landau,
> With Lord Wood for a Man,
> For a Maid Lady Anne,
> And Alderman Wood for a Beau.

John Wood's 'sallery' as chaplain to the Princess was small and irregular. His next job as chaplain to the Duke of Sussex was less glamorous and probably did not pay enough either. However, in 1824 he was appointed by the Corporation of London to the rectory of St Peter's, Cornhill. The *Essex Chronicle* reported that there were four other candidates and that the living was worth from £700 to £800 a year. This was a good salary at a time when many people supported families on 8 shillings a week, but John always found it a struggle to support his large and growing family. As he was an accomplished classical scholar, he was able to supplement his income by being a reader for the publishers Chapman and Hall; and in 1832 he was appointed also to the vicarage of Cressing and moved his family to Essex where they were to remain.

He was an active man and in Essex became involved in Whig politics and local government. He became Chairman of the Board of Guardians which administered the Poor Law, and he was a magistrate, magistrates usually being drawn from the ranks of the gentry but mercifully generally better educated than those of Fielding's day. Katie, who doted on her father, described him thus:

> My father was a tall, handsome old man with merry blue eyes and a ready smile. He had a cheery word for all, a gentle wit that never found pleasure in another's discomfiture, and a natural dignity that kept him his friends and made no enemies. He troubled himself not at all about the differences between religious parties. Highly cultivated as he was, he possessed the unquestioning piety of a child and the simplicity of faith that 'thinketh no evil' and loveth all good.

The family was able, interesting and cultured. Emma now exhibited with the new Water Colour Society in London, Constable was one of her many friends, and Tennyson, Trollope and Meredith were visitors. Although Katie was born into the aristocracy, her father having inherited the new title two years before her birth, it was a minor aristocracy. The ambience was really upper-class gentry, the same class which had supplied Jane Austen with material for her novels a generation earlier. Unlike Tudor and Stuart times, the Church of England now generally recruited its clergy from the gentry, often second or younger sons, who since the eighteenth century had tended to be well educated; the dissenting churches, of course, recruited from other classes. Along with the aristocracy, the gentry patronised the arts and sent their sons on grand tours of the continent on leaving college. Country houses had large libraries whose books were read and not merely for show. There were, however, fewer books around than today, but they were the classics, and it would not have been unusual for an educated person to be familiar with Virgil, Horace, Shakespeare and Milton. Trevelyan, one of the most readable historians of the age, describes the English rural gentry by remarking, 'It had faults, of which drunkenness and gambling were the worst, but it lived a life more completely and finely human than any perhaps that has been lived by a whole class since the days of the freemen of Athens.' And, unlike the French nobles of the day, the English gentry did not refuse to intermarry with the new middle classes or to send their younger sons into trade. Katie's great-uncle, for instance, had made a fortune in brewing, and her uncle was a London merchant.

Although John and Emma Wood were apparently happily married, *A Century of Letters*, the family history compiled by Minna Evangeline Bradhurst, occasionally gives the impression that John could be irascible. Maria, for instance, wrote of him, 'John sometimes complains about the misery of having married an artist, while he is as proud as a peacock of her handiwork.' In later years, he actually bought up all of Emma's available paintings and hung them at Rivenhall, the family home. Nevertheless, for most of his life John Wood was chronically short of money and does not seem to have borne the situation with the same stoicism as his wife. The Woods were much like the Bennets of Jane Austen's *Pride and Prejudice*. In both cases, there was a family of girls to marry off. There was the same shortage of money, and the same hope of money in the background. In pure Austen fashion, Baron Western, the Woods' landlord and a wealthy MP for Essex, promised to leave his money to the eldest son, Frederick. However, as the boy died in early manhood the money was left elsewhere. Sir John's father, Matthew, had also been left a fortune, but it was eaten up by Chancery after a long, Dickensian law case. However, there was still in the background the money of Benjamin and Maria Wood who were constantly helping John and Emma with their many children. Perhaps because of this, several of the children, Katie included, turned out to be rather casual about money.

However, if Sir John was something of a Mr Bennet, Lady Emma was by no means a rattle-pated Mrs Bennet. Emma seems to have been a remarkable woman and the dominant partner in the marriage. Her portrait when young shows her to have been a dark beauty, if rather plumper than we would consider perfection today. Katie describes her in old age as 'still a very attractive woman with large grey eyes and jet-black hair that she kept to the end of her days – a woman scorning throughout her life all the cosmetic adjuncts to feminine beauty, she was rewarded by nature with the preservation of her good looks in old age.' As well as being beautiful and talented and a devoted mother, Emma was also a vicar's wife and a Florence Nightingale to the poor. Her sister Maria wrote of her:

On the morning of the 13th of January a messenger came in breathless haste to beg John would go to the wheelwright of the village who had cut his leg very badly. Emma, being nearest dressed, ran to the house and found the housewife useless from fright and distraction, and the poor man unhelped, bleeding profusely. Seeing that it was a case past their skill, she sent a man and horse for a surgeon, and closing the wound with her fingers and thumbs held the edges together for an hour and five minutes. When the surgeon arrived he was obliged to remove her hands himself as they were so benumbed.

Maria also recounts another heroic anecdote:

She was sent for to a poor woman who had given birth to a child but a few hours and who was seized by cholera. All the disgusting symptoms of this dreadful malady were exhibited, and Emma saw the poor woman knotted up by cramp from her feet to her throat. She proposed giving her laudanum, but the mother of the sufferer, an old woman past eighty, refused to let her daughter take it, saying that she should have brandy which was an excellent medicine. Knowing that it was sometimes given, and not knowing herself what to prescribe, Emma waited until the doctor whom she had sent for arrived. He prescribed strong emetics, and Emma then turned her attention to the newborn infant and taking it up proposed to the grandmother to feed it. This she refused to do, saying she was sure it wanted nothing as she had given it plenty of gin. Leaving then the poor sufferer, the mother of eleven children, to the care of the doctor, Emma took the infant in her arms and carried it home. Her nursemaid declined touching it, so she put it into the cradle and washed and dressed and suckled it for five days, when the poor mother being out of danger she carried it home to her. To estimate the heroism of her benevolence fully, you must know that she was at the same time suckling her own beautiful child and had always trembled at the very name of cholera, while she had five children at home, four of whom she had recently nursed through the scarlet fever. The woman and her child are now both well and strong.

This incident occurred while her husband was away from home, and Emma used to describe with much amusement his horror when he returned and, hastening to see his child, beheld two little heads in the cradle. 'Good gracious, my dear Emma,' he exclaimed, 'you never said there were two.'

Cholera first struck England in 1832, when it claimed 18,000 lives. It came from the East and was an absolutely dreaded disease because there was no cure. The germ could be caught from water or excrement. So it spread rapidly through the slums, which then had no drainage or clean water. The symptoms were terrifying: acute stomach pains and vomiting. The victims felt intensely cold and their skin turned a blueish hue. Sometimes they died within hours. So Emma's attention to the woman and her baby were remarkably Christian and courageous.

According to Maria, Emma's own fecundity rivalled Sarah's in the Bible. She had six children in quick succession, of whom four died. Then she had seven more. Eight were alive at the time of Kate's birth, but two years later Emma suffered the deaths of her eldest surviving son, Frederick, and of her 17-year-old daughter Clarissa. Katie's six living siblings, then, were Maria, Francis, born in 1834, Charles, born in 1836, Evelyn, born in 1838, Emma and Anna. This listing from *Burke's Peerage* typically does not give the birth dates of the girls, only the dates of their marriages.

Maria, who was always called Polly, married a Lieutenant-Colonel in the army who took her to India soon after Katie was born. Frank joined the army as an officer in the 18th Foot and married when Katie was 9. Later, he was greatly to influence her life by introducing her to a young cornet in the 18th Hussars called William Henry O'Shea. Charlie, although a good scholar, became a farmer because his parents thought an outdoor life would be good for his health. Emma married the wealthy Sir Thomas Barrett-Lennard when Katie was eight and went to live in a mansion called Belhus, near Rainham in Essex. Anna married Charles Steele, a Lieutenant-Colonel in the 17th Lancers, when Katie was 13. The marriage did not work out, however, and Anna bolted home after only a week of it, becoming the constant companion of Katie's childhood. Of all the Wood children, Anna was the most talented and, along with her mother, was to become a minor Victorian novelist.

At the time of Katie's birth, the family lived in a house called Glazenwood in Bradwell, Essex, about forty-five miles from London. The family had moved there because the vicarage at Cressing was too damp, and they were soon to move again, this time to Rivenhall Place, a beautiful old house dating back to Tudor times, with forty rooms and its own park of 100 acres and a lake. According to family legend, soon after Katie's birth Sir John sent his son Charles out on horseback to find a larger house for his many children. Presently the boy returned, saying he had found the house his mother would love 'because it has a waterfall down the front stairs'. Rivenhall was owned by Lord Western, a friend of Sir John, who rented it to him on a long lease as he was willing to carry out the many necessary repairs. Katie's first conscious memories are of this house, and she tells us, 'The beautiful old place was a paradise for growing children and the space and beauty of this home of my youth left me with a sad distaste for the little houses of many conveniences that it has been my lot to inhabit for the greater part of my life.'

A person, so the psychologists tell us, is shaped by his background and birth. So, given the facts of Katie's childhood and the changes going on in the England of her and her parents' day, what sort of person was she likely to become? Like all upper-class Victorians, she grew up with a sense of privilege and confidence. Not only did she live in a mansion and her father have a respected position in society, but the British flag then flew in many countries of the world. All this was bound to affect her outlook on life. And, as the youngest of a large family, she was cosseted and expected people to come to her rescue. From her father and brother she learnt to expect much from men and how to please them. And in her mother she had the example of kindness, unconventionality and the woman's role. It is unlikely that, as a child, she understood matters like the Irish Famine or the repeal of the Corn Laws or the £10 vote, but she did grow up in a political atmosphere. Indeed, she belonged to a family that did not banish its children to nurseries like other Victorians, but expected intelligent conversation from them. And although she was to have no formal education, she was her father's constant companion from early childhood and travelled with him to political meetings. Later she wrote:

> In politics he was a thoroughgoing Whig, and as he was an able and fluent speaker, and absolutely fearless in his utterances, he became a great influence in the county during election times. I remember, when he was to speak at a political meeting, how he laughed as he tied me up in enormous orange ribbons and made me drive him there, and how immensely proud of him I was (though, of course, I could not understand a word of it all) as he spoke so persuasively that howls and ribald cries turned to cheers for 'Sir John's man'.

She was later to understand a great deal about politics.

CHAPTER 2

CHILDHOOD

As a child I used to waken to the dawn growing slowly into day, when the mist was rising from the lake and floating in soft clouds through the trees which overhung the water. I heard the faint, uncertain call of the wild duck and the flapping of the wings of the half awakened swans. Then came the soft swishing of the cart horses, as they stood in the water to drink before beginning the day's work, and I listened with delicious fear in the gloom, wondering if it would be safe to creep downstairs without waking anyone, and out under the great trees where the sun was beginning to tip the golden leaves; then on over the bridge to the other side of the lake to feed the swans.

In many ways Katie had an idyllic childhood, and she begins her memoirs with this lyric description of awakening before the rest of the family at Rivenhall. It was a huge square house, standing on a slight hill and overlooking the open country, with a lake to one side. A granddaughter of Lady Emma was later to describe it as 'one of the stately homes of England'. Somehow, since moving in, the Woods had found hundreds of pounds for the repair of its forty rooms and miles of passages. The water flowing down the stairs had been staunched, and so something must have been done to the roof also. But big as it was, the house seems quickly to have been made comfortable and lived-in. In her memoirs, Katie tells us that there was a large hall with logs burning in great open fireplaces. A smaller hall opened out of this, from which broad, shallow oak stairs led to the upper rooms. Katie describes her fear in crossing these halls by the flickering light when she went from the dining room to her father's study in the evening. The huge drawing room had a grand piano, and its walls were filled with Lady Emma's paintings, while Sir John's library was crammed with books.

Outside, the beautiful old-world garden was dominated by a huge cedar tree. There were peony bushes in the flower beds with pink blossoms the size of dinner plates. As the summer wore on, they were replaced by scarlet and oriental poppies, and in the autumn by yellow and wine-coloured double dahlias. Lady Emma was the gardener in the family and had planted these flowers, which she tended in all weathers.

There was an old sundial there, made from one of the piers of old London Bridge which Sir John had bought. And there were peacocks wandering about the lawn. The place must have been a paradise for a young child.

As she was considered delicate, Katie was kept out in the fresh air as much as possible. Horse riding was prescribed by the doctor, for she had a weakness of the 'heart and lungs'. So she spent many hours galloping side-saddle on her pony Eugenie. At other times she would ramble the countryside. Or, when the lake froze in winter, she would join the people from the neighbourhood who came to skate there.

When she was old enough, she was allowed to fetch the letters before breakfast from the new post office half a mile away. On the way back she would linger, sometimes stopping to chat to cottagers on the estate or to her father's curate whose letters she also collected. The curate was to teach her about astronomy, an interest which she later passed on to Parnell. For delaying so long with the letters, she would be scolded by her mother and sisters, but her father always took her side, explaining that while he and she liked their breakfast better than their letters, 'grown-up ladies wanted their letters more than their breakfast.'

The Victorians went in for huge breakfasts, and that of the large Wood family was probably on occasions not greatly different from that of Trollope's archdeacon and his family in *The Warden*:

> The tea consumed was the very best, the coffee the very blackest, the cream the very thickest; there was dry toast and buttered toast, muffins and crumpets; hot bread and cold bread, white bread and brown bread, homemade bread and bakers' bread, wheaten bread and oaten bread; and if there be other breads than these, they were there; there were eggs in napkins, and crispy bits of bacon under silver covers; and there were little fishes in a little box, and devilled kidneys frizzling on a hot-water dish; which by-the-by, were placed closely contiguous to the plate of the worthy archdeacon himself. Over and above this, on a snow-white napkin, spread upon the sideboard, was a huge ham and a huge sirloin; the latter having laden the dinner table on the previous evening. Such was the ordinary fare at Plumstead Episcopi.

After breakfast, Lady Wood would have attended to her housekeeping, giving orders to the cook about the food for the day. These and other domestic tasks efficiently accomplished, she would then answer her letters or work at her painting or writing, while Sir John occupied the library. If either of them went out in the morning, they changed, and, as it was then considered bad form not to change for lunch, they did so again when they came in. If they were going out again, they would change back into outdoor tweeds. A frock was always worn for drawing room tea, and, if there were guests for dinner, the family would usually dress.

Like many youngest children of large families, Katie was brought up with a mixture of spoiling and neglect. Normally in the Victorian era, a child of her class would have spent a lot of time with servants, and, although the Woods did not exile their children to the nursery, it seems that Katie's nurse Lucy had a great deal to do with her early childhood, and Katie in later years was still very fond of her.

If Katie had come from a wealthier family, she might have gone to a small, private boarding school at the age of 9 or 10, or else been taught at home by the family governess. But Katie had no formal education. She never went to school, and due to financial difficulties the governess who had taught the older Wood children had been let go shortly after Katie's birth. In a haphazard way she was taught by her father, but there is the definite suggestion from her memoirs that she was neglected by her mother, or that there was some conflict in their relationship. For instance, although Katie makes a great deal of fuss about the death of her nurse in her memoirs, she never even mentions her mother's death. There is no indication that Lady Emma did not love her youngest daughter, but it could simply have been that, as she was 43 when Katie was born, the novelty and delight of small children had worn off. She was, after all, a talented and busy artist who had to supplement the family income, first with her paintings and later with her novels. Lady Emma was considered a saint by all who knew her, but even saints have their faults. Hers seems to have been a habit of making favourites among her children. The first object of this maternal fixation had been John, her clever little son who had died years before. Then it was the angelic Clarissa who had died at 17. And the last was her son Evelyn who was seven years older than Katie. In her memoirs, Katie says quite bluntly:

> As a matter of fact, my mother was so entirely wrapped up in Evelyn that I think I was jealous, even though I had my father so much to myself. My mother was most affectionate to all her children, but Evelyn was her idol, and from the time when, as a mere lad, he was wounded in the Crimean War, to the day of her death, he was first in all her thoughts.

Evelyn was a lively and clever boy who was to rise to great heights in the army. According to family tradition, he had little schooling until he went to Marlborough Grammar School at the age of nine. Then, at the still tender but usual age of 14, he went into the navy and, as a young officer, was severely wounded in the Crimea. His injuries were complicated by the endemic typhoid fever, and when Lady Wood heard this she travelled all the way to Scutari to see him. There she found him 'a living skeleton, with ulcers on his poor spine and hips, caused by lying so long on skin and bone' – bedsores in our language of today. His mother, who could act as decisively as Katie herself did in later years, announced that she was bringing her son home to Rivenhall to nurse him back to health herself. Florence Nightingale, who was in charge of the army hospital, tried to oppose this. But she had met her match in Emma Wood, and in the end the determined mother got her way and took her son back to England.

Evelyn recovered from his wounds and later made the unusual switch to the army. There he had a brilliant career, winning a Victoria Cross before he was 21 and eventually becoming a Field-Marshal. As a boy, at home on holidays, he had like all big brothers the habit of teasing his small sister. Katie tells us:

> Evelyn was especially adroit in bewildering me, and used to curb my rebellion, when I was reluctant to fetch and carry for him, by drawing a harrowing picture of my remorse should he be killed 'in the next war'. The horror of this thought kept me a ready slave for years, till one day, in a gust of temper, I burst out with: 'I shan't be sorry at all when you're killed in the war cos' I didn't find your silly things, and I wish you'd go away and be a dead hero now, so there!' I remember the horrified pause of my mother and sister and the howl of laughter and applause from Evelyn and Charlie. Evelyn was very good to me after this, and considered more, that even little girls have their feelings.

If Katie was somewhat neglected by her mother, she was her father's pet. She tells us that her father was her 'dear companion and friend always, and to him I took all my little troubles and griefs and all my joys'. From early childhood, he took her everywhere with him – to the political meetings when, as we have seen, he decked her out in the colours of the party, to court when he sat on the magistrates' bench, to prison when he visited, to church services in Cressing, and even all the way to St Peter's in London when he went to do duty there. At those times she stayed asleep in a hotel while he took the Evensong.

Although Katie's lessons were haphazard, they must have been far more interesting than those any school could provide. Her father would direct her reading in the evenings, 'gently substituting Scott for a less edifying author'. And in the daytime he would take her for long walks in the countryside, drawing questions out of her in a Socratic manner and never failing to answer them. His special interest was botany, and Katie tells us:

> My happiest days were when we took long walks and hunted for wild flowers together. My father knew a good deal about Botany, and taught me the names of flowers I collected, their old English names and the derivations of them. I have still the books he gave

me, that I might learn more of the flowers which grow without cultivation, and the power of observation he awoke in me then has been a great solace to me through life.

Sir John was a most popular vicar who believed a sermon should never last more than twenty minutes. He loved children, and when he took the Sunday service at Cressing the boys would rush to pick up his cigar butts and finish them as a 'treat before singing in the choir'. Cigars were not considered a luxury at the time and were more popular than the cigarette which by the time of the Crimean War was considered 'fast'.

Sir John delighted his own children by putting their sayings and doings into doggerel and setting them to music. An exploit of Charlie's made him known for some time as Jaunty July:

Jaunty July, Jaunty July
Shot a squib in his Father's eye.

And for his eldest daughter, Maria, he wrote:

Maria was a picture book
To little Emma showing.
Says I, 'Don't give it to her.'
Says she, 'I aint a-going.'

And, when the children insisted on a rhyme for himself, he wrote:

John Page Wood be it known to all men
Can write a good hand
If he has a good pen.

Despite the companionship of her father, Katie missed children of her own age to play with. She tells us in her memoirs of playing cricket with a boy who looked after the 'boots and knives' in Rivenhall: 'I thought this youth a marvellous player, and when on one occasion I won the game, I threw a stump into the air in my joy. My triumph was short-lived, for it came down on my head, and cut it very badly.' The poor, stammering boy dragged her bleeding to the house where Katie's nurse attended to the wound. When quizzed about what had happened, Katie conveniently fainted. The unfortunate boy must have been blamed because Katie tells us, feeling sorry only for herself, that the 'little episode led to the banishment of my chosen ally, the bootboy; and I was thrown more than ever on my own resources'.

In the days before radio or television, people had to rely on their own entertainments – hence the popularity of novels in the Victorian age. The young ladies of the family were often accomplished musicians and would entertain the guests after dinner in the long evenings by singing or playing the piano. Lady Emma was a fine musician, and, as Katie grew older, she longed to play the piano as well as her mother. She started to pick out tunes on the big grand piano in the drawing room, but, when she asked her mother for music lessons, the answer was, surprisingly, a firm no. Lady Emma said, 'There is the piano, go and play it if you really want to learn.'

The reason given for this refusal was that the eldest daughter, Maria, had announced after years of expensive lessons that she detested music and, if she could help it, would never play a note again. But it is also indicative of other things: firstly, that it was Lady Wood who held the purse strings, and secondly, that there was no money in the purse for such pursuits as music lessons, especially for a young and insignificant daughter at the end of a big family.

But Katie was undeterred, and in time she could pick out tunes by ear, and she even began to compose a little. Eventually she persuaded a church organist in nearby Witham to give her lessons, but whether he was paid or not she does not say. She made progress, however, and soon discovered she had a pleasant singing voice. Singing lessons from a French teacher were now allowed by her mother who liked Katie to sing French operatic songs. But her father wanted nothing but Handel, and Katie tells us, 'I used to sing "God is For Us", "Comfort Ye" and "How Beautiful are the Feet" very creditably.'

She must have delighted her parents and their visitors. In later life, one of Lady Wood's friends, an editor of *The Times*, was to describe her singing in a letter:

I used to think – indeed still think Katie a wonder of wonders. I admired her strength of character immensely. Shall I tell you what first of all made me discover she was weak and mortal? She could not stand still to sing. She must fold her arms and walk about the room in and out among the furniture like a dreamer.

Katie's interest in music led her to set to music any verses that appealed to her. One of these was Longfellow's 'Weariness', which Lady Emma praised so highly that Katie sent it to the poet. He wrote to thank her, saying it was 'the best setting of his poem he had ever read'. So, on her next visit to London with her father, she brought the manuscript to Boosey's, the music publishers, and asked them to bring it out.

'Quite impossible, my dear young lady,' their representative answered at once. 'We never take beginners' work!'

Katie plaintively remarked that even Mozart was a beginner once.

This brought a burst of laughter from the man who smilingly consented to look at the manuscript.

Then Katie says he tried some of it, finally agreeing, much to her joy, to publish 'Weariness' and a couple of her other songs.

Katie does not tell us how old she was when she had this unusual distinction, but she was probably about 15. Her coup certainly delighted her father, and her mother was the type of woman who would have encouraged her to write more music, yet there is no record of her having done so ever again. In later life she was to be very restless and constantly on the move, so perhaps she did not have the sticking power necessary for any real artistic accomplishment. After all, the family friend had aptly described her as a dreamer. In any event, her parents, like all upper-class Victorians, brought up their daughters to marry, not to have careers. If she dabbled in the arts and became accomplished in some, that was fine. But an unmarried woman was looked down on and generally considered a problem in Victorian times. Shaw's Vivie Warren was not to strike out on her own for a career for another generation, and she seemed rather monstrous to most theatregoers even then. Katie's main object in life was to find a husband, if possible a rich one.

In her memoirs, Katie tells us that she was the unwitting initiator of her mother's novel writing. In the longer winter evenings at Rivenhall, while her father read *The Times* and her sister Anna read or sketched, Katie would sometimes write the plots of stories for her father to read. As the characters were all involved in violent actions and had a flagrant disregard for convention, he called them 'bloodstained bandits'. Her mother and sister Anna, however, later offered to buy one of her plots to write up into a novel. At this time Katie must have been in her teens, because Lady Emma did not publish her first novel until 1866, the year of Sir John's death, when Katie was 21. Or it could have been that this early work was published in one of the magazines of the day, where many Victorian writers got their start. At any rate, Lady Wood was writing long before her first book, *Ephemera*, a collection of poems and line drawings in collaboration with her daughter Anna, came out in 1865. Katie tells us that one of her chief pleasures as a girl was to sit on the swing under the old cedar tree, 'gently swinging backwards and forwards', reading her mother's and Anna's manuscripts. Later, to her great pride, they would listen carefully to her comments and suggestions for changes.

Anna was considered the better writer of the two women, and in later life was thought one of the cleverest women in England. As girls, she and Katie were great friends, although there was a considerable difference in their ages. Katie tells us that her sister had 'soft, brown hair and a lovely skin, blue eyes that were mocking, gay, or tender in response to many moods, and a very pretty figure. And I solemnly decided that she was really pretty and quite "grown-up" enough to be loved by the "beautiful ones".'

One of these was Colonel Steele of the 17th Lancers, whom Anna married in 1858, when Katie was 13. He was a dark, handsome man and one of Evelyn's many friends who on visits paraded around Rivenhall in 'beautiful uniforms and jingly spurs'. Katie tells us that she was in awe of these 'magnificent beings' and would gallop past the drawing room on her pony, Eugenie, imagining herself a maiden from a fairy story and the young officer a handsome prince. Another of the 'beautiful ones' gave her her first grown-up book, a first edition of *Vanity Fair*, and one cannot but wonder if Becky Sharp's wise comment on life made any impression on the young reader: 'I think I could be a good woman if I had five thousand a year.'

But the heroes of romance will not always stand the harsh light of reality, and Anna ran away from her handsome husband after only a week of marriage. According to Wood family tradition, she was horrified at the idea of sexual intercourse. But it is impossible to know what goes on between people in their private lives. The Steeles were never divorced, and Anna was always known as Mrs Anna C. Steele. Her family were very supportive of her decision to leave, and there were often violent scenes at Rivenhall as her husband tried to get her back, with Anna running out of the back door and Colonel Steele dashing in the front. On one occasion, Evelyn was actually sued for assault after knocking Colonel Steele down.

Anna was reputed to have been highly acerbic about men, and to have said, 'All men can be won by flattery and liquors.' It was rumoured that she lived and died a virgin, but Katie, for one, did not think this true in later life. Indeed, she seems to have suspected her sister of having an affair with her – Katie's – own husband, Willie O'Shea. Certainly, Anna was popular and extant letters show that she was at least on friendly terms with a number of eminent men, among them Anthony Trollope, George Meredith and the Irish novelist and MP Justin McCarthy.

Trollope came regularly to Rivenhall during Katie's girlhood. He particularly liked hunting and was a daring and courageous rider. This was a source of anxiety to Lady Emma because Anna loved to follow him. The hounds frequently met at Rivenhall, but hunting was not to Katie's taste. She always felt sorry for the victims of the chase and, while the hunt was having breakfast, would sometimes creep off and tramp about the covers to spoil the scent. Later she would wait until the quarry got away and then shout 'view holla' in the wrong direction. Her father never hunted either, although there was a painting of him in the drawing room as a young man in hunting dress. This used to puzzle Katie but, on asking why, she was told it was because he was so old. Later she understood that, with so many children to educate, her 'sporting parson' had to grow 'too old' early in life.

Visiting was an important part of life in the days of the great country houses. Friends or relatives might come to stay for weeks, and members of the same family constantly visited each other. It was on a visit with Anna to their brother Frank that Katie first met Willie O'Shea. Frank was married, and the two girls stayed with him and his wife in the officers' quarters. As part of their entertainment, they watched a military review and were delighted with the spectacle of so many men in full military dress. Afterwards some of the officers came to call, and among them was Willie O'Shea, then a cornet in the 18th Hussars. Later in the evening, the girls were brought to a play acted by the officers and were flattered by the attention they received. Katie does not say whether Willie was in the play or even at it. In fact, he hardly seemed to register with her at all because she noted in her memoirs, 'I found the elderly and hawklike Colonel of the Regiment far more interesting than the younger men.'

The photographs of Katharine and Willie, however, bring these two young Victorians to life for us. At the time of their first meeting, Katie was about 16 and small for her age, with dark Italian looks. Her eyes were big and full of fun, her mouth generous and rather sensuous, and her nose aquiline. She wore the looped crinoline, which had come from Paris in about 1854 and was to stay in fashion for the next twenty years, and her hair was braided and tied behind. Willie was about 21. He was of average height, and handsomely Irish-looking with thick wavy hair and a full moustache. He looked confident and slightly superior. And in his braided Hussars uniform, with his plumed helmet under his arm and his sword jangling as he walked, he must have been very striking.

The next time they met was at Katie's sister Emma's country house, Belhus, near Rainham in Essex. Emma had married Sir Thomas Barrett-Lennard when Katie was eight, so there was a big age gap between them. Despite this they always got on well. Indeed, throughout her childhood Katie constantly visited her older sister and greatly enjoyed the Barrett-Lennards's lavish hospitality. The couple were wealthy and their house lay in hundreds of acres of parkland. Emma was reputed to be the nicest of all the Wood children. She also inherited her mother's musical ability and wrote numerous songs, among them 'Plymouth Hoe' which was very popular in its day. Like Katie, Emma was fond of setting poems to music, and among these were works by her mother and Anna, as well as Tennyson's 'Crossing the Bar' and William Allingham's ever-popular 'Fairies'.

Emma's husband, Thomas, was fascinated by horse racing. He kept a stable and had heard from his brother-in-law Frank Wood that young Willie O'Shea was an excellent rider and would probably be willing to ride the Barrett-Lennard horse, Honesty, in the Brentwood Steeplechase. Accordingly, Willie was asked and instantly agreed to ride the horse, and was invited for the weekend to Belhus. Katie remembered the occasion:

> My first sight of Willie then, as a grown-up, was on this evening, when I came rather late into the hall before dressing for dinner. He was standing near the fire, talking with the eagerness that was not in those days bad form in young men, of the steeplechase he had ridden and won on Early Bird.
>
> I had been so much the companion of older men than he that I

was pleased with his youthful looks and vivacity. His dress pleased me also, and, though it would appear a terrible affair in the eyes of a modern young man, it was perfectly correct then for a young officer in the 18th Hussars, and extremely becoming to Willie: a brown velvet coat, cut rather fully, sealskin waistcoat, black-and-white check trousers, and an enormous carbuncle and diamond pin in his curiously folded scarf.

When introduced to me he was most condescending, and nettled me so much by his kindly patronage of my youthfulness that I promptly plunged into such a discussion of literary complexities absorbed from my elders and utterly undigested, that he soon subsided into a bewildered and shocked silence.

All his life people were to comment on Willie's dandified appearance, and it seems, by the standards of the day, that he was then dressed to kill. Although Katie tells us that his dress was perfectly correct, it was only usual for the Swells of the Sixties to wear diamond pins and elaborately folded scarves. At any rate, he seems to have stood out in contrast to his well-bred and conventional hosts. One also gets the impression that he was rather gullible, if not a little stupid, for all his dazzling appearance. For although six years older, he was stunned when Katie launched into her literary discussion and failed to realise that she was only showing off.

Then Thomas asked jokingly, 'Who is Katie to go in with, Milady?' 'O she will go in with O'Shea,' was Emma's reply.*

Willie always pronounced his name O'Shee, so this brought a ripple of laughter which mildly ruffled Katie's 'sense of importance'. It might also suggest that the Barrett-Lennards did not take their young guest too seriously, but as a bit of a joke. After all, he had only been invited because he was a good rider, and his dinner partner was a schoolgirl not yet 'out'.

* All dialogue quoted is taken directly from Katie's memoirs, *Charles Stewart Parnell: His Love Story and Political Life.*

CHAPTER 3

COURTSHIP

Willie O'Shea belonged to a family of 'Castle Catholics'. In Ireland this was a term used to describe those members of the new middle class, or the old Norman or Gaelic aristocracy, who identified more with the English Protestant ascendancy than with their fellow-countrymen, the mere Irish. Although English in aspiration, they were usually fervent Catholics; and, much like the upper-class Irish and English Catholics of today, they sent their sons to top English Catholic schools to be educated. Their daughters were often sent to continental convents. Indeed, there was a long tradition of Irish emigré connection with the continent. Down through the centuries, Irish patriots had fled English Protestant domination to Catholic France, Spain or Portugal. The most notable groups were the Earls of Donegal and the Wild Geese, that famous band of Jacobins led by Patrick Sarsfield who had held Limerick for James II in the historic siege after the Battle of the Boyne. The Earls fled after the Elizabethan Wars in Ireland, and the Wild Geese were allowed to flee to the continent with their arms, where many of them settled, often joining the continental armies or marrying into the aristocracy. A branch of the O'Shea family had fled after a rebellion, settling in France in the middle of the seventeenth century to become the Ducs de San Luca.

Willie's immediate family came from the south-west of Ireland. His grandfather, William O'Shea of Rich Hill, Limerick, had three sons, Henry, John and Thaddeus. Henry, who became Willie's father, was apprenticed to a Dublin solicitor. John emigrated to Spain at an early age, where he prospered and founded a bank. And poor Thaddeus became the black sheep of the family, according to Katie, 'wasting his substance in gambling and in breeding unlikely horses to win impossible races'. Willie, as a boy, was kept well away from the influence of this wild, ne'er-do-well uncle and was hardly allowed even to know him. Nevertheless, the uncle's prodigal instincts were to flower in the nephew.

Willie's father, Henry, was anything but wild. At the death of his father, as the eldest he had taken over the family's affairs. Finding his family estate heavily mortgaged and his childhood home, Rich Hill, in a state of collapse, he went to Dublin. There he eventually qualified as a solicitor and set up his own practice which specialised in the problems of bankrupt estates, a particular Irish problem at the time. Business flowed in, and Henry became a wealthy man. He married Catharine Quinlan from Tipperary who, according to the Catholic custom of the day, had been granted a temporal title of 'Comtesse of Rome' by the Pope. The couple had two children, Mary and William Henry.

In her memoirs, Katie speaks highly of Henry O'Shea, but she describes the Comtesse O'Shea as a 'bundle of negations wrapped in a shawl – always a very beautiful shawl'. The woman was prematurely feeble and a grimly rigid Catholic. Her only other definite characteristic, Katie tells us, was 'her profound sense of my undesirability as a daughter-in-law'. Katie had a liking, however, for Willie's sister, Mary, and says that they might have got on well except that Mary too thought she was unsuitable as a wife for Willie. Mary would have been pretty, but a serious illness had badly marked her skin. And, according to Katie, she was humourless and a rather tiresomely religious person who wore herself and her friends out in her 'endeavours to make bad catholics out of indifferent protestants'. Also she says that Mary 'was a human library of solid information and was as ignorant – and as innocent – of the world at twenty-eight as she must have been at eight.' Mary had also been largely educated in France, and so she sounded more French than Irish. On one occasion when the three members of the O'Shea family got together, Katie was much amused at Henry with his rich Irish brogue, Willie with his plummy public school accent and Mary with her lisping French.

Henry had spared no expense on his children's education. They had both spent time in France and Spain, so were accomplished linguists. Willie had been sent off to boarding school at St Mary's College, Oscott, in Warwickshire in 1850 when he was about ten. The school then prided itself on a liberal rather than a commercial or professional education. Foreign languages were studied, as were the usual upper-class accomplishments: English elocution, drawing and music. Katie writes that 'Willie had no natural taste for learning', but he must have had some because he did well in school. In her biography of Katharine, *The Uncrowned Queen of Ireland*, Joyce Marlow says that 'surviving mark books show that during his five years at Oscott O'Shea was well above average in scholastic ability, usually second in a monthly class placing, never less than fifth'. George Moore, the Irish novelist, who attended the school about ten years later, describes it in *Confessions of a Young Man* as a 'hateful Roman Catholic College'. Unlike Willie, he did not do well there, but was expelled at the age of 16 for 'idleness and general worthlessness'. The school, however, was one of the best available for the sons of the Irish and English Catholic upper and middle classes. John Henry Newman preached there during Willie's time, and Wilfrid Scawen Blunt, the poet, was a contemporary. Blunt was later to record in his diary, 'I was at school at Oscott with O'Shea and hated him as cordially as the Irish do today. He was older than me, a bit of a dandy, a bit of a bully.'

After Oscott, Willie travelled to France and Spain where he perfected his languages and gained even greater self-confidence. He then entered Trinity College, Dublin, where he did not do at all well. So, in 1858, his father bought him a commission as cornet in the 18th Hussars. This was a famous sporting regiment, and as an accomplished rider Willie fitted in well. On his departure, his doting father's instructions were, 'First become a smart officer; secondly do what the other men do and send the bill to me.'

And Willie did just this.

Bills poured in for uniforms, mess expenses, gambling debts. And soon the fond father was protesting at the enormous expense of keeping his son in such a costly regiment. Willie was contrite, but made no perceptible attempt to mend his ways. He continued to live beyond his means, and so as a last resort his father bought him a captaincy, hoping that this at least would increase his sense of responsibility.

Alas, it did no such thing.

So the evening that Katie saw him across the hall that second time in Belhus, looking the dandy in his brown velvet coat, check trousers and sealskin waistcoat, he was already a hardened spendthrift and a reckless gambler. But qualities which are tiresome in someone older are acceptable enough, and even charming, in the young. After all, Willie had plenty of time to settle down. For now it was all right, even quite the thing, to be a little reckless. Wasn't he handsome, gay and amusing? And renowned in the regiment for his quick Irish wit? Such a guest would enliven any dinner table or weekend party. Over that particular weekend, Katie and he became good friends, and on his departure he presented her with one of his conventional poems praising 'her golden hair and witsome speech' – not very observant, surely, when Katie was usually admired for her thick black curls.

The next episode in their courtship could be taken from the pages of Jane Austen's *Mansfield Park*. Katie describes in her memoirs how one day at Rivenhall when her brothers were home, someone suggested they form a theatrical group to do plays, a common enough pastime among the well-to-do. In the Wood family there was a lot of talent under one roof, and in Rivenhall there was plenty of space to put on a play. Everyone immediately became excited by the idea, and people from the surrounding county were roped in to help. Lady Wood left her own painting and writing and took over the painting of the set. There was much friendly squabbling about what play to do and who would get what part, but Lady Wood adjudicated from the high ladder, and finally two skits were decided on called *Amy Robsart* and *Betsy Baker*. Katie, to her delight, was chosen for the part of Amy in the first, and Anna played Betsy in the second. Willie was given the part of Queen Elizabeth in *Betsy Baker*, but he does not seem to have been much of an actor. The sight of him dressed in skirts and a red wig prompted a fellow officer to quip on his name, 'O she is a jolly good fellow!'

Willie was flustered and fuming at this, and soon the whole house broke into singing, 'O she is a jolly good fellow!'

So Good Queen Bess stalked off the stage in a temper.

Not perhaps the expected response from one so renowned for his wit and humour, but something of a foreshadowing of the pomposity and egotism which were to be such a part of his character in later years.

After their initial effort, the company were soon rehearsing another comedy to be presented at Belhus. This was so successful that they named themselves the Belhus Dramatic Corps and presented their plays publicly. Throughout the 1860s, they appeared in Chelmsford, Colchester, Brighton and even London. They had professional coaching and direction, and received rapturous notices in the leading newspapers of the day. Charlie Wood's children presented bouquets of flowers to the actors after the performances, and all their friends came. Anthony Trollope wrote to Anna Steele, 'Of course we will come. Will you get three stalls for myself, wife and one of my boys.'

Willie attended these performances, but his acting was not considered good enough to take part. Katie always acted though, and after the show he presented her with beautiful bouquets. He was now very much the attentive young man, and she was by this time considered old enough to have her own sitting room at Rivenhall. She tells us that she received many valentines, but there does not seem to have been any other serious suitor in her life. And, although they were not engaged, Willie was always around.

The next summer she spent a great deal of time with him at Belhus where he was now a welcome guest and not merely tolerated for his riding ability. Katie describes that summer very romantically in her memoirs. The rest of the family were busy with their own affairs, so the two young people were left to themselves much of the time and took long walks under the great limes of the avenue, or explored the 'cool depths of the glades, where the fallow deer ran before us, or the kitchen garden, where the high walls were covered with rose-coloured peaches, warm with the sun as we ate them. What we talked about I cannot remember but it was nothing very wise I should imagine.'

It all sounds idyllic.

Of the two, Willie seems to have been the more in love because Katie records quite a telling episode in her memoirs of this time. She was attracted to a young officer called mysteriously ES who was very athletic and used to delight her by jumping over her pony. Emma, her sister, must have noticed this because she sent Katie to the barracks with an invitation for some young officers, ES among them, to come to dinner. Willie accompanied Katie in her pony cart, and when they arrived at the barracks jumped out to deliver the letter. Getting back in, he noticed that ES and some brother officers were looking out of the window. So he promptly leaned over and kissed Katie full on the lips. This was quite daring behaviour at the time, and she was furious at being compromised and vowed angrily never to speak to him again.

'But I only wanted to show those fellows that they must not make asses of themselves,' Willie protested apologetically.

So Katie forgave him.

And ES refused the invitation to dinner.

Tenaciousness was to be another of Willie's qualities in later life. If he got an idea into his head, he would hang on to it like a terrier in possession of a bone. And now he doggedly pursued Katie. Did he think he was marrying into money? The Woods lived in a big house all right, but there was no real money, except Aunt Ben's in the background. Willie, however, could not have been unaware of their powerful connections in political, military and artistic life – many of the youthful actors of the Belhus Dramatic Corps went on to high positions in the Empire.

Nevertheless, at this point in the story there is no need to attribute base motives to one of our principals. Willie was later to have his share of contumely, and to be remembered in Irish history as one of its worst villains. For now, however, he was just a young man in love, and his behaviour in claiming the girl of his choice as his own was typical of any young man.

Soon after the dinner party incident, Willie rejoined his regiment, and Katie returned to her parents at Rivenhall. One morning, she tells us, she was irritated at being awakened by her mother placing a thick envelope on her cheek and singing, 'Kathleen Mavourneen. . .'.

The letter was from Willie.

Katie was at a loss for the words to reply to the sheets of poetic prose he sent her. But she must have replied in some favourable manner because whenever he could get time off from his regiment he would come by train to visit her. She would collect him at the station, and they would drive to Rivenhall where they would spend hours fishing for pike in the lake or talking to her father, Sir John, who delighted in the young man's company.

Shortly after this, Willie was seriously hurt in a riding accident. He was in the habit of schooling young horses on the downs, and one morning when he was exercising Early Bird on a racecourse, the horse tripped over a chain across the course. Both horse and rider fell, but the horse managed to limp home. When Willie was missing from an early parade, his fellow-officers went to look for him. They found him unconscious about twenty yards from the chain and carried him back to the barracks on a stretcher. He had several broken ribs and concussion.

Katie writes that he was exercising his own steeplechaser, but one wonders if, in fact, it did not belong to the Barrett-Lennards because they went to Preston Barracks to nurse him and, as soon as he was well enough, moved him to their Brighton house. After six weeks, he recovered consciousness, and they took him then to Belhus to convalesce. His friend Robert Cunninghame Graham was invited along to keep him company, and Katie and Anna met the party in London, and all set off to Belhus together.

On the way, although still unable to speak, Willie slipped under cover of the rug a ring from his finger on to hers.

After Katie and Anna left Belhus, Mr O'Shea came from Ireland to nurse his son. When Willie became well enough to rejoin his regiment Katie came again to see him. On this occasion he presented her with a turquoise locket. Willie seems to have been truly smitten, but there is a distinct impression from Katie's account that her feelings for him were cooling. 'It was a lovely thing, and I was very happy to know how much Willie cared for me.'

It sounds very much as if she were now just flattered by his attention.

About this time Katie and Anna went to stay by themselves in Emma's Brighton house. The visit turned out to be reminiscent of a scene from comic opera. The two girls were delighted to be on their own in the 'great tall house' with only a caretaker to look after them. They spent their days by the sea and their evenings walking in the Lewes Crescent Gardens. As they preferred breakfast to dinner, they always dined on bacon and eggs. Cunninghame Graham, Willie's great friend, was a constant visitor, and Katie says in her memoirs that she realised in retrospect that he must have been in love with Anna. She then adds rather oddly, considering her own history, 'though, as she was already married, his suit was hopeless.'

One evening while the two girls were getting ready for bed, there was a thud on the balcony below. In giggling trepidation, they peeped out of the window to see two bouquets of flowers which had been thrown up from the road below. Cautiously they looked over the balcony and saw two young men standing on the road. At this, the girls fled back indoors and, still giggling uncontrollably, bolted the windows.

The next night the same thing happened.

And it went on for another week.

Anna was going mad with curiosity. So one evening she disguised herself as a maid and, as Katie signalled from the window that the two young men were coming round the corner, went out the front door to 'post some letters'.

The young men fell into the trap and begged the maid to take the bouquets in to her young ladies.

'It's as much as my place is worth if it gets to my lady's ears,' Anna said, disguising her accent and pretending to be very shocked.

The two young men assured her that the flowers were acceptable and 'that her lady need not know'.

'Ha!' exclaimed Anna. 'And their ma away and all.'

But she gave in, returning home with the flowers, a big tip and a packet of verses. When Katie opened the door, Anna fell into her arms helpless with laughter. The suitors' cards were in the bouquets, and the girls found out that the Romeos were brothers, belonged to a London club, and in true romantic fashion meant to pursue the girls 'to the end'.

Lady Emma was suitably shocked but the flirtation must have continued for some time because the two swains were later found in the grounds of Rivenhall. She sent them packing.

Back at Brighton, Anna and Katie received a telegram one evening saying that their mother was seriously ill. There was no train that night or the next morning, so in the end the two of them daringly hitched a ride in the engine of a goods train. However, when they arrived at home, Lady Emma was better. In any event, both of these incidents suggest perhaps some of the unconventionality and individuality that was to be a part of Katie's adult character.

All this time Willie was running up debts which he duly sent home to his father. When he sent a bill for £15,000, a terrible amount of money at the time and the equivalent of about £300,000 today, his father paid without complaining. But he told Willie that if there were any more debts, his mother and sister would have to go short. So Willie again promised to try and live within his means, and as a first step resigned from the regiment. His poor, long-suffering father died soon after this, and Willie returned to Dublin.

Katie then did not see him for some time, and when they finally met again at a London party, she tells us that she did not recognise him as he had grown whiskers, which were then highly fashionable. She writes:

> I had now known Willie very well for three years, but I was very young, and a curious distaste for my 'love affair' had grown up within me. I felt a desire to be left free and untrammelled by any serious thoughts of marriage; and, though I had not grown to dislike Willie, I wished him away when he looked fondly at me, and half-consciously I longed to get back to the days when men were little more to me than persons to be avoided, as generally wanting something to be fetched or carried. I fancied my mother understood me better than anyone, for the day after the dance she interviewed Willie when he came; and I only remember a feeling of relief as he merely said goodbye to me in passing down the stairs, where I was childishly sitting, yawning violently to attain to the mistiness of outlook that I felt was expected of me!

Katie wrote her memoirs in old age, but there is no reason to suspect her account of her young feelings. She had definitely got over her infatuation for the gay young captain.

Willie departed to Valencia, and Katie did not see him for a long time. But his feelings at being rejected can be inferred from a poem he sent to her:

FAREWELL

1

In lightly turning o'er this page, may pause
*   A woman's hand awhile, which mine hath prest*
In more than common clasp; for here I was
*   More than a common guest.*

2

Here, at the casement whence, 'mid song and laughter
*   We watch'd the buds whose bloom should deck thy hair,*
Too wise to cast a more defined thereafter —
*   Throughout a spring so fair.*

3

Alone, I write farewell within this book,
*   The summer sun is streaming o'er the park;*
Oh, for the sunshine of a last fond look
*   Over a heart so dark!*

4

Farewell! I know not if a merry meeting
*   For such a parting e'er shall make amend.*
Harsh words have stung me; is their venom fleeting,
*   Or hurtful to the end?*

The verses are conventional and fairly trite, but they do reflect Willie's hurt at being dispatched so abruptly. Of Katie's parents, Lady Emma was the one who objected to Willie. As the Woods were so liberal, it was hardly that he was a Catholic. Most probably Lady Emma discerned even that early that Willie was irresponsible and unstable. But the main reason for dismissing him seems to have been Katie's changed feelings for him.

While Willie brooded in Spain, Katie gaily went off to Belhus with her parents for an extended visit with her sister and brother-in-law, the Barrett-Lennards. Life at Belhus was always jolly, and there were plenty of visitors to provide stimulating company. That winter John Morley was among them. He was later to become Gladstone's chief lieutenant and to play an important role in the Parnell drama. The kindly Woods found conversation with this brilliant, intense young man very wearing indeed. So Emma hit on the idea of palming him off on her young sister, saying, 'You, dear Katie, don't matter, as no one expects you to know anything!'

So the 'fool of the family', as Katie called herself, invited the genius to walk in the park with her, and found that she could quite easily engage him in conversation. 'With the ready tact of the really clever, he could already adapt himself to great or small, and finding me simply ready to be interested, was most interesting, and I returned to my family happily conscious that I could now afford to ignore my brother Evelyn's advice to "look lovely and keep your mouth shut!" '

But things were soon to change drastically for the Woods.

While the family were at Belhus, Sir John died. Katie nursed him night and day during a lingering illness, and held his hand as he took his last breath. Afterwards she seems to have had some sort of nervous collapse. She tells us in her memoirs that a sedative was poured down her throat, and she awoke to see Willie and her sister looking down at her. To her delight, Willie took a white King Charles spaniel out of his pocket. She seems to have been more delighted by the dog, however, than by the sight of Willie. 'I was too much worn out and miserable to wonder at the presence of Willie, whom I believed to be in Madrid, but contented myself with curling round in bed with my new treasure.'

Later she learned that her mother and Anna had telegraphed for Willie to come from Spain. In those days it would have taken several days to travel so far, but if Willie were not considered suitable husband material, why send for him to make a long journey now in Katie's worst hour? Either the Woods lacked consideration for Willie's feelings in the matter, and were using him as the Barrett-Lennards had used him to race their horse – after all, he was gay and amusing and might cheer Katie up. Or else they had changed their minds about him. Given the strict conventions of the day, the second interpretation of the events is the more likely.

Willie returned to Spain almost immediately, and the Woods busied themselves with arrangements for Sir John's funeral. Katie went to Rivenhall and destroyed all his papers, as he had asked her to do. She was afraid of causing a fire by burning them, so she sank them in the lake. She tells us of her state of mind at this time:

> The loss of my father was my first real sorrow, and I wandered miserably around his study, where everything was as he had left it, including the things he had so lately touched – the letter-weight, pressed down on the unanswered letters and those now never to be answered; his sermon case; his surplice folded on his table ready for the next services at the Church, now for him never to take place. I felt that I could not bear the sadness and longing for him, and as soon as I could I returned to the warmer glow of the family circle at Belhus.

There she found considerable talk about money. 'We must sell the cow, and of course, the pig,' her elder sister Emma announced cheerfully. This brought a round of rueful laughter. But, as always, Aunt Ben came to the rescue, settling a yearly income on her sister. Katie spent the next year living quietly with her mother and Anna at Rivenhall. They threw themselves into their writing and generally lived the literary life, inviting many writers and critics to Rivenhall, among them George Lewes, the lover of George Eliot, Mr Chapman of the publishers Chapman and Hall, and various writers from *The Times*.

Katie, however, had no such interest to absorb her, and we can only imagine the sense of loss that would surface when she was not busy helping with the visitors. She had never been her mother's favourite. And she had, after all, lost her best friend and constant companion in her father. Had his death brought on a nervous breakdown? Katie says as much in her memoirs. Certainly it was a difficult age to lose a father. And he had liked Willie. By sending for him, it can plausibly be assumed that her mother had now changed her mind about the feckless Irishman. Why? Was it in some deference to the dead man's memory? Or did she believe that Willie had now abandoned his rakish army ways? Or was it simply that a change in the Wood family fortunes had brought about a changed view of Willie? There was no other suitor in sight. Perhaps he was simply better than nothing? Katie was pretty, but she had no unusual talents. Also she was bereaved and a depression might seriously hinder her future marriage prospects.

At any rate, Katie went with her mother and Anna to stay with Emma at Brighton in the late winter of 1866. And during their visit Willie O'Shea, just returned from Spain, called with his friend Cunninghame Graham. Katie says quite simply, 'I now yielded to Willie's protest at being kept waiting longer and we were married very quietly at Brighton on January 25, 1867.'

She does not sound like a joyful bride.

CHAPTER 4

MARRIAGE

At the time of her wedding, Katie was nearly 22, and by mistake she was almost married to the wrong man. The best man, Cunninghame Graham, was standing in the groom's place, so the vicar asked him, instead of Willie, if he would take this woman to be his wife.

'No, no, no,' said the startled Cunninghame Graham.

So the situation was saved — even if Katie did not in the end marry the right man in Willie.

Willie's Catholicism was always merely social. Although his pious mother and sister disapproved of Katie and did not attend the wedding, it did not appear to cost him anything to marry Katie in a Protestant church. At the time, the English hierarchy did not insist that Catholics had to marry within the Church. Their souls were not damned so long as some of the children were brought up as Catholics. Often in a mixed marriage, if the father were Catholic and the mother Protestant, the boys would be brought up Catholic and the girls Protestant. But Katie agreed to all of her children being baptised and brought up as Catholics. Certainly, as her father's daughter she was liberal in such matters.

What the Whiggish Woods thought we will never know. Katie does not say in her memoirs if her mother attended the wedding, but some of the Woods definitely did. Anna was a bridesmaid, and Emma gave Katie a trousseau.

Willie was deeply infatuated with his bride. As an Irishman, he would have been considered by the English, if not a parvenu, at least socially inferior to the Woods. But if he were a fortune hunter, he would have done better elsewhere. True, Aunt Ben had settled £5,000 on all of the Wood children, except Evelyn, on marriage, so Katie was coming into a small fortune in today's terms. There was no guarantee, however, of anything more. Katie was only one of a large family, and at that time there was no question of her inheriting more than the others. In addition, Aunt Ben was unpredictable and eccentric. She had, for instance, refused to give Evelyn a marriage settlement because he had married an Irish Catholic in a Catholic church. There is no need, then, to suspect Willie's motives.

Katie's are perhaps another matter. Indeed, reading between the lines of her memoirs, one gets the impression that her little dog, Prince, now meant more to her than Willie. But marriage had its advantages. She had got away from home where her status as the youngest and as an unmarried daughter was low. Marriage would also give her some independence and a place in society.

Whatever Katie was later to feel about Willie, in the early days of the marriage she certainly came to love him. Indeed, she seems whole-heartedly to have enjoyed the prospect of her new life, and she was quite childishly delighted with the wedding presents. An Aunt H had given her a gold and turquoise bracelet, and Anna, who was not at all wealthy, a carbuncle locket with a diamond centre. Katie was especially touched by Anna's gift, but she says in her memoir, 'Willie merely remarked of it: "That is lovely, darling, and this," taking up Aunt H's bracelet, "this will do for the dog," snapped it round the neck of my little Prince.' Later, much to their chagrin, the O'Sheas forgot to take the bracelet off the dog when they visited the same aunt.

Honeymoons are often an anti-climax because people expect too much, or they are tired out after all the fuss of the wedding, or they are simply not yet used to each other. The O'Sheas' honeymoon was no exception. Katie was too much the Victorian to say anything about their sexual relationship in her memoir, but she was bored. A friend had lent them his house, but she says, 'it was a kindness which proved unkind.' As it was January, the weather was too bad to go out, and Willie was too much in awe of conventions to invite anyone to visit and cheer them up. Also, the large retinue of servants got on Katie's nerves. 'I think that no two young people,' she wrote, 'were ever more rejoiced than we were when we could return to the life of the sane without comment.'

It was surely a bad omen for the future.

Before marrying, Willie had sold his army commission for £4,000, and his Uncle John now promised a partnership in his Spanish bank if Willie would invest in it. Willie agreed, and he and Katie immediately set out for a new life in Madrid. On the way, they stopped in London where, Katie says, the Comtesse O'Shea and her daughter Mary were staying:

> They were very nice and kind, and so gently superior that at once I became politely antagonistic. They brought me some beautiful Irish poplins which were made into gowns to wear in Madrid to impress the Spanish cousins, and a magnificent emerald bracelet, besides £200 worth of lovely Irish house-linen. My mother-in-law and sister-in-law were most generous indeed, and I then, and always, acknowledged them to be thoroughly good kind-hearted women, but so hidebound with what was, to me, bigotry, with conventionality and tactlessness, that it was really a pain to me to be near them. They admired me, and very plainly disapproved of me; I admired them for their Parisian finish (for want of a better term) and for their undoubted goodness, but, though I was rather fond of Mary, they wearied me to death.

On the crossing to Boulogne Katie was ill, so they had to remain there for several days before going on to Paris. Here Willie displayed the conventionality and jealous possessiveness which was to be so prominent an aspect of his early relationship with Katie. Both qualities had appeared before: the conventionality on his honeymoon, and the jealousy when he kissed her publicly in front of the officers' mess at Purfleet. At Boulogne, he wanted to go out to *déjeuner*, but Katie was too ill to accompany him. Accordingly, he ordered her food to be brought to her room by a maid. However, in France room service was customarily by a waiter; and, rather than let a man enter Katie's room in his absence, Willie locked the door. He had just gone out when the waiter unlocked the door and brought in a tray, saying, 'Madame should eat and recover herself'. When Willie returned, he was annoyed to discover the waiter taking her tray away. The incident is unimportant in itself, but it indicates Willie's basic stupidity.

In Paris, the antagonism between Katie and her in-laws flared into a row. While sightseeing, Katie insisted on bringing Prince, her dog, everywhere with her, even into Notre Dame cathedral. The other two women had not noticed the little dog hidden under her cloak, but when Katie let him down again outside, the Comtesse was horrified.

'You took the dog into the *church*! Oh Katie, how wrong, how *could* you? Mary! What shall we do? Do you not think − ?' and turning a reproachful glance on me, Mary responded. 'Come, mother,' and, leaving me amazed and indignant on the steps, they passed into Notre Dame again. With some curiosity I peeped in after them, and beheld them kneeling at prayer just inside the door. They came out almost at once, and the old Comtesse looked happier. 'You did not understand, dear,' said Mary kindly, 'it is better not to take the little dog into a church.' I was young enough to resent being told I did not understand, and promptly returned, 'I understand, Mary, that you and the Comtesse consider it wicked to take Prince into Notre Dame. Well, I don't, and you must excuse me if I remind you that God made the dog; and I seem to remember something about a Child that was born in a stable with a lot of nice friendly beasts about, so you need not have gone back to pray about me and Prince, I think!' And, scooping up Prince, I stalked off with a dignity that was rather spoilt by my not having sufficient French to find my way home, and having to wait at the carriage for them. We drove home with much stiffness, and only thawed sufficiently to assure Willie how much we had enjoyed ourselves!

It is little wonder that the spirited Katie did not get along with her pious in-laws, but in fairness the dog does sound like one of those pampered little yappers heartily hated by all except its doting owner. Katie's new

French maid, Caroline, apparently spent as much time brushing and washing Prince as she did attending her young mistress. Afterwards the dog would be rewarded by having a pale blue ribbon tied around his neck for staying still.

After Paris, the young couple set out for Biarritz on their way to Spain. On the way Katie fell ill again, coming down with whooping cough and pneumonia. She was nursed back to health by a hotel chambermaid, a young Basque girl who was so devoted that Katie gave her a ring from her finger before she left.

While she was recuperating the Duc de San Luca, one of Willie's relatives, called on them, and he too came under Katie's spell. They also met Willie's old schoolfriend Wilfrid Scawen Blunt who recorded in his diary that, while Katharine was attractive, he still did not like Willie with his 'pretentious, affecting, English ways'.

Madrid was to captivate Katie, but when they first arrived, travel-weary and dusty, Willie's fussing Spanish relatives proved too much for her, and even Prince responded grumpily to their cheerfulness. However, Willie at last dragged them away and left Katie to sleep in her hotel bedroom. The next morning she was up early and, ignoring Willie's warning that 'Only the English and dogs go out in the day,' went downstairs and ordered herself a big breakfast. Then she went out to explore the deserted streets, finding the pavements warmer than England on a hot summer's day but the air not as 'breathless'. She ended up cooling off in the Prado Gallery where she could delight in being alone as it was the unfashionable time of day 'for walking'.

The next day a party was given in her honour, and indeed Madrid proved to be one round of parties. Life for Katie was suddenly filled with colour and spectacle. She admired the beauty of the O'Shea women and the charm of the men – even if she was curious about their odd Spanish table manners. John O'Shea turned out to be charming and witty, but an incurable gambler, and thus a great trial to his wife and family. Fortunately, he was lucky and did not lose too much money. His greatest fear was of getting cholera, and Katie was warned not to mention it in front of him. 'A necessary warning,' Katie tells us, 'as rumours of cholera were as prevalent in that year as those of the expected revolution. . . .'

Indeed, the political situation in Spain was like a time bomb set to go off. Katie and Willie were once even caught in crossfire as a mini-revolution broke out. But on the whole the unrest did not affect them. Katie may have marvelled at the weeds growing untidily in the Queen's courtyard, but otherwise life ran smoothly. Her days were filled with parties to attend, the engagement of a cousin, and on Shrove Tuesday a pancake feast under the trees at the Prado. Of that feast, she writes:

The oil was of the rankest, and the smell horrible, but I managed to eat a pancake to please my Catholic friends. It was a very interesting scene, the well-dressed people and the peasants all mingled together eating the greasy pancakes that they would not have touched at their own table. Beautiful women in their soft draperies and white and black lace mantillas, the waving fans and the handsome dress of the peasants made an animated picture I have never forgotten.

Katie and Willie's favourite walk was to the Retiro gardens with its acacia trees and wild flowers. There they saw Spanish children playing, and Katie remarks, 'Willie, who was fond of children, used to wish that he might have many, though I was too young to find them interesting.' There was as yet no sign of Katie becoming pregnant, but that was not a cause of any anxiety to the young couple. In fact, they seem to have been idyllically happy.

Then they had their first quarrel.

An elderly Spaniard had for some time paid attention to Katie. At first she took his compliments and gifts as the tiresome and unwelcome attentions of an old bore. But, one evening at the Prado, he suggested that Katie should hang a blue ribbon from her balcony as a signal for him to come to her rooms. Katie, highly insulted and furious, told Willie, who had just come up with another woman of their party, to take her home at once. He did but was angry at her abruptness, and, when she told him the reason, he merely laughed and said that she was imagining things. This typical male reaction resulted in a row, and Katie wrote:

> I was very angry, and did not sleep well, and when I rose late in the afternoon of the following day I found that Willie had gone out. I was looking rather mournfully out of my window when I saw the flutter of a blue ribbon on the opposite balcony. For a moment I drew back in disgust, then a happy thought seized me and, dashing into my bedroom, I pulled out several yards of pale blue ribbon which I cut into long lengths. Stepping out on to the balcony, I looked carefully and ostentatiously up and down the street before tying each ribbon to one of the ornamental heads of the balcony. This done to my satisfaction, I threw on my mantilla and ran down-stairs, only stopping to leave a message with the porter to the effect that if the Señor — called he was to be told that Señor O'Shea awaited his visit with pleasure and yards of ribbon on a stick.

Katie spent a carefree day with the O'Shea cousins, and when she came back the ribbons were gone from the balcony and Willie was in a friendlier mood. She never knew what had happened between the two men, but from then on the elderly Don Juan pretended not to see either herself or Willie.

It was not long till the quarrelsome Willie quarrelled again, this time with his uncle. In her memoirs, Katie only says that it was 'some dispute about the business arrangement of Willie's partnership'. But whatever the cause, the result was that the young people were on their travels again, this time back to England.

When Katie and Willie returned, they decided to invest their money in a stud farm. After all, horses were Willie's passion, and Katie had been raised in the country, so horse breeding would be a pleasant occupation. Eventually they found a suitable estate to rent, Bennington Park in the heart of Hertfordshire, about three miles from Stevenage and eight from Hertford. The house was large and comfortable, the grounds were attractive, and there were stables, cottages for the groom and gardener, and the usual endless kitchen gardens, rose gardens and glass houses. It was to be Katie's only real married home, and, when she moved there in the spring of 1868, she says the park was 'a carpet of snowdrops'.

The young couple had high hopes for the success of their venture. Willie had bought some excellent brood mares with names like Alice, Maud, Scent and Apricot, and soon, to Katie's delight, foals began to appear. She spent many happy hours watching them in the meadow and feeding them bowls of warm milk. Life was very pleasant now. Her own pony was sent over from Rivenhall, and would pull her in the pony cart through the lanes of Hertfordshire to return her neighbours' calls. Her old nurse, Lucy – Loolee to the Wood children – came to live with her, and although the old woman was very jealous of Caroline, the French maid, Katie promised she would never again live away from her. Loyalty, as we shall see, was always one of Katie's strongest points.

Around this time some cracks began to appear in the marriage. Willie was now often away from home. In her memoirs, Katie just remarks that he was 'at the races, etc.' What 'etc.' means we will never know. Was it drink? Or women? In all of the abuse and vilification that was later to be heaped upon Katie for her affair with Parnell, no one was ever to say anything about Willie's affairs – although at the time of her divorce in 1890, Katie was to compile a longish list of them. And considering his erratic behaviour, we might safely assume that he was up to something at this stage. For instance, he would insist that Katie invite people to dinner and then inexplicably not turn up himself. Or he would accept invitations to dinner parties but then make her go on her own – a habit much frowned upon by the stodgy Hertfordshire neighbours.

As she was so much alone, Willie did have the decency to suggest that she keep a large retriever dog inside for protection. When it savaged a tramp, however, Katie got rid of it. Willie then bought her a gun, but having a loaded gun in her bedroom made her nervous

until I hit on the happy expedient of getting out of bed and discharging it (in the air) through my always open window the first time I woke in the night. I am sure this had an excellent effect in keeping off wanderers of evil intent, and I heard, to my joy and Willie's, that a gardener courting one of the maids, found 'the Missis a perfect terror with that gun'.

Despite Willie's absences, Katie was to look on Bennington Park as the happiest time of their marriage. She threw herself into work. With Willie rarely there, she had to supervise the stud groom, Selby, and the twenty 'lads' whom Willie had hired at the low wages of the day. There was also the garden to be seen to, the household chores, and sometimes entertaining the friends Willie unexpectedly brought home. There were frequent parties to attend. She writes:

> The chief form of social intercourse in the county was the giving of long, heavy, and most boring dinners. People thought nothing of driving eight or even ten miles (and there were no motor-cars then) to eat their dinner in each other's houses, and this form of entertainment used to produce such an absolutely painful boredom in me that I frequently hid the invitations from Willie, who liked to 'keep up with the county'.

Although Katie complained of boredom, the O'Sheas were popular with their neighbours. Mischievously, she took great delight in mixing prim and conventional young county ladies with Willie's rakish and impoverished racing friends. Sometimes the girls' parents were shocked, and Willie, conventional as usual, urged her to be more careful. But Katie says, 'the girls enjoyed themselves, and that any reasonable human being should enjoy a county dinner party is an achievement of which any young hostess may be proud.'

As well as breeding their own horses, the O'Sheas boarded horses for other owners, and sometimes Katie had to make important decisions on her own:

> One evening, when Willie was away, the stud groom rushed to the house to say that one of the horses, a very valuable stallion named Orestes, belonging to Mr Porter, the trainer, of Alfriston, Sussex, had slipped in his box while being groomed and broken his leg. I sent frantically for several veterinary surgeons, but there was nothing to be done, and I had to give the order to have the horse shot to end his sufferings. I then sat, horribly frightened, awaiting Willie's return, for the stud groom's gloomy reiteration of 'It's your responsibility, ma'am; your responsibility,' was not reassuring. However, Willie, while much upset at the accident, and the necessity for shooting the horse, quite agreed that I had done the only thing possible in the circumstances, as did the owner – Mr Porter.

Her responsibilities at Bennington taught Katie that she had considerable resources. She was, for instance, far more practical than Willie, and she helped keep down the huge expenses of running the stables by sending large quantities of fruit, vegetables and butter into the Hertford weekly market. But her efforts made little impression on the huge debts that Willie was beginning to amass. He was hopeless, Katie tells us, at 'dunning friends' for money owed on stabling their horses. Everything seemed to be going out, and little coming in; and eventually Willie could see no option but to sell his brood mares to try and get out of debt. Katie wrote:

> As I urged against the sale of the mares, which he so often threatened, their happy, peaceful maternity, in the long lush grass and shade of trees by day, their comfortable boxes at night, and their fondness of me, he used to stare gloomily at me and swear gently as he wished there were more profit than peace in their maternity and my sentimentality. But he could forget his worries in the pleasure of schooling the yearlings, and we agreed always to hold on as long as possible to a life we both found so interesting, and with the facile hope of youth we thought to get the better of our expenses in time.

To complicate matters, Katie's eldest surviving brother, Frank, was dying of consumption, and Katie, at his urgent request, went back to Rivenhall to nurse him. She found that he had become a drug addict from the morphine given to relieve his pain. This often happened in Victorian times, as doctors were barely aware of the addictive nature of drugs. With the help of a saintly doctor, Katie nursed her brother through the horrors, often putting 'candles in every window that he might not see the shadows – the terrifying shadows which delirium and continual doses of morphia never failed to produce'.

When Frank died, with typical good-heartedness Katie took his servant back to Bennington. The man, she said, 'was a useless encumbrance, as it turned out, but relieved my mother of his presence at Rivenhall.'

When she returned home, Katie was pregnant. She discovered, also, that while she had been away the feckless Willie, to try to get out of debt, had gone on a gambling spree. Up to this time he had been able to keep the bailiffs at bay by wining and dining the local bank manager. But now that canny man refused to accept any more hospitality and demanded that the overdraft be cleared immediately. There was now nothing for it but to sell the mares, and Katie was miserable:

> As the long string of throughbred mares was led away to the station and I kissed their muzzles for the last time I cried bitterly. Poor Willie watched them go with a miserable face, which became

even more so when a sympathetic old groom explained pitifully: 'Ah, dear ma'am, maybe you'll cry more when they all comes back.' And come back they did, escorted by Tommie, the pony, for not a bid of any importance was made for any of them. Though I was glad to see my favourites again, it of course meant more trouble in the immediate future, our affairs getting into a worse state every day till bankruptcy became imminent.

Then the Woods came to the rescue. Katie's brother-in-law, Sir Thomas Barrett-Lennard, the man who had first introduced her to Willie, bought all of the mares for £500 and turned them into the park at Belhus. With this sum, Willie was able to pay off all of the servants, except the faithful stud groom, Selby, old Lucy and the French maid, Caroline, who decided to throw in their luck with the O'Sheas and the hope of better times ahead. Then Willie declared himself bankrupt, and his goods were seized and sold over his head.

Katie does not moan about the collapse of her hopes and the loss of her home. She only relates how a neighbour 'very kindly' took her pony across the fields at night so that it would not be sold with the rest of their goods.

It was the end of a chapter.

CHAPTER 5

UPHEAVAL

The next four years were unsettled, troublesome and lonely for Katie. Not only did she and Willie move house four times, but he was also increasingly absent. However, after the loss of Bennington, other Wood relatives besides Sir Thomas Barrett-Lennard came to the O'Sheas' aid. Aunt Ben rented them a house beside Emma's in Brighton, and Uncle William, then Lord Chancellor of England, sent a large cheque. However, he politely refused their lawyer's request to find Willie a job. And, indeed, finding a use for Willie's dubious talents is from now on a constant theme in our story.

The first Brighton house was big and expensive. The O'Sheas settled in with Caroline, Lucy and Selby, their three loyal servants. In Victorian times, the duties of household servants were strictly categorised; for instance a lady's maid would never be expected to do housework or to cook, and an outdoor servant would never work in the house. So it says a lot for Katie's charm, and most probably Willie's, that these upper servants cheerfully took on what then would be considered menial duties. They were also to prove invaluable in looking after the O'Sheas' baby son, Gerard, who was born there.

Katie was ill for some time after Gerard's birth and still depressed by the loss of Bennington, all her animals and country life generally, but the baby was a great consolation. She was, in fact, to prove a doting but sensible and conscientious mother to all of her children – at least until the death of Parnell when her own health drastically broke down.

The psychologists tell us that we are the parents to our children that our own parents were to us. If so, then Katie had an excellent role model in her mother, Lady Emma Wood, who came to stay and help her over her first birth. Emma Wood was then 68 years old, but age had neither dimmed nor slowed down this remarkable woman. She was still painting, and during her visit delighted Katie with the present of a water colour. Since her husband's death in 1866, she had published four novels, two of them in three volumes. One, *Sorrow on the Sea*, an exposé of the evils of farming out illegitimate babies to cruel foster mothers – the solution to unwanted pregnancies at the time – had created so much of a stir in 1868 that her conventional brother-in-law,

Baron Hatherly, was appalled and bought up every available copy and burnt them.

In the next nine years Lady Emma was to write six more novels, all in two or three volumes. Lady Emma's granddaughter, Minna Evangeline Bradhurst, Charlie Wood's daughter and the compiler of the Wood family history *A Century of Letters*, describes Emma Wood's table in the window of the Rivenhall Library as being 'blackened by age and somewhat old'. In her book Mrs Bradhurst remembers a visit to Rivenhall and draws this picture of Emma Wood around this time:

A soft mist hovers over the emerald carpet of the park, the trees, bare of leaves, are outlined like lace against the grey sky. Two children race their ponies towards the stone porch of the Georgian house.

At the sound of their gay voices an old lady hurries out. Her smooth white hair is parted on one side and looped round her small ears. A maul stick is in one hand and palette and brushes in the other; her blue eyes sparkle as she stands in the portico and waves to the boy and girl, signalling them to gallop past her to the lake to show off their steeds. This is my most vivid recollection of my grandmother, Lady Wood. How proud we used to be as my father on his hunter joined us, with a whispered 'sit up', which was strictly obeyed, and we galloped together from the lake, past the porch, to the stables where we put up our ponies before going indoors. I can see her when the times came to say good-bye, standing at the door of her beautiful old home watching us as we rode over the park out into the highway, and left her in the dusk and grey mists with the moon rising behind the trees.

Mrs Bradhurst goes on to descibe daily life at Rivenhall:

Grandmamma and Aunt Anna were busy people; both wrote many successful novels, which stole so much of their time that they used to call them their 'bandits'. We never stayed to tea when we drove over, and as we were leaving used to look with great interest at two large blue china bowls of milk on the tea-table, for them to skim off the cream as they wanted it into their cups. The cook Fanny's voice screaming, 'Yes, Miladi,' 'No, Miladi,' down the long stone passages seems to echo in my ears sometimes to-day. Fanny was kind and would sometimes take us to see some of grandmamma's smaller pictures, which were very finely executed in water-colour. Little velvet curtains on tiny brass rods were hung in front of them to keep them from fading. The subjects were mostly classical. One was 'Actaeon surprising Diana and her Nymphs', which Fanny used to call 'Diana and her daughters'. We wondered why grandmamma laughed when we repeated this scandal of the chaste goddess.

As a goodbye gift grandmamma would give us pink fondants out of a blue satin box painted with pink roses, wrapping them in half-sheets of her thick white gold-edged notepaper. We began to wish for them as soon as we arrived.

Emma Wood had never made any secret of her ambivalance about Willie. She, after all, had sent him packing only five or so years before in London. At that time she had considered him to be irresponsible and, without a job, unsuitable husband material. Whatever the reason for her change of heart in agreeing to the marriage, now, with the loss of Bennington and his continual absences, she could have had the satisfaction of being right in her initial doubts. While it is unlikely that a woman of her character would gloat, the growing frostiness between herself and Willie can easily be imagined. Indeed, there is evidence to support the theory that while visiting at the time of Gerard's birth, she tried to influence Katie to leave Willie once and for all, and that Katie's refusal drove a wedge between mother and daughter, or at least drove Katie to side with Willie. Lady Emma wrote to a friend, 'Katie did not pay me the compliment of leaving O'Shea. He only gets there once a week.'

No doubt Lady Emma was right, but it is easy to be right, and the human reality is often more complex that any simple 'right' solution would suggest. For one thing, it is never easy for any woman anywhere to leave her husband. To do so is to admit failure in one of life's biggest decisions. And Katie was proud. Moreover her best quality was her loyalty, and it still went to Willie. Besides, she was a Victorian, and a Victorian middle-class woman's only social outlet was through her husband; a single woman was regarded at best as a liability, and at worst as a bit of a joke. A husband was also a married woman's sole source of income. As the Married Women's Property Act did not become law until 1882, any money she might have had in her own right automatically became his on marriage. It is true that divorce had been available to women since 1857, but they did not have equal rights with men in a divorce suit until 1923. Thanks to the sufferings of Caroline Norton in being denied access to her children, the law regarding custody of infants had been changed as far back as 1839. So if Katie could *prove* that Willie had deserted her and that *he* was in the wrong, she might possibly have been granted custody of her child – as long as the child was under 7. In 1873, the age of the child in question went up to 16, and in 1886 the actual welfare of the child began to be considered. But in 1870, when Lady Emma was pressing Katie to leave Willie, the father was the sole legal guardian of the child, and this was to be the law until the Guardianship Act of 1973.

And even if Katie had got custody of Gerard, how was she going to support him? It was hard enough as it was to get money out of Willie. At present they were living on donations from her relatives. All of their money, which consisted of Willie's inheritance from his father, the cash from the sale of his army commission, and Aunt Ben's marriage settlement on Katie, had been lost in the Bennington venture. Probably Katie would manage well enough living apart from Willie. Her relatives would come to the rescue again. But where would she go? Back to Rivenhall to be in the power of her mother? And what would she do there? In those stuffy Victorian times, the only acceptable job for a woman of her class was as a governess or a companion, or a few women might succeed as artists. However, Katie had not the talent of her sister Anna, and her education had been too patchy and haphazard to take on the education of others. And, after all, how could she be a companion with a small child of her own to look after? Although she was lucky enough to have her maid Caroline and her old nurse Lucy, Katie was not the sort of woman to give others total control of her children. So the only role in life allowed her was that of 'angel in the house'.

This was the situation of all middle- and upper-class women. Working-class women had, of course, always worked outside the home, but they could not vote; only single, propertied women had some municipal suffrage. It was to take another fifty years and a horrific world war before all women of all classes could both vote and work. Their status was to change gradually, and emancipation to come through different avenues. As Raymond Chapman says in *The Victorian Debate*:

> Emancipation was gained not only by the few who campaigned directly for it. It came largely from the achievements of women who showed they could outdo men in every field, who overcame the supposed inferiority of women simply by ignoring it. Emancipation was the gift to their sex of women as diverse in accomplishment as Florence Nightingale, Harriet Martineau, Mary Kingsley and Mrs Humphrey Ward. It also owed something to the growing popularity of the Queen, who had no patience with it at all.

Katie's attitude to emancipation was probably not far different from the Queen's. Although she was to behave unconventionally in a conventional age, she was no trailblazer. Like most of her contemporaries, she was class-bound and isolated from the concerns of leading feminists of the age, such as the fight for female suffrage and trade union organisation. And later she was too busy looking after Aunt Ben and her children to volunteer for charitable work. Although in her youth she was close to two of her sisters, she does not seem to have had other close female friends. She was always defined by her relationships with men, first her father, now Willie and later with Parnell. Besides there is one fact that her mother ignored in trying to pry her loose from Willie: Katie still loved her feckless husband. She loved him enough to try and please him in every possible way, even in the way she wore her hair. For instance, as she tells us in her memoirs, at this time the Franco-Prussian War was being waged, and Brighton was full of French emigrés. The foreign women wore their hair braided low on the neck, a style that Willie admired. So, much as she hated the fashion, she bought extra braids of hair to please him.

What Willie was doing in London is not known. Katie does not say in her memoirs, and no letters survive. It is possible that this immature man found married life simply too dull after his rackety, hard-riding, hard-drinking days in the officers' mess. One incident which Katie does describe illustrates the sort of company Willie was keeping. To save Aunt Ben money, the O'Sheas had moved to a cheaper house in Brighton's Marine Parade, and soon afterwards Willie brought a steeplechaser friend and his wife to stay. During dinner the man became ill, and in a few hours was raving in delirium tremens. Katie says that the petrified wife hid in one bedroom while the demented man knocked the doctor flat in another. Was Willie drinking as much as his wild, racing friends? Was this why he stayed so often in London? Although his contemporaries were later to say many terrible things about Willie, no one ever mentioned alcoholism. However, at the time of the divorce Katie did accuse him of being unfaithful with a long list of women.

The O'Sheas soon moved again, this time to Patcham, a village outside Brighton. The other Wood relatives now began to comment on Willie's frequent absences, and Katie herself began to be irritated. To pass the time, she often drove her old pony in to Brighton to see her sister Emma, or she took lonely walks on the downs. On one of these walks, she met a strange woman rider:

> I made her acquaintance, and found her a very congenial companion. Quiet and rather tragic in expression, she thawed to me, and we were becoming warmly attached to one another when Willie, in one of his now flying visits, heard me speak of my new friend. On hearing her name – it was one that a few years before had brought shame and sudden death into one of the oldest of the 'great' families of England – he professed to be absolutely scandalised, and, with an assumption of authority that at once angered me, forbade me to have any more to do with her. He met my protests with a maddening superiority, and would not tell me why she was 'beyond the pale'. I explained to him my own opinion of many of the women he liked me to know and almost all the men, for I had not then learnt the hard lesson of social life, and that the one commandment still rigorously observed by social hyprocrisy was, 'Thou shalt not be found out.'

It was a lesson that Katie was to learn to her cost.

Willie's attitude to the 'strange woman rider' was typical. Anyone who broke the iron moral code was an outcast and unfit company for a 'respectable' woman. The respectable woman was idealised, as was family life. Historians have suggested that one reason for this was the insecurity brought by the decline of religious faith as a result of Darwin's theories about evolution. People had to have something to cling to, so they clung to the solid institution of family life. Now we might watch television together in the evenings, but then a father would read to his family. He took his role as provider and pillar of society seriously. The irony was that, outside family life, he could do as he liked. Indeed, it was almost expected of him. Yet, despite widespread prostitution, prudery pervaded family life.

At Patcham, Katie became more and more depressed and lonely. Finally she suggested to Willie that she and Gerard should join him in London. Surprisingly, he agreed and they moved into a small house on the Harrow Road. In her book Katie states another reason for the move was that they wanted to shake off the unwelcome attentions of a Mr D, a business partner of Willie. When she was quite properly 'not at home' to him, he would leave her expensive presents of Spanish lace which she was tempted to keep.

She tells us:

> This 'Romeo' was more than middle-aged, and, when he wrote that for safety's sake he would address messages to me through the 'agony' column of the newspapers, Willie's wrath was unbounded.
>
> He wrote to poor 'Romeo' in sarcastic vein, alluding to his age and figure, his insolence in addressing 'a young and beautiful woman' with his pestilent 'twaddle'. He told him, too, that he withdrew from all business transactions with him, and would have much pleasure in kicking 'Romeo' if he dared call at the house again. I almost felt sorry for the foolish old man; but it was wasted on him, for he continued, undeterred by Willie's anger, to address 'Juliet' in prose and verse in the daily papers. As he said, the 'Daily Press was open to all, and the Captain could not stop that!' I used to laugh helplessly as Willie opened the morning paper at breakfast, and, first gravely turning to the 'agony' column, would read the latest message to 'Juliet' from her devoted 'Romeo', becoming so angry that breakfast was spoiled to him.

Katie comes across here as girlish and rather silly. But she obviously enjoyed getting her own back on Willie for his infidelities. Otherwise there was not much to be happy about. Harrow Road was to prove another low point in the O'Sheas' fortunes. Not only was the house depressing, with funeral processions passing constantly on the way to Kensal Green cemetery, but Willie developed a lump in his neck which had to be operated on by the doctor with Katie assisting. Gerard also became ill, and Lady Emma wrote to a friend, 'Gerardie is in great danger – Kate's baby – and Kate is half mad with terror'. In addition to having to cope with the sickness of her husband and baby, Katie was short of money for daily household expenses. She describes her dealings with a kindly Jewish moneylender who was so captivated by her that he tore up Willie's IOU notes, saying, 'Don't worry yourself, Captain O'Shea, but pay me when you can, and add six per cent interest if you are able.'

Katie says that they were able to clear their debts within a year, for inexplicably, in 1872, things got better. Katie does not explain how in her memoirs, and there are no clues in *A Century of Letters*, the Wood family history. As the O'Sheas had not yet entered the public arena, we can only assume that Willie, who was always embroiled in some cracked financial scheme, had persuaded some poor unfortunate person to invest in one of them. In any event, the result of improved fortunes was another house move, this time to Beaufort Gardens in Chelsea. The faithful groom, Selby, left the O'Sheas now, realising that the Captain was not going back into horses, but Caroline stayed to reign over a staff of new maids.

They were now back in the social swirl of smart dinner parties on which Willie thrived, but which Katie detested. Willie would even employ a French hairdresser to come in and dress her hair for a party, but Willie's concern often only lasted until the party was over when he would leave her home and go out again to 'finish up the night'. Katie's one small solace at this time was that she finally won the hair war.

> One evening when we were going out to some stupid function Cunninghame Graham came in, looked at my hair, and cried aghast, 'Do take it down, Youngest. You look awful!' As my own conviction was similar I lost no time in doing so, and afterwards used Cunninghame's opinion in defence of my own personality.

In these years the O'Sheas entertained many visitors from France and Spain whom the gregarious Willie had met through London embassies. They also saw a lot of Anna, now a successful author, who had rented a house at Buckingham Gate. Willie surprisingly got on very well with Anna, and she and Katie were later to fall out seriously over this. It was a pity because Katie was to need her sister. An indication of their early closeness is that *Gardenhurst*, Anna's first novel, is dedicated to 'My Sister Katie (Mrs O'Shea)'. This novel, which had been published in 1867, was quite a success and ran into several editions. Although it was considered her best work at the time, it is typical of the middle-brow, romantic Victorian woman's novel in which the saintly heroine suffers and suffers, and suffers. This genre was also favoured by Caroline Norton and countless other women writers. Like theirs, Anna's characters in *Gardenhurst* are one-dimensional stereotypes. They are either unbelievably good or unbearably bad. A wicked husband dies and then inconveniently turns up alive. An angelic lover, who is ridiculously accident-prone, fails to turn up with fatal results for the heroine. The minor characters, however, provide an interesting insight into the Woods' family life. The setting is somewhere in 'X—shire', and most obviously Rivenhall. There is a mother who paints, a father who retires into his study at the first whiff of trouble, a rich and crotchety old aunt who likes to read Greek, a brother who gambles, and a sister who has to fetch and carry for him. There are also constant money troubles, hopes of an inheritance, and a heroine who sings beautifully in the drawing room. It was all very familiar.

Another of Anna Steele's novels, *Lesbia*, is much better in structure and characterisation. It was not published until 1896, several years after Katie's own divorce, and attempts to say something serious about the role of women in Victorian marriage. The heroine, Lesbia, is a flighty butterfly who is torn between her loyalty to her dull, hard-working husband and her infatuation for a supercilious lover with the unlikely name of Lord Ulick O'Neill. In the end, after much melodrama, she chooses the better man, her husband, and he in turn learns something about the fallible nature of women.

Whether Anna and Willie had an affair at this time, or later, or ever, is unclear. Certainly Anna lent a sympathetic ear to Willie's complaints about Katie, but certainly also Katie and Willie were now still sleeping together. Two more children were born in Beaufort Gardens, Norah in January 1873, and Carmen in August of the following year.

In the period following Norah's birth Katie thought seriously about becoming a Catholic, but finally rejected the idea. To get away from Willie, she would go for long walks in the London parks, and on the way home would drop into the Brompton Oratory 'for a few minutes peace and rest of body and soul'. However, like many Anglicans of the time, she seems to have been more attracted to the ritual of the Catholic Church than to its doctrine. Also she tells us:

> I had before me two types of Catholic in Willie and his mother and sister, and both were to me stumbling-blocks. The former was, as I knew, what they call a 'careless Catholic', and I thought that if he who had been born in that faith that means so much, made so little of it, perhaps it was more of a beautiful dream than a reality of life. Yet when I turned and considered those 'good Catholics', his mother and sister, I found such a fierce bigotry and deadly dullness of outlook, such an immense piety and so small a charity, that my whole being revolted against such a belittling of God-given life.

So when Carmen, her youngest daughter, was baptised, Katie did not go into the Oratory for the ceremony but waited in the porch, feeling 'that my children were taken from me and that I was very lonely'.

By now Willie's neglect of Katie was the subject of gossip and even open comment among her relatives. Her uncle, Baron Hatherly, the Lord Chancellor, often invited the O'Sheas to functions. Willie would always find an excuse to wriggle out of these, but insisted on Katie going 'perfectly gowned'. There, she tells us, relatives would remark, much to her chagrin, 'Dear Katie, alone again! Poor, dear girl, where does he go? How odd that you are so often alone – how little you know!'

And, to make matters worse, her Aunt Charlotte would always greet her with eyes shut and head to one side, saying, 'Poor dear! Poor lovely lamb!'

However, despite Katie's disintegrating marriage, there were some compensations in life. Her favourite sister, Emma, had taken a house in London for the season, as her daughter had reached a marriageable age, and Katie found great consolation in her own children.

The winter after Carmen's birth, 1874–5, was bitterly cold, and Katie's health became a cause of anxiety. In her memoirs she says she was threatened by consumption, then a killer disease, but it is more likely she was having some sort of nervous collapse. Aunt Ben's doctor recommended opium injections, but her own doctor luckily interfered, saying, 'The man's mad, or wants to get rid of you!' After a conference, it was decided that the family should go to the Isle of Wight so that Katie could recuperate in the slightly warmer southern climate. As Willie was again typically short of money, faithful Aunt Ben sent a cheque to cover expenses. At first the family stayed in a hotel where they had a happy Christmas. But to save money Willie soon moved Katie and the children into lodgings at Ventnor, and then, as the place was too dull for him, he fled back to London.

At Ventnor, Katie had trouble sleeping due to the stormy weather and the constant fog horns. A local doctor persuaded her to try meat extract instead of drugs for insomnia, and this remedy was so effective that she used it for the rest of her life. But despite getting more sleep, Katie's health did not improve. Willie was 'too busy' to visit her, and she became so depressed by the 'many poor consumptive people' around her that she decided to move nearer home, to Hastings. At this stage, Willie seems to have disappeared completely because Katie's nephew had to escort her and the children and nurses to their new lodgings. However, she says, as soon as Willie heard where she was, he came down.

It was while the O'Sheas were at Hastings that Katie renewed her relationship with her Aunt Ben, who was then 82. As the old woman did not allow gentlemen visitors to stay overnight, the O'Sheas went daily. Katie says that she did not know her aunt very well before, and that as a child she would have been 'wild with terror' at the idea of being left alone with her. But now she was fascinated by the old woman who still dressed in the 'fashions of her early Victorian youth' and would not allow any noise in her strictly regulated house.

Maria Wood, Aunt Ben, was Emma Wood's older sister. She had married Matthew Wood's wealthy brother, Benjamin, and although the marriage had been very happy, it had to their mutual regret been childless. Consequently, Benjamin was always helping his brother's family and had even considered adopting one of them. After his death, Aunt Ben had scrupulously carried out his last wishes and continued to help.

She now lived alone except for her servants and was regarded locally as an eccentric recluse. Although not talented like her sister Emma, she was a great intellectual and well read in several European languages. Katie says that up to the last week of her life she translated Greek verse. Describing the pleasure this gave her, Aunt Ben wrote in a letter to a friend, 'No one with whom I associate cares about a passage in Homer or in Greek tragedy and the interest I feel in puzzling over them is so unparticipated, so unassisted and unknown that it must be genuine, and believing it to be so satisfies my conscience when it would reproach me with the inutility of my occupations.'

To have some intellectual company, Maria Wood paid the novelist George Meredith to come to Eltham once a week to read and talk to her. There are different accounts of what she paid him – Katie says it was £300, Wood family tradition £150. But whatever the amount, the association soon grew into a friendship.

Seemingly Aunt Ben was very strict about her polished floors and people had to hopscotch from rug to rug. However, Meredith did not always obey her instructions, and Katie leaves this account of his visits:

> On days of rebellion against these forms and ceremonies he would hesitate for a moment just inside the door, and, with a reckless uplifting of his head, begin a hasty stride across the sacred places; a stride which became an agitated tip-toeing under the scandalised gaze of the footman. Before he began to read to my aunt the following dialogue invariably took place: –
>
> 'Now, my dear lady, I will read you something of my own.'
>
> 'Indeed, my dear Mr Meredith, I cannot comprehend your works.'
>
> 'I will explain my meaning, dear Mrs Wood.'
>
> 'You are prodigiously kind, dear Mr Meredith, but I should prefer Molière today.'

Readers of his novels today, with their convoluted style, might well agree with Aunt Ben's opinion.

There are many other stories about Aunt Ben's staunch individuality. Although, for instance, she subscribed generously to charities and encouraged her servants in religious belief, she herself was an agnostic. Once, when a local clergyman offered to read her the scriptures, she replied, 'I thank you, Mr —, but I am still well able to read, and the Scriptures do not interest me.'

And when asked if she did not wish to go to heaven, she replied tartly, 'Not if it is inconveniently crowded.'

According to Wood family tradition, one morning her maid asked if she would please go down the back stairs to her breakfast. When Aunt Ben insisted on knowing why, the maid had to tell her that the cook had hanged herself over the front stairs and that the body was still there. Aunt Ben merely said, 'Why should I go down the back stairs because my cook has committed a crime? Go and cut down poor Sarah.'

The same rather grim sense of reality led her to keep her coffin in readiness outside the back door of her house. And when she heard that her nephew, Evelyn, who acted as her almoner towards the end of her life, had given money to a house for incurables, she was angry and said, 'They do but cumber the earth and are useless.'

A less tough but more eccentric characteristic was her fear of heights. To conquer it, she always walked down the stairs backwards. Indeed, even getting her into her coach for her daily drive was quite a ritual. As there were steep steps from her hall down to the drive, she had a narrow bridge built, one end of which rested on the top step and the other in the carriage. On the drive she would sit bolt upright looking neither to right nor to left.

However, Katie tells the story of how one day, returning from the drive, Aunt Ben said to the coachman, 'I observed that you and Henry saluted a lady during our airing.'

'Yes, ma'am, the Empress Eugenie, ma'am.'

'Never do that again, Frost. I forbid my servants to salute that lady.'

In Aunt Ben's legitimist view, the emigrée Empress Eugenie was but an upstart. However, her hauteur could extend also to officials of the crown. Her home, Eltham Lodge, which was surrounded by beautiful countryside, was the property of the crown, and the house was one of the finest examples of the Wren style of English domestic architecture. Aunt Ben held the lease for life, but several times there were efforts made to move her. On the occasion of the marriage of the Duke of Connaught, a deputation came to suggest that she terminate her tenancy so that the house could be offered to the Duke and his bride.

She received the deputation in her large upstairs drawing room which was sparsely furnished but hung with magnificent tapestries. While she sat at one end in her high-backed chair, they had to walk the bare length of the highly polished floor. Greatly awed, they delivered their message, and when they were finished she asked if that were all?

'Yes', mumbled the foreman.

'Gentlemen,' she said with great deliberation, 'it seems to me that you shelter yourselves behind the fact that you are a corporation and therefore have neither a body to be kicked nor a soul to be damned. Good morning.'

Aunt Ben was intelligent, acerbic and, above all, very rich. Still it is unlikely that Katie, whom she always called her 'Swan', was fortune hunting by visiting so frequently. More likely she was both attracted by the old woman's personality and grateful for so much immediate help with money.

As Aunt Ben was childless, Katie often brought her children, probably thinking they would cheer the lonely old woman up. However, Aunt Ben regarded children as 'immature little animals' and wrote to a friend, 'Dear Swan seemed to expect me to kiss the infant, so I did, but had to go upstairs afterwards and rinse out my mouth and nostrils, as I like not the odour of milk.'

Perceptive as she was, it is likely that Aunt Ben quickly saw through Willie. She wrote to a friend, 'The irrevocability of the marriage vow makes it frightful, unless there be every chance of it being always considered a silken cord instead of a rusty chain.' However, even if Katie had wanted to leave Willie at this time, for which theory – despite what she wrote in old age – there is no proof, Aunt Ben was so proper and so conventional about morality that she would probably not have countenanced it. Instead, soon after the O'Sheas' first visit, she proposed to make Katie's tie a silken cord by suggesting the following arrangement: in return for Katie's companionship in her old age, Aunt Ben would buy her a house, pay her a regular salary and educate her children. Katie says that the suggestion was made when Aunt Ben saw how alone she was with Willie always away, trying to make money, but Lady Emma might have sown the seed. It was her style. But whoever suggested that Katie be Aunt Ben's companion, the arrangement suited everyone and was legally contracted. What nobody realised, however, was that it was to last for the next fifteen years.

Wonersh Lodge, the house Aunt Ben bought for Katie, was just across the park from Eltham Lodge, and, so that Katie could have easier access to her, the old woman had a gate built between the two properties. Eltham is only eight miles from central London, but in 1875 it was a small country town with a few shops in the High Street. Wonersh Lodge, which Katie described as a 'comfortable villa', was built in the 1860s and seems typical of the solid redbrick Victorian family houses being built at the time all over the suburbs of London. There were four reception rooms downstairs, as well as a large conservatory which Katie later gave over to Parnell. The front garden was small, but the back bigger with stables at the end. Aunt Ben also furnished the house, so Katie and the children were very comfortable and delighted in their new-found space. As well as having the run of a bigger house, the children now had the whole of Eltham Park to play in.

Although neither of the O'Sheas considered that their marriage was yet over, Willie had now quite cavalierly abdicated his financial responsibilities for his family. He had always been willing to accept money from Katie's family, but up to this time had kept up certain pretences of independence. Now all pride seemed to be gone, and, although at first he spent a lot of time in Wonersh Lodge with his family, he was soon off to London again, this time to persuade friends to invest in yet another scheme, a Spanish mining business. Katie remained the devoted mother and divided her time between Aunt Ben and the children. Gerard was now five, but Norah and Carmen were still babies of two and one. However, thanks to Katie's new independence, there was no problem about employing help.

Life went on evenly for a few years until Norah came down with scarlet fever and diphtheria. In those days both were highly infectious killer diseases, so Katie immediately dispatched the other two children to their grandmother in Paris, and asked Willie to stay in London to avoid infection. Then she nursed Norah with such devotion that she became ill herself. However, both mother and daughter eventually recovered and went to Folkestone to recuperate. There they were joined by Gerard and Carmen. As Katie later wrote:

> The two children had been away from me for some months, and I hastened on to the steamer to greet them. I laughed as I caught sight of the very formal little Frenchman into which they had turned my sturdy young son and, ignoring his polite lifting of his hat in greeting, had in two minutes rumpled him into the noisy, rough little sinner whom I loved. My little Carmen was more difficult. She looked like a little fairy in her French frills and laces, and bitter weeping was the result of my trying to take her from her nurse. This exquisite little mortal did not thaw to me for some days, but with the help of Elfie, the collie, I gradually won her affections from the Paris of her baby-heart.

Motherhood was always very important to Katie, but Aunt Ben also needed her, and she says she was glad to get back to the old woman. From now on, she began to realise, the children would be with their governess and would have less need of her. Indeed, around this time, Gerard proved to be too difficult to teach at home, so he was sent to boarding school at Blackheath. At the time he was only eight and two years younger than the usual acceptance age at the school. Katie describes him as a 'gusty child' in her memoirs, and from an early age this boy had serious temper tantrums, throwing himself down in the middle of London traffic or down the stairs at home. Now, with Willie continually absent, he must have been even more difficult. Still, Katie must have missed him when he went to school. He was, after all, her firstborn child and only son.

Willie, meanwhile, had been successful in getting investors for his Spanish mining business. That he did testifies to his considerable charm and persuasive powers. One of the investors was the wealthy Christopher Weguelin, an old friend from the happier days of the Belhus Dramatic Corps. Tim Healy, the man who was later to lead the fight against Parnell, claimed that at the time of the divorce in 1890,

O'Shea presented letters to his solicitors in which Katie had written, 'You did not object to Christopher,' and to which Willie had replied, 'Christopher is dead. Parnell is not.' However, as Joyce Marlow points out, 'these particular letters were not produced in evidence and have not proved traceable.' She thinks, as do I, that there is no solid evidence for the accusation that Katie was unfaithful to Willie before she met Parnell. Infidelity was not in her character, and in any case the risk of pregnancy was too great then. And the accusation came from two quite unreliable sources – Healy, who was vehemently biased against Katie, and Wilfrid Scawen Blunt, who was much too careless about simple facts to be given much credence.

Even after Katie began to dislike Willie, she retained a good deal of wifely loyalty. So if she was seeing a lot of Christopher Weguelin at this time, it is more likely that she was doing it for the benefit of Willie's mining company. To his delight, as he loved life abroad, he was sent to Spain as manager at a high salary. Consequently, he had to rely on Katie to arrange contracts and orders for machinery from London companies, and she threw herself into the matter with her usual enthusiasm.

Unfortunately, the venture failed, and Willie returned to Eltham. Katie says that she was pleased to see him again, but she also realised how incompatible they now were. They mutually agreed, then, that he would have permanent rooms in London and visit her and the children at weekends. The weekends soon dwindled into mere Sundays when he came regularly to take the children to Mass at Chislehurst.

However, Willie urged Katie to come to London and host dinner parties for him. As always, she found entertaining and being entertained intensely boring, but her willingness is further proof of her loyalty and of some lingering affection between them. On one occasion, Willie bullied her into accepting an invitation to a ball. Accordingly she went to Thomas's Hotel in Berkeley Square, her childhood haunt, to meet him. Typically he forgot about the appointment and did not turn up until the next morning.

Having failed hopelessly at everything he had so far attempted, Willie decided in 1880 to run for a seat in Parliament as a member for County Clare. He had inherited land there, and the present member for the county, an old man called the O'Gorman Mahon, is credited with having persuaded Parnell, the Irish leader, to accept Willie. The O'Gorman Mahon was now nearly 80 and had been elected to Parliament at the time of O'Connell. Before Parnell, Daniel O'Connell was Ireland's greatest leader. He is called 'The Liberator' because, without shedding a drop of blood, he persuaded the English Parliament to grant Catholic Emancipation in 1829. Basically this gave Catholics equal rights with Protestants, allowing them to vote and to enter Parliament. It opened the way to men like Willie O'Shea and the O'Gorman Mahon who did not belong to the ascendancy class. The O'Gorman Mahon had also been a soldier of fortune under many flags and a personal friend of several European kings and princes, including the Czar of Russia. As Jules Abels says in *The Parnell Tragedy*, 'He was a conqueror of hearts, too, and had fought for love as well as honor, informing Gladstone on one occasion that he had fought twenty-two serious duels in all of which he was the aggressor.'

Willie wrote to Katie to find out what she thought of the idea. He would like it all right, he said, but would the expenses be too much for them to manage? Katie writes quite frankly in her memoirs, 'I wrote back, strongly encouraging him to stand, for I knew it would give him an occupation he liked and keep us apart – and therefore friends.'

With the help of the O'Gorman Mahon, Willie was easily elected. However, the old man had not a shilling to his name, and so Willie, with typical extravagance, guaranteed the election expenses of both. It was now Katie's job to try and get the money out of Aunt Ben, but as always the old woman paid up without complaining. Seemingly she would pay anything to have her 'Swan' by her side. She also had to fork out for Willie's London rooms, and, as salaries for Members of Parliament were not proposed in the House of Commons until 1911, Katie most probably had to supplement him out of her salary from Aunt Ben. But at least Willie was now busy and out of her hair. Now she might at last have some peace. But peace was to prove not enough. As an old woman, she was to describe her feelings at this time:

> Why should I be supposed to have no other interests than Willie and my children? Willie was not, as a matter of fact, at all interesting to me. As to my children, I loved them dearly but they were not old enough, or young enough, to engross my whole mind. Then there was dear old Aunt Ben, who was so old that she would not tolerate any topic of conversation of more recent date than the marriage of Queen Victoria. What a curiously narrow life was mine, I thought, narrow, narrow, narrow, and so deadly dull.

It was the plight of so many women of the time. The Victorian pieties of hearth and home were obviously not enough. Women, like men, needed to have their minds and bodies challenged in some useful work. And Katharine was no exception. She was utterly bored. It was time for the entrance of the hero of the drama, Charles Stewart Parnell.

CHAPTER 6

PARNELL

In the early pages of *A Portrait of the Artist as a Young Man*, James Joyce describes how a genial Christmas dinner in Ireland suddenly degenerated into a ferocious political argument.

> At the door Dante turned round violently and shouted down the room, her cheeks flushed and quivering with rage:
>   – Devil out of hell! We won! We crushed him to death! Fiend!
> The door slammed behind her.
>   Mr Casey, freeing his arms from his holders, suddenly bowed his head on his hands with a sob of pain.
>   – Poor Parnell! he cried loudly. My dead king!

Charles Stewart Parnell, whose final political defeat evoked this angry scene, was the most eminent Irishman of his day and Ireland's most commanding political figure since Daniel O'Connell. His great political triumph was in welding the disparate political factions of his country into one united body in the Westminster Parliament, and then, by concerted pressure, in bringing the Liberal Party to support Home Rule, or the re-establishment of its own Parliament, for Ireland. In the view of many historians, by 1890 Parnell had brought this movement to the very verge of success.

The dramatic fall of Parnell, his hectic struggle to regain control of the Irish Party, and his sudden death in 1891 had at least two profound consequences. Firstly, a vehement and intractable bitterness, which was to last for years and which is ably caught in Joyce's scene, was injected into Irish life. And, secondly, Irish nationalism was reduced to a state of impotence that was to remain unchanged for a quarter of a century, and with effects that are still vividly apparent in the embittered turmoil over Ulster today.

Towards the end of 1889 Parnell was riding the crest of the wave, but on Christmas Eve a petition for divorce was filed in London by Captain O'Shea, citing Parnell as the co-respondent. Less than twelve months later Parnell, as a result of the ensuing scandal, was repudiated by the majority of his party; and the last bitter struggle had begun. The catalyst that toppled the 'uncrowned King of Ireland' was Katharine O'Shea who was to be vilified even to this day under the journalistic sobriquet of 'Kitty O'Shea'.

Katharine first met Parnell on 30 July 1880. Despite the difficulties of their marriage, Katharine was still willing to help Willie however she could. After he had been elected as a Member of Parliament for County Clare, she agreed to arrange a number of political dinner parties for him at Thomas's Hotel in Berkeley Square, to which useful and prominent individuals would be invited. Katharine hated dinner parties but she probably still felt obligated to play the part of wife: it was after all the role to which she had been brought up. But another reason was that life would definitely be much better for her if Willie was occupied and a success. And for this to come about, it was necessary to cultivate the right people. As the leader of the Irish Party, Parnell was sent several invitations which, with his usual casualness about opening his mail, or with his aloof distaste for social functions, he ignored. Finally, when he did accept an invitation, he did not appear, and Katharine was twitted by one of the guests about 'the empty chair'. She then determined that at her next party Parnell would fill that chair.

Accordingly, she and Anna drove to the House of Commons, and she sent in a note, asking Parnell to come out and speak to them. This is how Katie described their first meeting:

> He came out, a tall, gaunt figure, thin and deadly pale. He looked straight at me smiling, and his curiously burning eyes looked into mine with a wonderful intentness that threw into my brain the sudden thought: 'This man is wonderful – and different.'
>
> I asked him why he had not answered my last invitation to dinner, and if nothing would induce him to come. He answered that he had not opened his letters for days, but that if I would let him, he would come to dinner directly he returned from Paris, where he had to go for his sister's wedding.
>
> In leaning forward in the cab to say good-bye a rose I was wearing in my bodice fell out on to my skirt. He picked it up and, touching it lightly with his lips, placed it in his button-hole.
>
> This rose I found long years afterwards done up in an envelope, with my name and the date, among his most private papers, and when he died I laid it upon his heart.

Charles Stewart Parnell belonged to a family that had been in Ireland since shortly after the Restoration, and that had already produced several persons of eminence. The first Parnell in Ireland was Thomas, the son of a mercer and mayor of Congleton in Cheshire. This Parnell, who was possibly a Cromwellian sympathiser, bought an estate in Queen's County and a house in Dawson Street in Dublin.

His first son, also named Thomas, was educated at Trinity College, received a Master of Arts in 1700 and was made Archdeacon of Clogher in County Tyrone in 1706. From 1710 to 1714 he was in London and a supporter of the Tory administration of Harley and Bolingbroke. Accordingly he fell in with Jonathan Swift and his circle, and was one of the five members of the famous Scriblerus club which included Swift, Pope, Gay and Arbuthnot. In 1716, on Swift's recommendation, he was made vicar of Finglas near Dublin, but died only two years later. His poems were collected posthumously and have since appeared in a number of editions, and he is still considered one of the more worthy of the minor eighteenth-century poets. He wrote devotional poetry as well as social verse, and his most famous poem, 'A Night-Piece on Death', may have initiated the school of graveyard verse which became so popular later in the century. By far the least able of the five Scriblerians and quite the most conventional, Thomas Parnell had, nevertheless, an Augustan tightness and control that may be seen in these lines from his 'Night-Piece':

> *The marble tombs that rise on high,*
> *Whose dead in vaulted arches lie,*
> *Whose pillars swell with sculptured stones,*
> *Arms, angels, epitaphs and bones,*
> *There (all the poor remains of state)*
> *Adorn the rich, or praise the great;*
> *Who, while on earth in fame they live*
> *Are senseless of the fame they give.*

Thomas's younger brother John became a barrister, a Member of Parliament, a judge and the great-great-great-grandfather of Charles Stewart. His son, another John, became an MP for Bangor, was created a baronet in 1766, and was described by that astute observer Sir Jonah Barrington as a 'crafty and prudent minor politician'. His son, the third John, however, became, as R. M. Foster remarked, 'Chancellor of the Irish Exchequer, an important Privy Councillor, and one of the most important Irishmen of his day'. Barrington called the second baronet the Incorruptible, and he became something of a national hero for his stand – which caused him to be dismissed from office – against the Act of Union. When Charles Stewart Parnell entered politics in 1874, he took care to remind his audience that:

If I appear before you as an untried man, my name and my family are not unknown in Irish politics. My ancestor, Sir John Parnell, in the old Irish Parliament was the active and energetic advocate of the removal of the disabilities which affected his Catholic fellow-countrymen. In the evil days of corruption he lost a great office and refused a peerage to oppose the fatal measure of Union.

In actuality, The 'Incorruptible' was a strong spokesman for the Irish Protestant landowning class and a vigorous opponent of measures that would alleviate the plight of the Catholic peasantry. In 1792, for instance, he had defended the Penal Laws, and his uncharacteristic opposition in 1800 to the Union was really based on his feeling that the Act would effectively diminish the power of the Protestant landlords. As an Irish patriot, Sir John was an anomaly indeed.

However his third son, William, the grandfather of Charles Stewart, was, in Foster's words, 'as radical a theorist as it was possible for an Irish Protestant landlord to be'. Indeed, Foster suggests that William Parnell may have exerted a considerable indirect influence upon Charles: 'though he died long before his grandson was born, he left behind several provocative pamphlets, an absorbing propagandist novel about Irish rural life, and a considerable reputation as a controversialist.'

Some of Parnell's biographers, such as St John Ervine and Jules Abels, discuss William Parnell only sketchily and do not even mention his able and controversial novel *Maurice and Berghetta, or The Priest of Rahery*, published in 1818. However, this political novel as well as William's various pamphlets investigated the plight of the Irish peasant and suggested remedies for its improvement. For a Protestant landlord to have such empathy and to espouse liberal views that ran quite contrary to the interests of his own class was most unusual; and it is William much more than the incorruptible second baronet who paved the way for Charles Stewart Parnell's own political opinions and career.

Like his predecessors, William was a Member of Parliament, but his son John Henry was basically a private gentleman and a typical Wicklow landowner. John Henry's third son, who was named after him, described him succinctly:

> After his marriage he settled at Avondale as a quiet country gentleman, keeping fine horses and hounds and hunting with all the Wicklow gentry. He was very fond of agriculture, at which he was recognised as an expert, and gave great employment to the people in reclaiming the land at Avondale. He was a prominent magistrate and D. L. for Wicklow. High-tempered when aroused, he was of a quiet disposition as a rule. He was fond of shooting and preserving the game all over the country and had his shooting-lodge at Aughavannagh, an old military barracks in the mountains of Wicklow, where he often went to shoot. He was a very fine cricketer and maintained a first-rate cricket club.

John Henry died in 1859 when his fourth son, Charles Stewart, was 13. However, it may not be far-fetched to say that the private preoccupations of John Henry were as deeply engrained in the character of his most famous son as was the social engagement of his grandfather

William. In Charles Stewart, these antithetical strains were both active. The private individual warred with the public leader. In later days, during the most delicate and absorbing moments of his political life, Parnell could hardly be torn away from the more absorbing contemplation of his sawmill, his mining operations, or even his tinkering with model boats. And in the most personal sense, his love for Katharine saw the triumph of the private man over the public man, and ultimately destroyed his political career. Parnell fought tenaciously at the end to save that career, but, had it ever come down to a choice between the career and the private life, he probably would have thought the world well lost.

His father, John Henry, had diverged from the pattern of the Wicklow landlord in one notable way. He did not marry into one of the county families. On a trip to America which he made with Lord Powerscourt during several months of 1834 and 1835, John Henry met Delia Tudor Stewart whom he was to wed in May 1835. The Tudors had settled in Boston in colonial times, and Delia's grandfather, William Tudor, had studied law with John Adams and become a judge, Advocate General of the Revolutionary Army and Secretary of State for Massachusetts. His son William was editor and proprietor of the prestigious *North American Review*, and his youngest daughter, Delia's mother, married Admiral Charles Stewart, the naval hero of the war of 1812 who was known as 'Old Ironsides'.

Delia Stewart, the daughter of 'Old Ironsides' and Charles's mother, was considered highly eccentric by all who met her, particularly in later life. Indeed it is impossible to find a favourable comment about this woman. Katharine Tynan describes her as 'a flamboyant person, very American, obviously "a handful" who must have been a trial to her grave and dignified son'. In 1880 Tim Healy wrote to his brother from America, 'They are the most extraordinary family I ever came across. The mother, I think, is a little "off her nut" in some ways, and, for that matter, so are all the rest of them!' And T. P. O'Connor, another party member and a loyal friend to Katharine in later life, wrote in his memoirs, 'I found her a very strange being. She talked slowly and deliberately, but almost perpetually. . . . It was hard to say whether she could be described as wholly sane.' Whether Delia was always so odd is impossible to ascertain. Although she comes across in her own writings as very confused and full of the most awful snobbery, her children seem to have been very fond of her. Her daughter Emily wrote sympathetically, 'The sudden transformation from having been the belle of New York to the solitudes of Avondale appears at first to have been a great disappointment to her.' However, Emily also said that with the births of her children she became less lonely, 'though she never took kindly to the country or country pursuits.' Delia is portrayed by many historians as having been rabid in her anti-English politics. Her son John wrote, 'Our mother was American to the core, a burning enthusiast in the cause of

1. Portrait of Katie in 1880. Parnell always carried it with him in a locket.

2. Lucy Goldsmith, Katie's nurse when she was a child. Afterwards she lived with Katie until she died.

3. Rivenhall Place, Katie's childhood home.

4. A portrait of Willie in a cornet's uniform.

5. Aunt Ben's house at Eltham. *(Blackheath Golf Club)*.

6. Wonersh Lodge. The house Aunt Ben bought for Katie and her children in North Park, Eltham.

7. Parnell in 1880. This photo was taken by his nephew and given to Katie shortly after they met.

8. Parnell photographed by Katie. 'His horses, Dictator and President were stabled nearby. His dogs, Grouse and Ranger were lying at his feet. His two young daughters were upstairs in the nursery. Nothing could have seemed more domestic or more permanent.'

9. A portrait of Katie from a miniature.

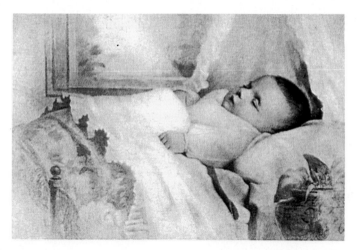

10. Claude Sophie, Katie and Parnell's first child who died at three months old.

11. Parnell about 1886.

12. A cartoon of Pigott from *Vanity Fair*. Katie wrote of his suicide: 'It was a painful affair, and Parnell was sorry for the poor creature.' *(National Library of Ireland)*.

13. A typical *Punch* cartoon at the time of Parnell. Notice the simian features of the Irishman. The Englishman is also satirized – this stereotype was later to appear in the stories of Somerville and Ross. *(Punch)*.

A LORD OF THE ADMIRALTY VERY MUCH AT SEA.

(An incident of Mr. Ashmead-Bartlett's recent Tour in Ireland.)

Mr. A. B. "Why Pat, my Lad, I see nothing to complain of here! These Potatoes are remarkably fine!"
Pat. "Bedad, Sor, but they're not Praties at all, at all. Shure

"EXCLUSIVE DEALING."

Irish Landlord (boycotted). "Pat, my man, I'm in no end of a hurry. Put the Pony to, and drive me to the Stat and I'll give ye Half a Sovereign!"

14. *Punch* comments on a boycotted landlord – again the Irishman is depicted as a gorilla. *(Punch)*.

15. A page from *Punch* makes fun of the balcony incident. *(Punch)*.

IN DIFFICULTIES!

16. *Punch* comments on Ireland's difficulties – the figure of Ireland has a distinct look of Katie. *(Punch)*.

17. Avondale, Parnell's family home. Today it is a museum. *(Radio Times Hulton Picture Library)*.

18. The house where Parnell died. 10, Walsingham Terrace, Brighton.

19. Katie's grave.

20. Kitty O'Shea's Bar, Dublin's famous hostelry of the Parnell era, in Upper Grand Canal Street, Dublin. *(Photo: Liam Blake/ Real Ireland Design Limited).*

Irish Liberty, and possessed of an inveterate hatred against England.'
But Roy Foster disputes this view:

> The reputation of a Fenian firebrand of the 1860's, which
> Parnell's biographers have attributed to her, seems to be based
> upon the most nebulous evidence; her political activity in the later
> part of her life only seems to have post-dated her son's rise to
> eminence, and to have mainly consisted of lending her presence on
> party platforms.

In any event, John Henry brought his new bride to the family home,
Avondale, near Rathdrum in County Wicklow, and, as Delia later
wrote:

> We had eleven children born, five sons and six daughters, all born
> at Avondale except Theodosia, who was born in Torquay, the
> place where the family first landed in England, and Henry, who
> was born in Paris. All born in the same room at Avondale except
> Anna. Five of the eleven children are now living [in 1891], three
> daughters and two sons. Ten of them grew up to majority. Hayes
> died of pleurisy and an affection of the liver at fifteen; and I lost
> an infant son, five years old, William Tudor, through bad
> vaccination.

However, as she spent the last years of her husband's life living apart
from him, it can plausibly be assumed that the marriage was not the
happiest. John Henry died on 4 July 1859, but Delia outlived him by
nearly forty years. She spent much time on the continent and many
years in America. She contrived to get through a good deal of money,
and was sometimes reported to be near destitution in her later years in
America. Always gregarious, she achieved some prominence among the
American Irish, but it was undoubtedly mostly for the importance of
her children, Charles, Fanny and Anna. It is very unlikely that Delia
Parnell influenced her son politically. Certainly as a young man Charles
regarded his mother's Fenian friends with irritation. As his brother John
wrote of him:

> I think he came to look upon most of the nondescript visitors to
> our house as tramps, as I did also to a certain extent. He finally got
> so tired of their constant visits that he used to wait for the so-
> called Fenians behind the hall-door in Temple Street and (like Sam
> Weller at Ipswich), directly the door was open make a rush for
> them and kick them down the steps.

As a mature politician, Parnell would sometimes make inflammatory
speeches, but they seem mainly occasioned by some necessity of the

moment rather than by real conviction; as a public man, he was basically a parliamentarian and much more moderate than many of his supporters.

The only other Parnell children who became notable public figures were his younger sisters, Fanny and Anna. Fanny was born in 1849 and became a prolific writer and political activist. It was she who conceived the idea of the Ladies' Land League in America in 1880, and her outspoken patriotic verse was widely read. John Boyle O'Reilly wrote of it, 'Crushed out, like the sweet life of a bruised flower, they are the very soul cry of the race.' In actuality, Fanny's verses are rarely poetry. Although formally fluent, they are usually hidebound by convention and utilise the most stale poetic diction. On just one or two occasions does the force of her statement carry her to success. For instance, in the second stanza of 'Hold the Harvest', a poem addressed to farmers in 1880, she wrote fiercely:

> The serpent's curse upon you lies – ye writhe within the dust,
> Ye fill your mouths with beggar's swill, ye grovel for a crust;
> Your lords have set their blood-stained heels upon your
>   shameful heads,
> Yet they are kind – they leave you still their ditches for your
>   beds!

She died in America at Old Ironsides's house in Bordentown, New Jersey, on 2 July 1882. After her death she became almost a cult figure. The crowds at her funeral were immense, and for some years after pilgrimages were made to her grave in Boston on Memorial Day.

Anna's career was also closely bound up with the Ladies' Land League, and she was persuaded by Fanny to return to Ireland at the end of 1880 and organise the League there. However, the fortunes of Anna and her League in Ireland are a later part of Parnell's own story and the subject of a future biography in this series.

His entry into politics was rather unexpected, even by his family, for little in his early life had suggested that his interests were much more far-reaching than the boundaries of Avondale which he had inherited upon his father's death. Parnell's character was always something of an enigma, not only to his many biographers but also to his closest associates. He was born on 27 June 1846, at Avondale, and was a headstrong child who tended to bully others. His older, quieter brother John bore much of the brunt of this, but the brothers always felt a considerable affection for each other. His early education was sporadic. At six, he was sent to a girls' school in Somerset, but in his second term was sent home after a bout of typhoid. When he was eight or nine, he was sent off to a school in Derbyshire, but after a year – at least according to St John Ervine's unsubstantiated statement – his parents were asked to remove him. After this he was tutored at home, and his recreations were those of a lively boy in well-to-do circumstances. In the early 1860s he studied at a crammer in Oxfordshire, and in 1865 he entered Magdalene College, Cambridge, where he remained until 1869 when he was sent down. His younger sister Emily, in her highly coloured and quite suspect memoir, *A Patriot's Mistake*, tells a story of how he seduced a farmer's daughter who then committed suicide. In fact, Parnell was sent down for being involved in a drunken brawl and for trying to bribe the policeman to let him off. Although this was only a temporary suspension, Parnell did not return to take his degree. Foster says that the Cambridge years only added 'to the sense of his inferiority in the matter of formal education which, according to his brother, he retained throughout his life'.

What Parnell retained from a rather casual education is difficult to assess. There are a number of stories which suggest that his grasp of Irish history and politics was, by 1874 when he entered the political arena, most lamentably sketchy. Henry Labouchere, the English Radical MP, wrote that the mature Parnell once showed him a letter which he meant to send to *The Times*: 'This was his own unaided composition, and never in my life did I see more astonishing English — confused, ungrammatical and passing comprehension.' On the other hand, the language of Parnell's public speeches, while hardly ever eloquent, is usually flatly clear. And his private letters to Katharine, although saccharine, are always plain and coherent. He seems, however, in mature life to have educated himself rather thoroughly about matters which deeply engaged him, such as mining, assaying and astronomy.

In 1871 he spent several months in America. The trip was partly to visit his brother John who was farming in Alabama, but mainly in pursuit of an American girl named Miss Woods whom he had met in Paris. She had seemed to return his affections, but when they met in America she turned him down because he was only an undistinguished private gentleman. John later wrote, 'His jilting undoubtedly helped to drive his energies into politics, for he was deeply hurt at the idea of being considered a country gentleman without any special abilities.' John was certainly in a position to know, for after his rebuff Charles spent several months with him in Alabama. Also, one constant quality in Parnell's aloof character seems to have been a stubborn and indomitable pride that would not admit defeat; and so it is quite possible that Miss Woods's rejection may have turned his thoughts to other pursuits than those of farming, cricket, sawmilling and hunting which had so far largely absorbed him.

At any rate, one evening early in 1874 Parnell was dining in Dublin with John, his sister Emily and her rakish and dissolute husband Arthur Dickinson. When the talk turned to tenants' rights, Parnell considerably startled his family by announcing, 'By Jove, it will be a grand opening for me to enter politics.' Even more startling was his determination not to align himself with the Conservatives or the Liberals, but with the Irish Party. Once earlier, when John had suggested that he take up the cause of tenants' rights and stand for Parliament as an Irish member, Parnell had replied, 'I could not, because I would not join that set.'

Whatever his motivation on this occasion, Parnell had always been a good landlord and was certainly sincere in espousing the rights of tenant farmers whose rents were entirely at the whim of their landlord and whose hold on land they might have farmed for years was at best tenuous. And although he may never have espoused the violence of the Fenians, Parnell was Irishman enough to have been deeply stirred by the recent execution of the Manchester Martyrs, and he was firmly committed to the principle of Home Rule.

'That set', at the time Parnell entered politics, was led by the genial, garrulous Isaac Butt, the head of the Home Rule League. As Paul Bew remarked, 'Butt and the majority of his followers devoted their energies to an unfailingly polite and almost totally ineffective parliamentary campaign to advance the Irish case for a moderate degree of self-government.' In five short years, Parnell was to displace Butt as the leader of the Irish Party in Parliament, and his rise to pre-eminence was as startling as it was odd. Whatever his drawbacks as an effective leader, Butt had great abilities, as also did other members of the party who were coming into prominence. Justin McCarthy was a popular historian and novelist; T. P. O'Connor was to be for years a popular journalist and editor; Tim Healy would be noted for his prodigious memory and his cutting wit; Joe Biggar devised the policy of parliamentary obstructions which Parnell took up and moulded into a formidable political weapon.

Among such varied and individual talents, Parnell in a very short time would stand as their acknowledged 'Chief', his authority unquestioned and his personal charisma utterly dominating the Irish Party. How did this country gentleman, so unprepared by education and interests and even opinions, achieve such an extraordinary feat? Intellectually, Parnell was hardly a match for the most notable of his colleagues but, having grasped a point, he was able tactically to pursue it stubbornly, tenaciously and unflinchingly. Then there was the implicit matter of class: perhaps even today the Irish dearly love a lord, and for years Irish people had been ground down to obey and the Anglo-Saxon land-owners accustomed to command. There was a good deal of this class arrogance in Parnell; it was an affectionate and benevolent arrogance, but one that showed itself even in his relations with his family. And, finally, there was a physical pre-eminence. Parnell has often been described as a strikingly handsome man. His photographs do not quite bear this out. His physique was not robust, sometimes his dress was startlingly bizarre, and in his forties his hair was notably thinning – indeed, his critics sometimes substituted for 'the uncrowned King of Ireland' the phrase of 'the uncombed King of Ireland'. However, for his day he was extraordinarily tall. In Avondale today there is a chair built especially for him, and it looks like the chair of a giant. He towered over the little Healy and the diminutive Biggar. All of these characteristics were combined with an aloof, even icy reserve, and the effect on his followers was overwhelming.

When Parnell was eventually elected to Parliament in 1875, he made no immediate impression. His speeches were sometimes halting and even painful to listen to. However, he assiduously studied the workings of Parliament and learned quickly, particularly from Biggar and the little man's long speeches which held up bills interminably. Obstructionism, Parnell quickly realised, could be the most potent weapon for the Irish Party; and on 31 July 1877 he, Biggar and John O'Connor Power instituted a debate that held up business all night and into the next afternoon. As F. S. L. Lyons wrote in his biography of John Dillon, 'This was in its way a historic episode, since it precipitated a final and decisive breach between Butt, who greatly deprecated such unseemly action, and the young activists who were now making all the running.' Dillon himself noted in his diary, 'This day I mark as the beginning of a new era in the history of Erin. And I wish to have in my room the portraits of the three men who pointed out to Ireland her way to freedom – Parnell, O'Connor Power, Biggar.' To Dillon and to most others, it was now clear that if the English 'vote down our land bill, why we will kill their education bill with amendments', and 'By means of following this policy of retaliation the Irish can, if they choose, very rapidly get whatever measures they desire – Home Rule included'.

By that day, then – 30 July 1880 – when Katharine met Parnell for the first time, and when he picked up her rose and pressed it to his lips, he had already become Ireland's uncrowned king. And he had no queen.

CHAPTER 7

LOVE

When jesting Pilate said 'What is truth?' he might have been voicing the lament of every historian and biographer. What might seem an easily substantiable fact is often the most elusive thing in the world to establish. And, of the various classes of facts, probably the most elusive and tenuous to discover is what really, specifically happened between a man and a woman.

In the case of Parnell and Katharine, certain points are abundantly clear, and the chief of these is his early, lasting and overwhelming attachment to her. What Katharine felt at one time or another is a bit more hazy, and there are other central issues that have long puzzled historians, and which have been interpreted quite differently.

The chief witness is Katharine herself, in the book *Charles Stewart Parnell: His Love Story and Political Life* which she published in 1914, nearly a quarter of a century after Parnell's death. There is much in the book with the stamp of complete authenticity, including many letters from Parnell himself. However, one commentator with some considerable claim to exact knowledge, Henry Harrison, has gone so far as to state that the book is a fabrication and a forgery. Harrison had been a young member of the Irish Party at the time of the 'split', and was also the man who conducted Katharine's business affairs in the months immediately after Parnell's death. In his 1931 volume, *Parnell Vindicated: The Lifting of the Veil*, Harrison wrote of Katharine's book:

> It is no less a forgery because some portions of it are genuine. And it is no less a forgery even though the weak fingers of the stricken authoress may have held the pen which stronger fingers guided — even though an enfeebled brain and wavering lips may have actually uttered some of that which a dominating mind dictated to it.

To Harrison, the villain in the case was Katharine and Willie's son Gerard who saw the book as an opportunity to vindicate his father.

In any event, in the two months after their first meeting, Parnell's attraction to Katharine quickly turned to love. Her first letter from him on 17 July explained that only the pressure of business had kept him from visiting her: 'And this notwithstanding the powerful attractions which have been tending to seduce me from my duty towards my country in the direction of Thomas's Hotel.' He also had to go to Paris to attend the wedding of his younger sister, Theodosia, but shortly after his return he accepted an invitation to dine. Katharine wrote:

> He arrived late, but apologetic, and was looking painfully ill and white, the only life-light in his face being given by the fathomless eyes of rich brown, varying to the brilliance of flame. The depth of expression and sudden fire of his eyes held me to the day of his death.

Parnell is now thought to have suffered from a kidney disease, and he impressed not only Katharine but everyone who met him with his frailness. During that dinner, he talked mostly to Katharine's sister Anna, but afterwards agreed to accompany the party to the theatre, a form of entertainment he rarely indulged in. On their arrival, Katharine wrote, 'he and I seemed to fall naturally into our places in the dark corner of the box facing the stage and screened from the sight of the audience, while my sister and the others sat in front.' In this first private conversation, the talk quickly became personal, but Parnell told Katharine about his near-engagement to Miss Woods, and how the last time that he had sought her out in America, he found himself becoming cold and disillusioned. He said that she had slipped a paper into his hand on that occasion, and on it was written a verse:

> Unless you can muse in a crowd all day
>   On the absent face that fixed you,
> Unless you can dream that his faith is fast
>   Through behoving and unbehoving.
> Unless you can die when the dream is past,
>   Oh, never call it loving.

Then, wrote Katharine, 'He asked me who had written the lines, and I answered that it sounded like one of the Brownings (it is E. B. Browning's), and he said simply: "Well, I could not do all that, so I went home."' He then added that he thought it was his own vacillation that had lost him Miss Woods, but that 'The strenuous work he had then put his whole heart into had driven out all traces of regret'.

It certainly seems probable that the memory of their first real talk remained fresh in Katharine's mind, even over the years, and that we may believe her reporting of it. If so, then Parnell's surprising account to a new acquaintance of a deeply personal matter, what had been thus far the one real love affair of his life, might well be ascribed to his already budding feelings for Katharine. Further, the ending of the story might have been meant as a warning not only to her but also to himself, that he was not interested in another such experience.

If Parnell was warning himself, however, it was a warning that went unheeded, for he and Katharine began to meet frequently. She would visit the Ladies' Gallery of the House, and, if the current deliberations were not important, he would then take her for drives into the country. Some of their conversation was about Willie's chance of being returned for Clare again, and Katharine secured Parnell's promise of support. On another occasion, Parnell and Justin McCarthy were lunching with Katharine and Anna, and, when Katharine had to leave early to return to Eltham, Parnell accompanied her to Charing Cross station. She had missed the train, so he hired a cab and drove down with her. She did not, however, invite him in because she did not know if the house was tidy, 'and he reluctantly returned to London.'

A few days later he was to dine with her at Thomas's Hotel, and he met her at Cannon Street station and suggested that they first have tea at the Cannon Street Hotel. Katharine described it:

> We went to the Cannon Street Hotel dining-rooms, but on looking in he saw some of the Irish members there and said it would be more comfortable for us in his private sitting-room. I was under the impression that he lived at Keppel Street, but he told me he had just taken rooms in the Cannon Street Hotel.

This, of course, all sounds very much as if Parnell had deliberately staged events so as to be alone with Katharine. In any event, she was already hopelessly compromised. It was not the thing for a Victorian married woman to be alone with a man in a hotel room, but from the beginning Parnell acted with a majestic disdain for the opinion of others. Katharine describes the occasion:

> We had tea in his sitting-room, and he talked politics to me freely till I was interested and at ease, and then lapsed into one of those long silences of his that I was already beginning to know were dangerous in the complete sympathy they evoked between us.
>
> Presently I said, 'Come! we shall be late!'; and he rose without a word and followed me downstairs. There were some members of his Party still standing about in the hall, but, as he always did afterwards when I was with him, he ignored them absolutely and handed me into a waiting cab.

They dined together at Thomas's that evening, and the next day he left for a visit to Avondale. Perhaps they had not become lovers, but something had passed between them, for immediately on arriving in Dublin Parnell wrote to her saying, not entirely unguardedly:

My Dear Mrs O'Shea, – Just a line to say that I have arrived here, and go on to Avondale, Rathdrum, this evening, where I hope to hear from you before very long.

I may tell you also in confidence that I don't feel quite so content at the prospect of ten days' absence from London amongst the hills and valleys of Wicklow as I should have done some three months since.

The cause is mysterious, but perhaps you will help me to find it, or her, on my return. – Yours always,

CHAS S. PARNELL

Distinctly the kind of letter a man would write in the preliminary stages of a love affair.

Katharine was already constantly on Parnell's mind. On 22 September he wrote from Dublin, 'I cannot keep myself away from you any longer, so shall leave to-night for London.' However, Katharine's old nurse, Lucy, who was 90 years old, was now dying, and Katharine was unable to meet Parnell in London even briefly. It was not in her loyal nature to leave the old woman alone, even for a lover.

On 24 September he wrote to her dispiritedly, 'I am very much troubled at not having seen you, especially as I must return to Ireland to-night – I came on purpose for you, and had no other business.'

Parnell was required in Ireland, for the Land League agitation was simmering to a boil. Abels writes:

The membership of the Land League skyrocketed to the mammoth figure of 500,000 and its president, Parnell, after the Parliamentary session, swept through Ireland like an avenging angel, speaking at New Ross, Kilkenny, Cork, Longford, Galway, Tipperary, Limerick, Athlone, Ennis. . . . At Cork he was greeted by a crowd of 100,000, and to an onlooker viewing the wild adulation he was 'like a Greek God come to take part in a festival organized by his votaries'.

To his admiring followers, he may have looked like a Greek god as he appeared on the platform, but his whirlwind of activity had exacted its toll, and Katharine saw him differently. As Ervine summarises it, 'They saw him as a man of resolution and vigour and unabatable strength, but she saw him as a worn-out man, perilously treading on the very verge of death.' And she had the opportunity to observe him closely, for 'In the autumn of 1880 Mr Parnell came to stay with us at Eltham, only going to Dublin as occasion required. Willie had invited him. . . .'

She found Parnell worn out, afflicted with a bad sore throat, and even falling asleep with exhaustion during the day. And she also experienced for the first time some of his superstitious idiosyncrasies. She had filled the drawing room with plants and palms for him, but found that he thought her daily watering of them was aggravating his throat. 'He was childishly touched when I at once had them all removed, and he sank happily on to the sofa, saying that "plants were such damp things"!' Another aversion was his particular loathing, unfortunate in an Irish leader, of the colour green. Katharine had a green carpet, and he believed that it too was harming his throat, so she even cut out a piece from the carpet and sent the harmless, unoffending material off to be analysed.

Nevertheless, he improved, both physically and mentally. Katharine wrote:

> I nursed him assiduously, making him take nourishment at regular intervals, seeing that these day-sleeps of his were not disturbed and forcing him to take fresh air in long drives through the country around us. At length I had the satisfaction of seeing his strength gradually return sufficiently to enable him to take the exercise that finished the process of this building-up, and he became stronger than he had been for some years. I do not think anyone but we who saw him then at Eltham, without the mask of reserve he always presented to the outside world, had any idea of how near death's door his exertions on behalf of the famine-stricken peasants of Ireland had brought him.

She began helping him cope with his flood of correspondence, and it seems certain that at this time they became lovers, if indeed they were not already. On 17 October, on a trip to Ireland, he began a letter to her, 'My own Love, – You cannot imagine how much you have occupied my thoughts all day and how very greatly the prospect of seeing you again very soon comforts me.' On 22 October he sent her two sprigs of heather from Avondale and 'also my best love, and hope you will believe that I always think of you as the one dear object whose presence has ever been a great happiness to me'.

In Ireland, mass evictions of tenants were being countered by violent reprisals from the evicted, and sometimes Parnell was dragged along by the force of his followers' feelings into speaking more violently than he desired. However, at a meeting in Ennis on 19 September he himself countered with a new policy of ostracism. Abels describes the meeting:

> After urging his listeners to keep a firm grip on their homesteads, not to bid for farms from which others had been evicted and to prevent 'grabbers' from doing so, he said, 'Now what are you going to do to a tenant who bids for a farm from which his neighbour has been evicted?' There were cries of 'Kill him!' 'Shoot him!'
>
> 'No,' Parnell went on, 'I think I heard someone say "shoot him." But I wish to point out to you a very much better way, a

more Christian and more charitable way, which will give the lost sinner an opportunity of repenting.'

'When a man takes a farm from which another has been evicted, you must shun him on the roadside when you meet him, you must shun him in the streets of the town, . . . you must shun him in the fair and in the market-place, and even in the house of worship, by leaving him severely alone, by putting him into a moral Coventry, by isolating him from . . . his kind as if he were a leper of old – you must show him your detestation of the crime he has committed; and you may depend upon it . . . that there will be no man so full of avarice, so lost to shame, as to dare the public opinion of all right thinking men . . . and to transgress your unwritten code of laws.'

Parnell's policy was to contribute a new word to the language – boycott. In Mayo that year there was continuous tension between Lord Erne's agent, Captain Charles Boycott, and his tenants. However, they applied social ostracism so effectively that Orange labourers had to be sent for from Ulster to harvest the crops under police protection – hence the origin of the word.

Although such tumultuous events in Ireland demanded Parnell's frequent presence, he constantly wrote to Katharine. Sometimes his letters were friendly but formal, as that written on 2 December which begins, 'My dear Mrs O'Shea' and concludes, 'Trusting to see you again next week on my way to Paris – Yours very sincerely, Chas. S. Parnell' – a letter obviously written with the expectation that it might be read by a third party, and from which we might plausibly conclude that at this early stage at least Willie had no idea that Parnell and Katharine were lovers.

Other letters, however, were for her eyes only and written in a quite different tone. For instance, that of 11 November:

My Dearest Love, . . . It is quite impossible for me to tell you just how very much you have changed my life, what a small interest I take in what is going on about me, and how I detest everything which has happened during the last few days to keep me away from you – I think of you always, and you must never believe there is to be any 'fading'. By the way, you must not send me any more artificial letters. I want as much of your own self as you can transfer into written words, or else none at all. – Yours always, CSP

The problem of Shakespeare's Antony was that matters of the heart displaced affairs of state. For a while, Parnell was still able to attend to affairs of state, but the 11 November letter certainly shows that already the centre of his attention was at Eltham.

Nevertheless, Ireland demanded much of his time. The Land League had become such a force that Parnell and fourteen of his followers were brought to trial 'for conspiracy to impoverish landlords'. He regarded these trials as a farce, for he knew that no Irish jury would convict him on such a charge. Such political matters did, however, necessitate a good deal of to-ing and fro-ing between Ireland and England, and Parnell now came to regard Eltham as his English base to which he repaired as often as possible.

On one occasion before the trials, when he feared that he might be prematurely arrested, he stayed secretly for two weeks at Eltham, in a small dressing room off Katharine's bedroom. Of this time she wrote:

> None of the servants knew that he was there, and I took all his food up at night, cooking little dainty dishes for him at the open fire, much to his pleasure and amusement. He spent the time very happily, resting, writing 'seditious' speeches for future use, and reading 'Alice in Wonderland'. This book was a favourite of his, and I gave it to him with the solemnity that befitted his grave reading of it. I do not think he ever thought it in the least amusing, but he would read it earnestly from cover to cover, and, without a smile, remark that it was a 'curious book'.

During this period, Parnell was immediately expected at an important meeting of the Land League leaders in Paris. However, he put it off for a week, and then finally, with Katharine accompanying him, he made his way towards Harwich by a devious route. At Lowestoft they had a good meal, and he capriciously decided to return to London and cross by the usual route to Paris the next day.

His actions were not always logical, but he sometimes feared that he was being watched by government detectives, and he adopted a series of subterfuges for writing to or meeting Katharine. Some of these were a bit absurd, and some of them were to surface to his discredit during the divorce trial. Ervine summed up his tactics:

> He had codes for communicating with her. He adopted false names — Preston, Stewart, Fox, Smith — and hired houses and rooms where he might take her. When he travelled to Eltham by road, he took a hansom to the Nelson public-house in the Old Kent Road, where he dismissed it, walked a little way, and took another hansom to Eltham. He arranged to have letters posted to her from various places when he was not there, so that Captain O'Shea, if by chance he should be at Eltham when they arrived, might believe him to be out of London. The whole apparatus was exceedingly silly, but Parnell had that simplicity of mind which made him imagine that such tricks deceived.

But, as Lincoln said, 'you cannot fool all the people all the time,' and Katharine had a new Irish cook from Tipperary. When the cook, Ellen, discovered that Parnell was in the house, she bought a gold locket and proudly displayed Parnell's picture in it. Soon the parlour maid, Mary, followed suit, and Parnell had to protest:

> Mary, that is a magnificent locket, and I see you are kind enough to wear my portrait in it. Mrs O'Shea tells me that Ellen has bought one also, but I just want you and Ellen not to wear them outside like that, for Mrs O'Shea lets me come down here for a rest, and if people know I'm here I shall be worried to death with politics and people calling.

After that, the women wore their lockets inside their blouses.

However, Katharine did take Parnell across the park and introduce him to Aunt Ben who was much taken with him and told him of how she had met Daniel O'Connell and had also heard him speak in the House. But she said, 'I much prefer your voice, Mr Parnell, for Daniel O'Connell's enunciation was startling to me.'

And Katie added:

> Parnell had a most beautiful and harmonious voice when speaking in public. Very clear it was, even in moments of passion against his own and his country's foes – passion modulated and suppressed until I have seen, from the Ladies' Gallery, his hand clenched until the 'Orders of the Day' which he held were crushed into pulp, and only that prevented his nails piercing his hand. Often I have taken the 'Orders' out of his pocket, twisted into shreds – a fate that also overtook the slips of notes and the occasional quotations he had got me to look out for him.

Whenever she could, she would go to hear him speak in the House, and he would make a sign to her 'by certain manipulations of his handkerchief' to meet him later. Whenever he was away in Ireland, they corresponded constantly, and his notes now began 'My dearest love' and 'My dearest Wifie'. In the body of the letters were now sentences like, 'If I return Thursday morning, my Queen may expect to see me about one o'clock.' And the conclusions were now signed 'Always yours, Charles' or 'Always your husband'.

Eltham became for Parnell a true home, and he gloried in its quiet domesticity. It was a place to retire to and potter around, pursuing absorbing hobbies. He took up book-keeping and astronomy; he spent hours making architectural drawings and assaying specimens of quartz from streams near Avondale. Indeed, he was so contented that Katie had ever greater difficulty in getting him to attend to affairs. 'Many a day I have let him work up to the last possible moment, and then literally pulled off the old "cardigan" jacket he worked in, and forced him into his frock-coat for the House. . . .' Sometimes he would have to catch the mail-train for Ireland, and she would have his clothes packed and ready, but he would sit down and say, 'You are in a hurry to get rid of me; I will not go yet. Sit down and let me look at you a bit, my Queen.' And then he would spend the rest of the evening talking to her 'of anything that came into his head – always watching me with that intent, considering gaze that was my bewilderment and my joy'. When she remonstrated that he must at least telegraph or write that he would be late or even not there at all, he merely replied, 'You do not learn the ethics of kingship, Queenie. Never explain, never apologise', adding, with his rare laugh, 'I could never keep my rabble together if I were not above the human weakness of apology.'

It did not occur to him to apologise even when Willie challenged him to a duel. When he was away, Parnell still took the occasional precaution of writing a formal letter to 'My dear Mrs O'Shea', such a letter as could be shown to Willie if need be. Nevertheless, it was often easy to forget Willie. In December he had been in Madrid, and ordinarily he had rooms in London, and there was an agreement with Katie that he would only appear at Eltham upon invitation. In January 1881, according to Katharine's memoirs he imagined that she had sent detectives to watch his movements, and he appeared angrily and unexpectedly at Eltham. Parnell was not there, but his portmanteau was in the room he used. Enraged, Willie stormed out of the house with the portmanteau – which he threw out of the window of a train. He went to Anna's house in London and vowed to 'challenge Parnell to fight a duel and . . . shoot him'. Parnell's immediate reply was one of the formal notes meant to cover his tracks: 'My dear Mrs O'Shea,' he wrote on 7 January 1881, 'will you kindly ask Captain O'Shea where he left my luggage? I enquired at both parcel office, cloak-room, and this hotel at Charing Cross to-day, and they were not to be found.'

Anna, however, managed to patch things up between Willie and Katharine, but Parnell was imperturbably preparing to go abroad to meet Willie and wrote to Katharine, 'He has just written me a very insulting letter, and I shall be obliged to send a friend to him if I do not have a satisfactory reply to a second note I have just sent him.'

Faced by Parnell's unruffled aplomb and given the explanation that he needed Katharine as 'a medium of communication between the Government and himself', Willie caved in, and as Katie said, 'merely made the condition that Mr Parnell should not stay at Eltham.' A public eruption had been averted, but Willie's action had one definite effect. As Katie wrote, 'From the date of this bitter quarrel Parnell and I were one, without further scruple, without fear, and without remorse.'

For some reason, at the time of his divorce suit, Willie gave the date of this business as being in July. Otherwise, his story is the same as Katharine's. It has always been a matter of contention among Parnell's biographers how early and how much Willie actually knew. And, indeed, the matter later became of considerable importance. If it had come out at the divorce trial that Willie had known early on and for years tacitly countenanced the liaison between Katharine and Parnell, the world would have put a considerably different interpretation upon events. In 1881, however, it is not implausible that his suspicions were truly allayed.

One good reason for his credulity may well have been the strong possibility that during this year sexual relations between him and Katie were at least intermittently resumed.

CHAPTER 8

DECEPTION

The popular notion about Parnell's career is that he was the Chief, the Uncrowned King, who, until Willie O'Shea instituted divorce proceedings at the end of 1889, was perfectly in control of the situation. The truth seems to have been that both politically and domestically Parnell was balancing precariously on a highwire that others were violently jiggling and twitching. Despite his magisterial hauteur and his incredible public charisma, events, both public and private, were in reality controlling Parnell. His unruffled aplomb was a mask, the aloof public persona of his own creation.

In his political career Parnell grappled with two great issues, the tenure of the land and Home Rule. In 1881 the land issue had become so inflamed that he was arrested and imprisoned for six and a half months in Kilmainham Gaol. The issue had come to a head because agrarian crime in Ireland had reached alarming proportions. Indeed, in the last three months of 1880 alone, nearly 1,700 outrages were reported. The government initially responded by a policy of coercion. In January 1881, as has been mentioned, the government prosecuted Parnell and other leaders of the Land League for conspiring to prevent the payment of rent and to encourage tenants to resist being ejected. That Dublin trial resulted, predictably, in acquittal, but in February the government arrested that major guiding force in the Land League, Michael Davitt.

In this tense time Parnell, as Paul Bew remarked, 'managed to be all things to all men.' Pushed by events, his speeches were sometimes inflammatory. At the same time he favoured a policy of conciliation to landowners, and he was basically committed to reform by parliamentary rather than by violent means. When the Executive of the Land League met in Paris to discuss its response to Davitt's arrest, it was Parnell who was the temperate voice. The alternatives were for the Irish Party to secede from Parliament and to come out for the non-payment of rents, and, on the other hand, to work within Parliament for an improvement in the situation of the tenants. For the moment, the parliamentarian Parnell won the day.

At the same time Parnell was finding that his personal life could not always be kept under control. Although he was urgently needed in Paris for the meeting of the Land League Executive, he turned up a week late because he could not tear himself away from Katie. There are not quite substantiated stories that Parnell's colleagues, wondering where he was, opened his mail. In Tim Healy's and John Dillon's versions, they found a letter from a barmaid in Birmingham who had had a child by Parnell and who needed money. In the versions of Michael Davitt, T. P. O'Connor and, indeed, of Katherine herself, the letter was one from Katharine, and this was the first intimation that the Irish leaders had of Parnell's attachment. However, Davitt, O'Connor and Katharine were none of them at Paris, and, according to F. S. L. Lyons, John Dillon's son recollected his father saying that a child was involved.

If Parnell was the man on the pedestal, it was necessary to keep the eyes of his followers trained upward towards his aloof and handsome face. But if their eye level were at his feet, it might prove difficult to prevent them noticing that the feet were of clay.

The re-opening of Parliament initiated a period of hectic activity about Irish matters and demanded Parnell's closest attention. Firstly, the government introduced a coercion law to deal with the problem of land agitation. The Irish bitterly but futilely opposed it, and on 2 March it was passed. Then Gladstone introduced his Land Bill which Parnell realised offered a vast improvement in the plight of the peasant, but which he could not quite overtly support. As Joyce Marlow put it:

> He knew this was the Land Bill Ireland wanted, that most of the peasants, the Catholic hierarchy and the moderate nationalists would gladly accept it, but boiling on his left flank was the Fenian element at home, and particularly in America which regarded the Bill as a minor stepping-stone, forced out of the Liberal Government only by the semi-revolutionary activities of the last year.

Parnell's precarious balance on the political highwire was becoming even more difficult to maintain.

But if for the moment he retained his political aplomb, he was becoming ever more indiscreet in his personal life. In May an old friend visited Aunt Ben, and so Katie had the opportunity to take her children on holiday to Brighton. At Brighton station she was met by a curious apparition:

> I was suddenly joined by a tall man whom I did not recognise for a moment until he said quietly, 'Don't you know me?' It was Mr Parnell, who had slipped into the train at Clapham Junction, knowing that I was going to Brighton, and who had cut off his beard with his pocket scissors in the train to avoid being recognised at Brighton. He had wrapped a white muffler round his throat, and pulled it as high as possible over the lower part of his face, with the result that the manageress of the hotel he stayed at was certain that he had an infectious illness of the throat, and

rather demurred at letting him in. It was only by the expedient of complaining loudly at being kept waiting in the draught with his 'raging toothache' that 'Mr Stewart' was reluctantly admitted. I could not bear his appearance – neither bearded nor shaven – so he went off soon after arrival, was properly shaved, and relieved the hotel staff by discarding the muffler and assuring them that he was free from pain now his 'tooth' was out.

Such naive subterfuges could hardly escape detection long.

Parnell stayed in Brighton for about ten days, and he and Katie regarded it as their honeymoon. Next month she suspected correctly that she was pregnant for the first time in eight years. It was then that Willie re-appeared upon the scene, and some sort of friendly relations were re-established between him and both Parnell and Katie. Although Willie was not allied with the Irish Party, Parnell now made use of him to relay opinions to Gladstone about the Land Bill. And it seems almost certain that Katharine accepted Willie again into her bed.

What really happened cannot be definitely established, and biographers have hotly debated the matter. Did Willie truly think he was the father of Katharine's child? Did Katharine really accept him again as her lover? Did Parnell know and acquiesce? In her memoir, Katie distinctly says that Willie thought he was the father and leaves the matter at that. Henry Harrison, realising the implications of the statement, heatedly asserts that it was inserted by Willie's son Gerard to whitewash his father's name, albeit at the same time tarnishing that of his mother. And even subsequent historians hashing over the matter have sometimes taken a lofty moral tone. Hence it is refreshing to note St John Ervine remarking:

> It was puerilely argued at the time of the divorce that Parnell could not be trusted in anything because he had lapsed in this, and that, therefore, his value to Ireland disappeared on the day when he first seduced Mrs O'Shea! To say that is as much as to say that a man cannot be trusted to drive a motor-car because on one occasion he was caught stealing his friend's cigars. It certainly does not become Irishmen, who boggle so little at murder, to boggle so much at adultery.

There are certain unimpeachable documents in the case – particularly some statements by Willie and some letters by Parnell – and from them some persuasive psychological probabilities can be inferred. Here, then, is one reconstruction of the events with some strong supporting evidence from Parnell's letters, from Willie's statements and from the substantiated actions of all three.

In January 1881 Willie had come to Eltham, discovered Parnell's portmanteau, and angrily thrown it away. Parnell's formal letter to

Katie, quoted on page 80, requested information concerning the whereabouts of the portmanteau and can only suggest that he and Katie at this time were keeping up the pretence that they were not lovers.

In May, Parnell stayed in Brighton for about ten days with Katie, and she became pregnant.

In June, Katie suspected that she had conceived, and it was then that certain decisions had to be made. Above all, a scandal had to be avoided, for it would entail two major consequences. It would muddy the political waters at what was a most difficult and delicate time, and it would certainly imperil Katie's inheritance of a very substantial amount from Aunt Ben. It is unlikely that the political threat would have had much weight with the politically imperturbable and even arrogant Parnell. On the one hand it would have seemed a challenge, and on the other there was the distinct appeal of retiring to an increasingly attractive private life. He could have returned to Avondale with Katie and pursued the tranquil domestic life that was so appealing and that left him abundant time to persue his engrossing schemes and hobbies. Nevertheless, Katie's expectations from the aged Aunt Ben involved an extraordinary amount of money. The proud Parnell may have been quite confident of supporting his new family at Avondale, but it was surely apparent to him that his schemes involved a considerable outlay of money, that his own resources were strained already to breaking point, and that what was at stake was a fortune. To avid Parnellites, particularly of an earlier day, it would have seemed heresy to attribute to him such venal motives. However, in December 1883 he imperturbably pocketed a national tribute of £37,000 to help him in his financial distress, and without vouchsafing even a word of thanks. And in later years he remarked to his brother John that another such tribute would be much welcome.

If, then, such reasoning impelled Katie and Parnell to carry out the deception, certain repugnant steps, at least for a while, were necessary. The chief of these was a rapprochement with Willie. He could either be told the whole truth and bought off by the promise of Parnell's help in his political advancement, or he could be deceived.

And it is here that Willie's character had to be considered, and here also that Katie's reading of his character would have carried most weight. Her years of marriage had utterly proved Willie's untrustworthiness. He was vain, self-seeking, irresponsible, egotistic and, despite some rudiments of canniness (or 'cuteness' in the Irish sense), he was both emotionally unstable and rather stupid. He was distinctly a person in whom to put no more trust than was absolutely necessary.

What, then, were they to do?

Immediately, Parnell began to employ Willie. As F. S. L. Lyons remarks, 'in early June an approach made to Gladstone by Captain O'Shea, who claimed to be speaking for Parnell, held out the prospect of a bargain whereby the land agitation would be ended in return of certain liberal amendments to [the Land Act].'

Despite Willie's co-operation with Parnell, there then occurred the matter of the abortive duel. It must be remembered that there is a discrepancy between Katie's and Willie's memory of the date of this event. But it was probably in July, six months *after* Willie's discovery of the portmanteau, and so obviously it was a new suspicion that had again inflamed Willie's ire.

Two strong possibilities have never been sufficiently stressed here by the historians. Firstly, if Katharine had allayed Willie's suspicions about Parnell by receiving him back into her bed after the January row, a new suspicion about her infidelity would very plausibly have enraged this self-important man. It would have seemed to Willie that, instead of being at the centre of dramatic domestic and public events, he was only being used as a cuckold and dupe. Secondly, after the affair of the projected duel had been damped down, Parnell and Katie continued to keep up the deception that they were but friends. As their liaison was not yet a public matter, they could only have been doing it for one person's benefit – Willie's. Throughout August and September Parnell wrote Katie both formal and private letters, sometimes enclosing them in the same envelopes. For instance, on 10 September from Morrison's Hotel in Dublin he wrote:

> My dear Mrs O'Shea, – Will you kindly address and post enclosed.
>
> I am quite recovered from my attack, and the doctor says that I shall be able to travel in a few days. – Yours very truly,
>
> CHAS. S. PARNELL

And in the same letter he enclosed the following:

> My own Wifie, – I know that you must have been much worried yesterday by my failure to send you a few words, but my Beauty will forgive her own husband.
>
> Your wire has been put into my hand as I write, and shall have an instant answer.
>
> It gives me so much pleasure to know that your trouble has not returned since I left, and that my wires give you pleasure. Your King thinks very often of his dearest Queen, and wishes her not to be sad, but to try and be happy for his sake. Everything is going on very well here, and your King is much satisfied.

Another letter which Parnell wrote on 7 October from Morrison's Hotel suggests even more overtly that Parnell and Katie had agreed to deceive Willie:

My Own Wifie, – I called to-day to see him [Willie] on my return
from Dungarvan, but he was out, and I waited for him three
hours. Calling again at eleven to-night, he was again out, but
returned just as I was writing to make an appointment for the
morning. He *says* that he leaves to-morrow (Friday) evening,
and stops to shoot on Saturday in Wales, and goes on Tuesday to
Paris to see the Papal Nuncio, who he says has requested him to
come. This, then, is the last letter I can send you for the present
through Eltham, so I hope to have the other address from you to-
morrow morning.

My dearest Katie must have been very lonely ever since. Did
she get my three letters? Her husband has been so busy he has
not even had time to sleep, but he has never been too busy to
think of her.

I can go over to London early next week if I may see you.
Should I remain in London or go down to you?

With numerous kisses to my beautiful Queenie.

CSP

Clearly stated here is the fact that, while keeping up an appearance of
political collaboration with Willie, Parnell was clandestinely corres-
ponding with Katie and contemplating visiting her while Willie was
abroad. We can further plausibly infer that Willie's self-esteem would
hardly have allowed him to go so complacently about his business with
Parnell had he any inkling that Parnell was the father of Katie's unborn
child.

In his letter Parnell remarks how busy he had been. Since the passage
of the Land Act in late August, his political balancing trick had required
the closest attention. As Paul Bew puts it:

Refusal to wind down the agitation implied the risk of imprisonment and the loss of 'moderate' support in Ireland. On the other
hand, refusal to maintain the agitation would have alienated
Irish-American feeling and the radical wing of the Land League.
Parnell tried to steer a middle course.

Actually it was not so much a middle course as a simultaneous attempt
to convince the moderates that he was on their side and the radicals that
he was on theirs. At a Land League convention in September, a
compromise of testing the new law was adopted. Such a compromise
would placate the majority who wanted to accept the new law, but at
the same time Parnell hastened to wire the reassurance to America that
tenants would still 'rely on the old methods to achieve justice' – that is,
upon violence.

The simplistic popular notion of Parnell's leadership was that he
moved inflexibly towards the achievement of certain fixed goals. The

reality was that time after time his real motives were masked from one group or another of his followers. To Parnell, this course of tacking and doubling was clearly necessary if he were to keep his hand on the tiller. It does not seem unrealistic, then, to suppose that the pragmatic politician would have greatly boggled at the use of similar tactics of concealment and duplicity in his private affairs. It is, then, quaint to find a professional historian like F. S. L. Lyons remarking that such a supposition about Parnell's private life was 'unpleasant,' when the same duplicitous tactics in his public life remain uncriticised and even admired.

St John Ervine believes that Parnell found it necessary to divert the attention of his divided followers from the Land Act to himself, and by appearing to inflame agitation to be actually courting arrest. Whether this was so, Parnell was quite aware that Gladstone thought he was attempting to undermine the Land Act, and he warned Katie that it was possible he would shortly be arrested. On 9 October he was in Wexford and, as Ervine relates:

> after his Wexford meeting was over, he sat at supper with two of his colleagues, one of whom, after much hesitation, timorously asked: 'Suppose they arrest you, Mr Parnell; have you any instructions to give us?' Mr Parnell looked through the glass of champagne he had raised to his lips, and said: 'Ah, if I am arrested, Captain Moonlight will take my place.' And Captain Moonlight did. It would seem that Parnell anticipated the advent of Captain Moonlight with pleasure, and perhaps at the moment he did, but there must have been a doubt in his mind. He did not like Captain Moonlight.

Indeed, Parnell's strategy is a little baffling, but arrest and imprisonment may have seemed one way of putting two dilemmas – public and private – at a distance until they had resolved themselves. Katie wrote in her memoir that he told her:

> the turmoil and rebellion he had brought to a head in Ireland must be very carefully handled to be productive of ultimate good, and that he could 'mark time' with the Land League better in Kilmainham than out, thus rendering this force more useful to the Home Rule campaign and less wanton in destruction.

And on 13 October, when he was finally arrested at Morrison's Hotel, he wrote to her, 'Politically it is a fortunate thing for me that I have been arrested, as the movement is breaking fast, and all will be quiet in a few months, when I shall be released.' What he did not say was that all might be domestically quiet in a few months also. He did write:

The only thing that makes me worried and unhappy is that it may hurt you and our child.

You know, darling, that on this account it will be wicked of you to grieve, as I can never have any other wife but you, and if anything happens to you I must die childless. Be good and brave, dear little wifie, then.

Your Own Husband

It is perhaps attributing somewhat ignoble and selfish motives to Parnell to suggest that the opting out by imprisonment would leave him still in the limelight, but also not quite responsible for whatever events were to occur both politically and privately. On the other hand, it must be remembered that both dilemmas seemed at the time insoluble, and also that Parnell himself was tired to the point of exhaustion.

For Katie, there was nothing to do but wait. She wrote:

From the time of Parnell's arrest onward until the birth of his child in the following February I lived a curiously subconscious existence; pursuing the usual routine of my life at home and with my aunt, but feeling all that was of life in me had gone with my lover to prison, and only came back to me in the letters that were my only mark of time. I had to be careful now; Willie became solicitous for my health, and wished to come to Eltham more frequently than I would allow. He thought February would seal our reconciliation, whereas I knew it would cement the cold hatred I felt towards him, and consummate the love I bore my child's father.

Her relations with the unsuspecting Willie were indeed difficult. As soon as the news of Parnell's arrest was announced in the papers, Willie appeared at Eltham to apprise Katie of the fact.

But Willie was so fiercely and openly joyful that my maids, who were ardent Parnellites, were much shocked, and I, being terribly overwrought, laughed at their disgusted faces as I went to dress for dinner. It was really the laugh of tears, but that laugh of jangled nerves and misery did me good service for Willie, and we got through dinner amicably enough, while he descanted upon the wickedness and folly of Parnell's policy and the way the Irish question should really be settled, and would be if it could be left in his hands and those who thought with him. He observed me closely, as he criticised Parnell and his policy, and reiterated his pleasure in knowing he was 'laid by the heels'.

The problem of Katie's evidence is which of two conflicting versions attributed to her is to be believed. In her book written in old age, she clearly states in several places that she and Parnell deceived Willie. For instance, she described the situation just before Parnell's arrest like this:

> I felt almost unable to cope with the situation; I was not strong and I was full of anxiety as to the probable effects upon Parnell's health of life in Kilmainham Gaol. In addition to my anxiety, the deception I had to practise towards Captain O'Shea, seldom as I saw him, told upon my nerves just now.

However, Henry Harrison, also writing many years after the events in his book *Parnell Vindicated*, flatly denies the validity of all such statements in Katie's book, and asserts that such passages were tampered with or even written by Willie's son Gerard. He then 'quotes' from several conversations that he had with Katie after Parnell's death when he was looking after her affairs, and in this version Willie had always been aware of the liaison. In fact, in Harrison's version, Willie even appears as something of a pander. The dates are all rather vague, but on one occasion, evidently meant to be in 1880 or 1881, Willie is supposed to have wanted something from Parnell and to have said to Katie:

> '"Take him back with you to Eltham and make him all happy and comfortable for the night, and just get him to agree." His air, his manner, made his meaning unmistakable to me. He knew too, of course, that Mr Parnell was staying with me when he [Willie] was not. How could he fail to know? Do you think it would have been possible to bind my children to secrecy? Would he not have heard it from the children when he saw them on Sundays? or the servants, if he cared to ask? I do not know exactly when he first learned of our love – we felt no obligation to tell him – but it cannot have been long before he knew it all. It was then, that was the only time, that I blurted the whole thing out, that I loved Parnell with my whole soul, loved him as I had never loved the husband whom I was defying. At one stage he made a tremendous fuss about it. He had been willing that I should have an 'affair' with him of conventional impropriety, transient, involving no ties, no upset, a mere *amourette*. He was more than willing that I should go to humiliating lengths occasionally to win him for O'Shea interests, but the idea of my giving him all my love, of my being engrossed, appropriated by him, was quite another matter. That infuriated him. He felt that he was losing something that was his, and it hurt his self-esteem. Ultimately he challenged Mr Parnell to a duel, and then when he found that Mr Parnell was quite willing to fight' – with a little derisive smile – 'he worked upon my fears for Mr Parnell to get him out of it. He sent my sister Anna, Mrs Steele to me – of course I hated the idea of a duel – and

between us we managed to settle it. We were on a perfectly clear basis from that onward, though he had known it well enough long before. Captain O'Shea's ambassadress received 'assurances' in the true diplomatic style. . . . My freedom was to be respected; appearances were to be preserved; scandal and all cause for scandal were to be avoided.'

The tone and some of the details, such as the characterisation of Willie and the slight imputation of contempt for Anna, have a ring of authenticity rather beyond the literary ability of Henry Harrison to concoct.

The attitude of Parnell also rings true in this version:

'He made no denials and he gave no assurances to Captain O'Shea. He was prepared – for my sake and reluctantly enough – to keep up appearances with the outside world and to avoid scandal, but he would have no ambiguities with Captain O'Shea. I will tell you one story of him which may help you to understand. One day Captain O'Shea came down to Eltham to discuss some important matter with Mr Parnell and the three of us dined together. As the night drew on, I retired before the others, and my door was still standing open when Captain O'Shea, who was the second to retire, came upstairs. He spoke to me, and the discussion of our evening's debate began afresh, and, in the course of it, he entered my room and the door closed. Suddenly, the door was banged violently open and Mr Parnell stalked in, his head held high and his eyes snapping; he said not a word but marched straight up to me, picked me up, threw me over his shoulder and turned on his heel; still without a word, he marched out of the room across the landing and into his own room, where he threw me down on the bed and shut the door.'

Mrs Parnell evidently derived some satisfaction from the episode in retrospect, for she smiled as she clinched her point. 'No, there were no words spoken, but I do not think that Captain O'Shea was left in doubt as to Mr Parnell's attitude. . . .'

If this account is correct, one can well understand the simmering anger that Willie would have had to stifle for years.

Which version, then, is correct? Historians do not agree, and there is not enough evidence to resolve the matter, but to my mind portions of both seem correct. My reading of the events can be summarised as follows.

In January 1881, Willie first suspected a liaison between Katie and Parnell, and threw Parnell's portmanteau out of the train. He was subsequently placated and his suspicions were allayed.

In June, Katie suspected her pregnancy, and she and Parnell decided to continue the deception by Parnell utilising Willie politically and by Katie occasionally resuming marital relations.

In July, as we have seen, there is the curious fact of Willie's flaring up again and challenging Parnell to a duel. What could plausibly have aroused Willie's ire is that, having been recently assured that his marriage was patched up, he chanced on some evidence, such as a letter, that reawakened his suspicions. In this case, the obvious thing that would have angered him to the pitch of issuing a challenge was the discovery that the new child was not his. Nevertheless, there are difficulties about this point, and Willie's concern about Claude Sophie, the child who was born in February 1882, indicates that he truly did think she was his child. Further, as the dead Claude Sophie was frequently mentioned in the divorce trial while Parnell and Katie's two later living children were not, probably because Willie knew they were not his, it seems likely that from early 1882 onwards, the deception among the trio was at an end.

Or almost at an end.

Until 1886, Willie continued to address his letters to Katie as 'My Dick', his pet name for her, and to sign them either 'Boysie' or 'Your Boysie', her pet name for him. Willie had, of course, a hold over them both, but his relations with Katie stayed, on the surface at least, amiable and even affectionate. He, of course, because of Aunt Ben's continued financial support, had every reason to remain on cordial terms. For Katie, the situation would seem to imply that she either had an abiding affection for Willie that her love for Parnell had not dissipated, or that she pretended to have such an affection in order not to rock the boat. Whichever was the case, it does not make her, to my mind, the hypocritical, designing woman out of Victorian or Edwardian or even much modern fiction. It only makes her a woman entangled in the laws, the customs and the mores of her time. Life and its issues are often much more complicated than they are portrayed in popular entertainment or even in classic works of art, and the ideal is often very far from the human practice.

CHAPTER 9

KILMAINHAM

On 11 October 1881, Parnell wrote to Katie from Morrison's Hotel in Dublin, 'To-morrow I go to Kildare, and shall try and start for London Friday morning; but I cannot be sure of this, as "something" may turn up at the last moment. . . .' The 'something' which Parnell expected did turn up two mornings later, and it was his arrest.

Despite the passage by the British Parliament of a Land Act which was certainly an improvement in the plight of the Irish peasantry, the agitation of the Land League had not in the least abated; and from the rather naive view of the British the arrest of Parnell and some of his principal lieutenants was a crushing symbol of how John Bull was prepared to squelch lawlessness.

The arrest, of course, had no such affect upon the Irish. It simply polarised matters further and even elevated Parnell to the status of a folk hero. One popular ballad which immediately appeared indicates how far the mythmaking process had already gone:

> Come, all ye gallant Irishmen, and listen to my song,
> Whilst I a story do relate of England's cruel wrong.
> Before this wrong all other wrongs of Ireland do grow pale,
> For they've clapped the pride of Erin's Isle into cold Kilmainham
>   Jail.
>
> It was the tyrant Gladstone, and he said unto himself,
> 'I niver will be aisy till Parnell is on the shelf.
> So make the warrant out in haste and take it by the mail,
> And we'll clap the pride of Erin's Isle into cold Kilmainham
>   Jail.' . . .
>
> But soundly slept the patriot, for he was kilt wid work,
> Haranguing of the multitudes in Limerick and Cork,
> Till Mallon and the polis came and rang the front-door bell,
> Disturbing of his slumbers in bould Morrison's Hotel. . . .
>
> Then up and spoke bould Morrison, 'Get up, yer sowl, and run!'
> Oh, bright shall shine in Hist'ry's page the name of Morrison!
> 'To see the pride of Erin jailed I never could endure!
> Slip on your boots -- I'll let ye out upon the kitchen door.'

*But proudly flashed the patriot's eye as he bouldly answered,
    'No,
It'll never be said that Parnell turned his back to face the foe!
Parnell aboo for liberty – sure it's all the same', says he,
'For Mallon has locked the kitchen door and taken away the
    key.'*

*They took him and they bound him, them minions of the law.
'Twas Pat, the boots, was there that night and tould me all he
    saw.
But sorra a step the patriot bould would leave the place until
They granted him a ten per cent reduction on his bill.*

*Had I been there with odds at my back of two hundred men to
    one,
It makes my blood run cold to think of the deeds that I'd have
    done.
'Tisn't there that I'd be telling you this melancholy tale,
How they clapped the pride of Erin's Isle into cold Kilmainham
    Jail.*

This is a typical Irish patriotic ballad. The dozens of others like it, commemorating Wolfe Tone and Robert Emmet and Father Murphy and Roddy McCorley and Kevin Barry, are all alike in elevating the defeated hero into a figure of intrepid and dauntless singleness of purpose. Even the real detail of how Parnell haggled over his hotel bill is apotheosised. The only problem was to be when the character of the folk hero was contradicted by the actions of the real man in real life.

The arrest of Parnell and his lieutenants brought rejoicing in England and riots in Dublin. To Parnell, as we have seen, the arrest was probably something of a mixed blessing – a blessing because it consolidated his stature while taking out of his hands the responsibility for events of which he did not entirely approve; a mixed blessing because Katie was pregnant.

He was able to scrawl a note to her before he was taken away from Morrison's Hotel and during his time in Kilmainham he contrived to write constantly to Katie, using various subterfuges, including invisible ink. His letters, which she published years later in her book, have sometimes been criticised as banal in expression and cloying in sentiment. They are full of expressions like 'My own little Wifie', 'My darling Queenie' and 'Your own loving King', and occasionally verge upon baby-talk. Their phrasing is not untypical of the romantic Victorian writing that might be found in a cheap novelette or popular melodrama. Any reference to physical passion is rare and phrased decorously as in 'With a thousand kisses to my own Wife, and hoping soon to lay my head in its old place'. However, Parnell's strength was not in the written word, and these letters, which were intended for Katie's eyes only, do simply and feelingly express his deepest emotions.

Katie's own plight was awkward and difficult. Not only was she worried about the effect that prison would have on Parnell's always precarious health, but she was also carrying Parnell's child and having to fend Willie off. She describes that strained meal on the night of Parnell's arrest when Willie jubilantly dined with her and gloatingly watched her reaction to the news:

> I was now quite calm again, and smiled at him as I reminded him that I was now as ardent a Parnellite as Parnell himself, and had already done so much hard work for 'the cause' that my politics were far more reactionary than when he had introduced Parnell to me: unlike his [Willie's] own, which were less so. My heart being in Kilmainham Goal with my lover, I was momentarily at peace, and could ask Willie questions as to the mode of life and prison discipline of political prisoners. Willie, as are so many men, was never so happy as when giving information.

The next months were a time of intolerable tension for her.

Politically, as many of the chief Irish leaders were now jailed with Parnell, there was a strong feeling among the Irish that some sort of retort ought to be made to the British. The retort took the form of a 'No-rent' manifesto issued to the Irish tenantry, to which Parnell reluctantly gave his assent. The non-payment of rent was sharply opposed by the Catholic hierarchy and doomed to failure, and also gave the government a reason for suppressing the Land League. However, the Ladies' Land League, of which Parnell's sister Anna was a leading spirit, quickly filled the vacuum and proved to be much more intransigent and difficult than its male counterpart. Foster writes that 'about this time Anna became a sort of folk heroine' and that 'she held a position in the popular imagination almost equal to her brother's'. And Margaret Ward says in *Unmanageable Revolutionaries*, 'Although resistance to landlordism had decreased, agrarian crime soared – there had been 2,369 "outrages" in the ten months before the Coercion Act and this number increased to 3,821 in the next ten months. The Ladies' Land League was given credit for having instigated this new wave of crime. . . .' Parnell, as presently became clear to the English, was a greater problem in prison and on the sidelines than he was at large and a restraining influence.

Kilmainham Gaol is a large, gloomy and depressing edifice now preserved as a national patriotic shrine. Its roll-call of political prisoners would finally include the most eminent of Irish patriots, among them Henry Joy McCracken, Wolfe Tone, the Sheares brothers, Napper Tandy, Robert Emmet, Michael Dwyer, William Smith O'Brien, John O'Leary, Charles Kickham the novelist, O'Donovan Rossa, most of the

1916 leaders who were executed there such as Pearse, Connolly, MacDonagh and Plunkett, and such later inmates as the Countess Markievicz and de Valera. Today the building houses mementoes of all of them, and one may even see Erskine Childers's yacht, the *Asgard*, which brought guns into Howth in 1914 – the story of which was told in the novel *The Riddle of the Sands*. And, of course, there is Parnell's cell.

Whitewashed as it is today, it is nevertheless a glum, depressing and constricting apartment, but Parnell was well-fed, able to read journals like *The Times, Engineer* and *Mining Journal*, able to rest, to talk to his colleagues and even to play handball. Save for the very nagging constant worry over Katie, it was probably a useful time of relief from stress for him.

Prison, nevertheless, was prison; and, despite Parnell's privileged position in Kilmainham, the incarceration began to take its toll, particularly a psychological one, as the months rolled by. One of his typical bothered letters was this one of 14 December:

> My Darling Queenie, – Your second letter reached me all right, and I can read them perfectly [a reference to the invisible ink]. But, my darling, you frighten me dreadfully when you tell me that I am 'surely killing' you and our child.
>
> I am quite well again now, my own, and was out to-day for a short time, and will take much better care of myself for the future. It was not the food, but a chill after over-heating myself at ball. But I do not intend to go back on prison fare, even nominally, again, as the announcement that we were on it has served the purpose of stimulating the subscription [a sum collected by the Ladies' Land League to provide better food for the prisoners].
>
> Rather than that my beautiful Wifie should run any risk I will resign my seat, leave politics, and go away somewhere with my own Queenie, as soon as she wishes; will she come? Let me know, darling, in your next about this, whether it is safe for you that I should be kept here any longer.
>
> YOUR OWN HUSBAND
>
> There can be no doubt we shall be released at the opening of Parliament, but I think not sooner.
>
> Dr [J. E.] K[enny] was allowed to be with me all night while I was ill, and we are not to be changed from our rooms.

As the weeks and months passed, Parnell chafed more and more at his imprisonment, and no time more than in February when Katharine's baby was due. On 14 February he wrote to her:

> I am very much troubled about my darling having become so thin, and fear that you have suffered a great deal more than you have

ever told me, and that you are not strong. I often reproach myself for having been so cruel to my own love in staying so long away from her that time, which has led to such a long, long separation.... At least, I am very glad that the days of platform speeches have gone by and are not likely to return. I cannot describe to you the disgust I always felt with those meetings, knowing as I did how hollow and wanting in solidity everything connected with the movement was....

I think Queenie ought to congratulate me at being away from the House instead of pitying me.

Two days later, on 16 February, Katharine gave birth to a baby girl, named Claude Sophie. Afterwards Parnell wrote to her:

I cannot describe to my little Wifie how hopeless and utterly miserable I felt until your little note came that all was quite right. I am very happy, my own, that our little daughter pleases you, and that you are not too much disappointed [apparently that the child was not a boy], and that she is strong and good-tempered. Does Queenie think she will be too big? I shall love her very much better than if it had been a son; indeed, my darling, I do love her very much already, and feel very much like a father.

But, although the baby was healthy at first, she shortly sickened, and, as Katie wrote, 'the doctors I called in could do nothing for her. Slowly she faded from me, daily gaining in that far-reaching expression of understanding that dying children have so strongly, and my pain was the greater in that I feared her father would never see her now.' However, Parnell's nephew Henry, the son of his sister Delia, suddenly died in Paris, and Parnell applied for parole to attend the funeral. This was granted, and he left Kilmainham on the morning of 10 April, and that evening found him at Eltham where, Katie wrote, 'I put his dying child into his arms.'

Parnell remained in Paris for about ten days, being laid up with a fever. In his absence Willie O'Shea, apparently with Parnell's knowledge, wrote to Gladstone, the Liberal Prime Minister, and to Joseph Chamberlain, a leading Radical member of the party, who was at that time thought particularly receptive to the problems of Ireland. Despite the absurd assertion in his letter to Gladstone that 'eighteen months ago Mr Parnell used every effort to induce me to take over the leadership of the Irish party', Willie succeeded in opening the door to negotiations.

When Parnell returned to Eltham on 21 April, he was closeted with Willie in the drawing room hammering out the details of a compromise which was to be known as the Kilmainham Treaty. Katie was upstairs with Claude Sophie and later wrote, 'when the daylight came and they went to lie down for a few hours' rest before Parnell left for Ireland, my little one died as my lover stole in to kiss us both and say good-bye.'

Willie disliked both Parnell and his Irish policies, but he was quick to sink his own feelings, for as the chief intermediary between Parnell and Gladstone he was for once at the very centre of important policy making, That was not only immensely gratifying to his own sense of self-importance, but who could tell what further opportunities for advancement it might lead to?

Back in Kilmainham, Parnell attempted to replace Willie with the more trustworthy party member Justin McCarthy, but Willie was not to be dismissed so easily. Parnell had already set out in a letter to McCarthy, which was to be communicated to the Liberal leaders, the terms he was prepared to accept. Refusing to be outflanked, however, Willie appeared at Kilmainham on 29 April and succeeded in wresting from Parnell another letter on the matter to him. The significant difference between the letters was the inclusion in O'Shea's of the statement that 'a practical settlement of the Land Question . . . would enable us to co-operate cordially for the future with the Liberal Party in forwarding Liberal principles and measures of general reform'. This was indeed a surprising admission, and Gladstone remarked, 'Upon the whole, Parnell's letter is, I think, the most extraordinary I have ever read. . . . I cannot help feeling indebted to O'Shea.'

There has been much speculation about why Parnell included such an unnecessary admission which, if it became widely known, could only cause harm and embarrassment to both the Liberals and himself. Obviously, though, it was given to placate Willie, and to offer him a titbit of vital information not in the McCarthy letter. Paul Bew concludes, 'It seems likely that O'Shea was only able to get such a result by means of compulsion. O'Shea had only one method of compelling Parnell to do anything – blackmail. O'Shea may well have given Parnell the alternative of the exposure of his relationship with Mrs O'Shea.'

This perhaps goes too far. Parnell himself wrote to Katie about the matter on 30 April, 'He came over to see me, so I thought it best to give him a letter, as he would have been dreadfully mortified if he had had nothing to show.' This does not seem as if Parnell had been blackmailed by a man who knew too much, but as if he were trying to stay on good terms with one who might become suspicious.

In any event, the outcome was the release on 2 May of Parnell and the other leaders in Kilmainham, and also the prospect of effective co-operation with the Liberals. Also on 2 May, Gladstone announced to the House that W. E. Forster, the recalcitrant Chief Secretary for Ireland, had resigned, that the onerous Coercion Act for Ireland would be allowed to elapse and, most important, that the arrears of excessive rent paid by Irish tenants would be dealt with.

Just four days later, on 6 May these hopeful prospects were dramatically shattered. Lord Frederick Cavendish, Forster's successor, and his Permanent Under-Secretary, Thomas Burke, were walking in Dublin's Phoenix Park when they were set upon by a small patriotic gang known as the Invincibles and stabbed to death.

When Parnell heard the news, he was with Katie at Blackheath station. She was seeing him off to London, but before he left he went to buy her a paper. As she later described the scene:

> From where I sat in the carriage I could see Parnell's back as he stood just inside the station door. I was watching him, and he half turned and smiled at me as he opened the paper – the *Sunday Observer* – to glance at the news before he brought it to me. He told me afterwards that he wanted to see what was said about Michael Davitt. He had now come to the top of the steps and, as he suddenly stopped, I noticed a curious rigidity about his arms – raised in holding the newspaper open. He stood so absolutely still that I was suddenly frightened, horribly, sickeningly afraid – of I knew not what, and, leaning forward, called out, 'King, what is it?' Then he came down the steps to me and, pointing to the headline, said, 'Look!' And I read, 'Murder of Lord Frederick Cavendish and Mr Burke!'

Cavendish's appointment had been a popular one, even in Ireland, and the effect of the murders was devastating. A crimes bill which Forster had prepared before leaving office was now passed by the House, the reformation of the Land Act was delayed for several years, and Parnell himself was so shaken – 'white as a sheet, agitated and apparently altogether demoralised', as Willie later wrote – that he had Willie forward an offer to Gladstone to resign. Gladstone was opposed to that, but Sir Charles Dilke wrote of Parnell, 'I never saw a man so cut up in my life. He was pale, careworn, utterly unstrung.' In the story of Parnell and Katie, one crisis was hardly surmounted when another, more terrible one, appeared.

After his release from Kilmainham, Parnell found himself plunged into activity. A new organisation to replace the banned Land League had to be set up, and in October 1881 the Irish National League was formed. Its policies were less narrowly agrarian than broadly national; its emphasis was on Home Rule more than on land reform, and on parliamentary action rather than agrarian outrage.

At this time, also, the Ladies' Land League was suppressed, a matter which Parnell managed by simply cutting off their funds. The dissolution permanently estranged his sister Anna whom Foster refers to as 'one of the most likeable, and possibly the most admirable, of the Parnells'. The incident has recently been re-examined by feminist historians who accuse Parnell of ruthlessness. However, although alike in many ways, the two Parnells were very different in their political aspirations: the brother was repelled by violence, but the sister saw it as a necessary means to an end. As Margaret Ward writes, 'While Parnell was courted by the English Liberals, his sister became an uncompromising nationalist, refusing to surrender political principles for short-term personal or political gains.' At any rate, they never spoke again and Katharine says in her memoirs that Anna even cut her brother dead in the street.

Parnell also now needed a new emissary to Gladstone. The contents of Willie's embarrassing letter had become public, and so it was impossible for Parnell and Gladstone to meet face to face without many of Parnell's more left-wing supporters becoming suspicious. Willie himself had, of course, proved impossible, but to an extent Parnell found a replacement in Katie. She wrote to Gladstone and had three meetings with him, and over the years continued to write many letters embodying Parnell's views to both Gladstone and Sir Richard Grosvenor, the Liberal Chief Whip.

In the summer of 1882 Katie again became pregnant. Parnell was much with her, although frequently travelling to Ireland. They were not greatly plagued by Willie who was still basking in the aura of the Kilmainham Treaty negotiations and who had great hopes for his future career. He himself bombarded the Irish Viceroy, Lord Spencer, and the Irish Chief Secretary with letters containing his views on Irish matters, and Katie, undoubtedly at his urging, wrote to Gladstone suggesting that Willie be appointed as Permanent Under-Secretary to replace the murdered Burke. Again she was ready to pull strings for Willie; the only trouble was, she had none. Spencer's view was, 'I can hardly think of a man more unfitted for the place.' Katie was persistent, and Gladstone's secretary referred to her as 'that bothersome woman', but there was no possibility really of Willie's appointment.

Willie must have realised that Katie only had Gladstone's ear because of her connection with Parnell, and he was in the years ahead to exploit the fact for all it was worth. A necessary part of the strategy, of course, was that he himself turn a blind eye to the affair; and he was in Ireland when Katie's new baby, Clare, was born on 4 March 1883. Although not mentioned in her memoirs, the child was duly registered, as Joyce Marlow notes, 'to the paternity of William Henry O'Shea, Member of Parliament for County Clare, Ireland'.

Domestically, it was a placid and even perfect time for Parnell and Katie. They walked and rode. He had his horses brought over from Avondale as well as his telescope and his assaying equipment. He practised target shooting, even with an air rifle in the sitting room until she installed a target for him outside in Aunt Ben's dried-up pond. She also rented a nearby field and set up a cricket pitch for him on which he played with the young O'Sheas and other neighbourhood children. Indeed, he was so content that she found it difficult to drag his old cardigan off him and push him away to Westminster. She would frequently come up to London and listen if he were making a speech, or she would wait for him or meet him if it were a late sitting, and they would drive back to Eltham together.

And there were moments like this one, during the bitterly cold and snowy Christmas of 1883 when they walked round the paths of Aunt Ben's estate listening to the local band and the carollers serenading the old lady:

> We walked up and down in the moonlight till the carols died away, and we heard the church clocks strike twleve. Then we stood together to listen to the Christmas bells sound clear and sharp from many villages on the frosty air, while Parnell again spoke to me of his belief that the soul after death resumed life in the planet under whose influence it was born. He spoke of his belief in a personal destiny and fate, against which it was useless for mortals to contend or fight, and how he believed that certain souls had to meet and become one, till in death the second planet life parted them until the sheer longing for one another brought them together again in after ages.
>
> I said, 'But it seems so lonely like that!' and he answered, 'It is lonely; that is why I am so afraid always of death, and why I hope with every bit of me that we shall die together.'

Despite such sombre moments, their life together remained a calm delight to both. The ruffled moments were caused by the great world outside. In 1883 Katie rented a couple of houses in Brighton, and Parnell had to appear there under the assumed names of Mr Smith and Mr Stewart. Once, returning from a late sitting of the House of Commons, they were shot at. Parnell's movements were watched by detectives. In the summer of 1884 Willie again became difficult, writing suspicious and protesting letters. One drew a heated reply from Katie on 24 July: 'Knowing what I do, it is very difficult for me to reply to your letters with patience. I don't in the least know what you mean or what "thing has to be done" – but this I do know – that I have put up with a great deal for a long time and I do not mean to any longer'. On 4 August Willie wrote to Parnell, 'You have behaved very badly to me', and urged Parnell not to stay at Eltham in his absence or a scandal could hardly be avoided. Parnell coolly and briefly replied that he did not know of any grounds for a scandal.

On 27 November Katie gave birth to her last child who was also called Katie, and again Willie was registered as the father. Neither Parnell nor Katie seemed to worry particularly about Willie at this time. After the birth of her new daughter, Katie had to spend some time recuperating in a nursing home. Shortly after she returned to Eltham, Parnell appeared in a hansom with a large invalid's couch for her. He arranged it in the sitting room, and then carried her downstairs to lie on it. All of this showed, writes Joyce Marlow, 'how unconcerned they both were about Willie's reactions'.

An even greater symptom of their unconcern was that Katie had a workshop and study for Parnell constructed off her sitting room. He even sent to Avondale for wood for the panelling and fireplace. Then in the spring he gave up his rooms in London and quietly moved in. Katie photographed him in his study, 'sitting in his own special easy chair, surrounded by his assaying paraphernalia and holding his pestle and mortar'. His horses, Dictator and President, were stabled nearby. His dogs, Grouse and Ranger, were lying at his feet. His two young daughters were upstairs in the nursery. Nothing could have seemed more domestic or more permanent.

CHAPTER 10

THE GALWAY BY-ELECTION

Willie was about to cause a great deal of trouble.

In November 1885, there was to be a general election. As it approached, it became quite clear that O'Shea could not again be returned for Clare. Nor, indeed, would he be acceptable for any other Nationalist seat. The reason, of course, was directly traceable to O'Shea himself. With his amazing blend of egotism, superciliousness and stupidity, he had succeeded in alienating the entire Irish Party. Katie wrote:

> From his first entry into the House he had refused to sit with the body of the Irish Party, and from his vantage point of the Ministerial benches kept up an undercurrent of sneering comment, or, still more galling, an appearance of deprecating amusement at the mannerisms, accents, or garments of his colleagues, which was the more irritating to them from its intangible air of tolerance.

On one instance after a sitting of the House, Parnell returned to Eltham, and Katie reported:

> After his supper, and while placidly lighting a cigar, he observed with a slight smile, 'A man was waiting in the Lobby to-night for Willie – to kill him.' 'To do *what?*' I exclaimed with horror. 'To kill him; it's all right; don't get excited! – he was much too drunk to be able to kill anyone; but I wish Willie would not annoy them all so much. From what I could make out Willie smiled at his pronunciation of "Misther Spaker, Sorr." Willie's smile is a bit of a twister sometimes!'

To make matters worse, Willie hardly ever attended any of the Irish Party meetings. When he did make an appearance at one in February 1884, after about a two years' absence, 'his ex-colleagues', as F. S. L. Lyons put it, 'seem to have regarded his attendance much as Macbeth regarded Banquo's ghost, an apparition as disagreeable as it was unexpected.'

Willie also made little secret of his allegiance to Joseph Chamberlain, the Liberal politician who was widely distrusted by the Irish Party. Chamberlain's 'henchman' and Chamberlain's 'jackal', Lyons calls him; and Willie's quondam colleagues in the Irish Party would certainly have espoused such terms.

But even if these matters had not told against him, there was the overwhelming objection of Willie's refusal to take the Party Pledge, which all bona fide members took as a matter of course: 'I . . . pledge that in the event of my election to Parliament I will sit, act and vote with the Irish Parliamentary Party.' At this critical election when every Irish politican recognised that party unity was essential, Willie's position was totally unacceptable. In a meeting in October with Parnell at Morrison's Hotel, James J. O'Kelly told Willie, 'it was not in the power of mortal man to get him in for any National constituency without the pledge and even [Parnell] could not do it.'

Parnell, despite his private loathing, was Willie's one supporter. But Willie, with his inflated self-importance, remembered his help to Parnell during the Kilmainham Treaty negotiations, and not only thought that Parnell was deeply in his debt, but also that Parnell was now ungrateful and treacherous. His detestation of Parnell is fiercely evident in this letter to Katie of 2 November from the Shelbourne Hotel in Dublin:

> All I know is that I am not going to lie in ditch. I have been treated in blackguard fashion and I mean to hit back a stunner. I have everything ready; no drugs could make me sleep last night, and I packed my shell with dynamite. It cannot hurt my friend [Chamberlain], and it will send a blackguard's reputation [Parnell's] with his deluded countrymen into smithereens.
> . . . He won't be of high 'importance' soon.
> I wonder the little girls have not written to me; no one cares a bit for me except my poor old mother.

One can only speculate about the nature of Willie's stunner. In his sleepless broodings was this romantic egomaniac already toying with the idea of exposing Parnell's liaison with Katie?

The question really throws into bold relief the historian's central problem, and not merely in this specific series of events, but in general. The problem is simply that in the charting of human emotions and public events inevitably only so much evidence is going to emerge. No matter how prominent the person or how public the event, some areas will always remain in shadow and others in a quite impenetrable darkness. Who murdered the young princes in the Tower? Was Napoleon finally poisoned? Was there a conspiracy to kill John F. Kennedy?

Often the most that can be done is to piece together something of the character of the protagonists, and in a broad sense understand their motivations. In the autumn of 1885, then, these were the ruling desires and leading motivations of our three main characters.

Willie was determined to be returned to Parliament at all costs, and the intensity of his determination rested upon his monumental self-esteem.

Katie was 'very anxious' that he be returned to Parliament and gave as her reasons:

> Politics were a great interest to him and gave him little time to come down to Eltham. When he did so the perpetual watchfulness and diplomacy I had to observe were extremely irksome to me. Years of neglect, varied by quarrels, had killed my love for him long before I met Parnell, and since the February of 1882 I could not bear to be near him.

Parnell was equally anxious and determined that Willie be returned to Parliament, and his motive was not, of course, any idea that the contemptible Willie could or would be of the least use, for Willie was distinctly untrustworthy and a proven political liability. Parnell's motive was clearly and ultimately his passion for Katie.

The leading lines, therefore, are perfectly clear, and it is also perfectly clear that the lines inexorably led to perhaps the most dramatic political crisis that Parnell had yet confronted. It was, in fact, a crisis that led him to stake his own political survival and, indeed, the future of the whole Nationalist movement upon the Irish accepting Willie O'Shea. It was quite a gamble.

It was also a gamble not worth taking unless it was pressingly necessary – and it is here, in the real reasons for the pressing necessity, that the historian enters into the shaded and the darkened areas of fumbling exploration and hesitant speculation.

Nevertheless, there are quite a lot of known facts.

Once it became apparent that no Nationalist seat was possible for Willie, it became necessary to find him some seat somewhere. Parnell first turned to the north of Ireland. Indeed, although he was now wooing the Tories rather than the Liberals, he actually proposed to Sir Richard Grosvenor, the Liberal Whip, that if Willie were accepted as the Liberal candidate for Mid Armagh, Parnell would promise to deliver the Irish vote to the Liberals in five other constituencies. Gladstone justifiably remarked that this was 'very curious'. However the Ulster Liberals, as Lyons wrote, 'showed a tiresome disposition to prefer one of their own sort,' and the whole plan fell through.

Parnell's manoeuvrings for Willie were indeed very curious to an outsider, but, according to Willie, Parnell's relations to him were those of a whipped dog. As Willie wrote to Chamberlain on 8 November:

Parnell called on me yesterday afternoon and began to mumble something about sorrow that I had not seen my way to contest Mid Armagh and hope than an English seat might yet be found for me. I soon cut matters short by telling him that I did not want any more beating about the bush, that no man had ever behaved more shamefully to another than he had behaved to me, and that I wished to hold no further communication with him. He enquired whether I wished him to leave and I replied, most certainly. He then crossed the room and held out his hand. I informed him that I would not touch it on any account.

I do not suppose he was feeling enough to have felt the blow long, but I never saw a man slink out of a room more like a cur kicked out of a butcher's shop.

We must make some allowances for Willie's usual self-dramatisation, with himself as the hero and everybody else as the ignominious villain. We must also note that the portrait of Parnell as a cringing Uriah Heep is quite ridiculous. Nevertheless, Parnell's demonstrable actions for several months show that there is a grain of truth in Willie's account, and the grain could only be that, no matter how much he disliked it, Parnell felt that he was in Willie's hands.

As both southern and northern Ireland had proved impossible, that left England itself for a constituency to be found.

Katie was particularly active in the matter, pulling what strings she could, even wiring Gladstone and 'grimly determined that I would make Lord Richard Grosvenor's life a burden to him until I had landed Willie safely on the Liberal benches'. Indeed, Katie was so anxious to serve Willie that she even agreed to forward the interests of his business associate, Samuel Montague, who was standing for Parliament in the Whitechapel Division of London. Accordingly she 'asked Parnell about getting the Irish vote for Mr Montague, and he had said he did not see what harm Montague could do, and it was just as well to get the Irishmen to support him as not.' She then wrote to a London agent of Parnell 'under such name as he would know the message emanated from him' to encourage the Irish to support Montague. The incident is not important in itself, but it certainly indicates the lengths she would go to at this time to placate Willie.

She did accomplish a good deal. Gladstone wired Willie authorising him to say that he had Gladstone's backing,' and Katie so harried Grosvenor that he came to Liverpool on Willie's behalf. Indeed, Parnell himself was in Liverpool, and despite his instructions to his followers to vote Tory when no Irish candidate was available, he was intriguing with the Liberals to elect Willie, and willing to give up a good deal to do it. When Grosvenor was asked about Parnell's curious behaviour, he replied in the presence of several persons, 'Oh, he sleeps with O'Shea's wife.' Grosvenor's knowledge of the liaison is also quite apparent in

Katie's account, and the matter was getting to be uncomfortably widespread knowledge.

Despite all the efforts on his behalf, Willie failed to be returned by a slim margin of fifty-five votes. 'The next day,' Katie writes, 'Parnell came back to me. I was suffering from a nervous breakdown owing to the sudden relaxing of the intense strain and work that I had been through, coupled with my bitter disappointment at Willie's defeat, and Parnell nursed, soothed and comforted me as tenderly as a woman.'

Willie had, however, an incredibly dogged persistence, and he went to Parnell insisting that his 'services in regard to the Kilmainham Treaty and also in acting between Chamberlain, Mr Gladstone and himself' warranted Parnell's supporting him for an Irish seat. There was just one available. T. P. O'Connor had been returned for both Galway and Liverpool and had elected to represent Liverpool. Hence there was to be a by-election to fill Galway's vacant seat.

However the objections to Willie that had prevented his nomination for Clare were just as potent for Galway, but Willie stubbornly refused to believe this and incredibly insisted that he was extremely popular in Ireland, although not with the 'rapscallion crew' that constituted the Irish Party. As Katie wrote, he 'fumed and urged his point with the deadly, nagging persistency that I had so often known and given in to, in the old days, for the mere sake of hearing no more on a subject.'

Finally Parnell said to him, 'And you will not take the pledge even?'

'No, I will sit where I like, and vote as I please.'

'Then the thing', said Parnell, 'is not worth discussing.'

It was not. The matter was flatly impossible. Yet Willie, encouraged by Chamberlain, continued to insist, and all through January 1886 Parnell brooded about the problem. He finally said to Katie,

> I can force Willie upon Galway, but it will be such a shock to my own men that they'll not be the same again. Or I can leave it alone, and ... and ... will do almost as much mischief with him there. Queenie, you must see him again, and tell him I'll propose him if only he will consent to take the party pledge. Tell him I cannot insult the others by proposing him without this.

But still Willie was adamant, and the result was that Parnell completely capitulated to him.

As Parnell said to Katie. 'I'll get him returned. I'll force him down their throats, and he can never again claim that I have promised and not performed. It will cost me the confidence of the party, but that much he shall have, and I shall have done with his talk of pledges.'

In considering Willie's actions, we have little documentary evidence to aid us, and we enter the dark and shaded areas. It is rather like a poker game in which a player raises the bet, and his opponent must then make a shrewd judgment about whether he is facing an ace in the hole.

Clearly Parnell thought that Willie had the ace, and so he folded his hand. Clearly he thought that Willie knew of his affair with Katie, and that he would publicly expose it.

This is the probability, and yet there are some nagging bits of evidence against it. Willie was a megalomaniac, and his view of the figure he cut in the political world very often had the most tenuous connection to reality. He saw himself as the protagonist when he was in reality a spear carrier; and it is not outside the bounds of possibility that he could have been truly ignorant of Parnell's love affair with Katie. His enormous self-esteem provided a terrific insulation, and it is just possible that he pushed himself because he had misread the cards in his hand, that he pushed himself because of his monstrously inflated idea of his self-importance.

There is a bit of evidence to support this view. None of his extant letters of the time, save the enigmatic one about his 'stunner', indicates that he was aware of the liaison. He does not tax Katie with it. His detestation of Parnell is amply evident, but his tone to Katie is familiar and even fond and he continues to use their pet names.

During the subsequent manoeuvres in Galway town, it was at least private knowledge that Katie was Parnell's mistress. 'The candidate's wife', Joe Biggar frequently asserted in conversation, 'is Parnell's mistress and there is nothing more to be said.' The problem, Tim Healy remarked, 'has its entire origin in a woman of evil character and is an abominable scandal.' However, Willie, in what Lyons calls a well authenticated story, 'absolutely denied to his proposer, Father Joseph O'Shea, OSF (who claimed to be a close relation), that Biggar's accusations about Parnell and Katharine had any truth in them.' Healy in his memoirs went further and reported that Bishop Thomas Carr of Galway had told him and Biggar that 'O'Shea had gone down on his knees before him and vowed there was no truth in any allegation which connected his wife's name with Parnell'.

This, then, is the available evidence. It is hardly conclusive either way. A pity, for the answer would throw a crucial light on the most significant dark and shaded area of this strange triangle. It would basically affect how and what we thought not merely about Willie but also about Parnell and Katie.

The events of the Galway by-election were the stuff of drama. When Parnell arrived by train on 9 February, with T. P. O'Connor and others, they were greeted at the station by an inflamed crowd that shouted slogans like 'To hell with O'Shea' and 'To hell with Parnell and Whiggery'. It was a startling reception for 'the Chief', but even so the crowd retained sufficient awe of him that they made for O'Connor instead, and Parnell had to whisk him quickly off to the hotel.

Biggar and Healy were already in Galway, whipping up opposition to O'Shea and support for the local candidate, Michael Lynch. There were tumultuous meetings, and Healy emotionally and Biggar bluntly attacked Parnell's support for Willie. Parnell deflated Healy by refuting the charge that he would resign his leadership if Willie were not returned. 'I have no intention of resigning my position. I would not resign it if the people of Galway were to kick me through the streets today.'

But even though Parnell said he would not resign, he made the real issue not the acceptance of the generally despised Willie, but the continued acceptance of him as leader of the Irish Party. He was not always an effective speaker, but on this occasion his remarks to a crowded meeting were electric. 'I have', he said, 'a parliament for Ireland in the hollow of my hand'. And he went on precisely to point out the effect in England if O'Shea, his choice, were beaten: 'There will rise a shout from all the enemies of Ireland, "Parnell is beaten, Ireland no longer has a leader."'

T. P. O'Connor wrote, 'It is impossible to describe the effects of these words on the audience. You could almost hear the shudder of emotion which they felt. Enough; Parnell had awed them into silence, into grudging and hateful obedience; it was one of the most complete subjugations of a crowd in history.'

The *Freeman's Journal* of 9 February, echoing Parnell's speech, hammered the point home:

> the issue is not between Captain O'Shea and Mr Lynch, but whether at the very acme of the crisis when the question of Home Rule hangs in the balance, when Mr Parnell almost holds it in the hollow of his hand, Galway will strike a blow at his prestige and at his authority, and do what in it lies to weaken his power with the English people and the English Government to press to a successful and immediate conclusion the united demand of a united people for Self-Government. Granted that Mr Parnell was completely in the wrong in recommending Captain O'Shea, the issue would remain unaffected. The power of Mr Parnell has consisted, and must consist, in English statesmen recognising that he is the personal embodiment of the Irish nation.

The message got across, and on polling day Willie received 942 votes and Lynch 54. Parnell's gamble had paid off. He had utterly won, and he was now able to return to Parliament with a united party behind him for what it was hoped would be the last, and the finally successful struggle for Home Rule.

And yet there was a price that would be paid in days to come. Part of it would be dramatically summed up in Tim Healy's bitter opposition to Parnell's final struggle for leadership. And, even more important, there was now the widespread, if still tacit, public secret of Parnell's liaison with Katie. The Galway by-election had established it firmly in the centre of things; and at any time, should the tacit public secret become overt public knowledge, the whole apparently impregnable structure that Parnell had built up could topple like a pack of cards. A pack of cards is probably the most appropriate metaphor for a gambler and, coincidentally, a gambler's purse is called the 'kitty'.

And was the drama of Galway finally worth Parnell's terrific gamble? He must himself have wondered, for in less than four short months the incredible Willie, rather than vote on the second reading of the Home Rule Bill, walked out of Parliament, and resigned the seat that he had moved mountains to get.

Why did he do it?

Abels suggests these reasons:

> After being elected a member from Galway, O'Shea's position in Parliament was not as comfortable as it had been before. Completely beholden to Parnell for his election, he nonetheless shunned his leadership, and this smacked of ingratitude even in the eyes of the English members. The tale being choice gossip, there was wide feeling that O'Shea had paid a price for his seat that was too high for a gentleman to pay. O'Shea felt himself slighted by many who had been his boon companions and hosts. By now the thought had finally penetrated his mind that the opinion was widespread, if not universal, that his wife was the well-established mistress of Parnell.

Whether Willie really knew that Katie was Parnell's mistress, and was pretending ignorance, is impossible to say. However, in the first months of 1886, it became difficult even to pretend ignorance, for various small items in the press were making uncomfortable innuendoes. In particular, there was a story entitled 'Mr Parnell's Suburban Retreat' that appeared in late May in W. T. Stead's *Pall Mall Gazette*, and remarked, 'During the sitting of Parliament the honourable member for Cork [Parnell] takes up residence at Eltham, a suburban village to the southeast of London. From there he can often be seen taking exercises round by Chislehurst and Sidcup'. Innocuous enough to the general public, but not to Willie.

He had already written to Katie questioning her about Parnell's proximity, and when reassured by her, replied on 26 April, 'With regard to Mr Parnell I believed your assurances, but I have scores of times pointed out to you that however innocent in themselves the frequent visits of a man to a woman during the absence of her husband is an offence against proprieties.'

It is plausible that it really was the 'Suburban Retreat' story that was the last straw for Willie, and that caused him to leave the House when the second reading of the Home Rule Bill came up in June. It had to be something dramatic that impelled him to this startling about-face. It is tempting to think that this mountain of self-assurance did not until then credit all the rumours he had heard, and it does make psychological sense in providing a motive for his throwing up what he considered his major occupation, being a Member of Parliament.

If this is so, then Willie thought that Katie's children, Clare and Katie, who were born in 1883 and 1884, were his. After 1886, sexual relations between Willie and Katie ceased. Before then, he was not often at Eltham, but he was sometimes there. There is very little evidence in the matter, and Katie's last two children are seldom alluded to. But a prime reason for Willie's incredible gullibility might well have been that he continued to sleep with Katharine from time to time until the early months of 1886. The last two girls, who were indisputably Parnell's, he might have later glossed over because of the galling but belated knowledge of his own cuckoldry.

This is a plausible scenario, and, if it has been glossed over, the reason may be that historians have not always been realistic reporters. Sometimes they have become as simplistically moral as romantic novelists.

CHAPTER 11

THE PIGOTT AFFAIR

The several playwrights who have treated the love story of Katie and Parnell have usually omitted the Pigott case, although it was famous enough at the time. However, its inclusion in the tight, constricted form of a play would have seemed simply a distraction from the lean, clean rise of the plot to its dramatic climax, and then its quick and tragic denouement. And not only did Katie never meet Pigott, but also that absurd tragi-comic figure belonged more to a Dickens novel than a romantic tragedy.

Nevertheless, Richard Pigott and his forgeries may have been a more determining factor than anything else in congealing Parnell's already stubborn intractability — and, therefore, in assuring the inevitability of the final grim incidents in the story of Katie and Parnell.

Richard Pigott was born about 1828 in County Meath, and became an Irish political journalist who owned several papers with patriotic titles like the *Irishman*, the *Shamrock* and the *Flag of Ireland*. St John Ervine cruelly but memorably describes him like this:

> He was a shiftless, moon-faced man who fell into villainy not so much because he was vicious as because he was incompetent. Generations of mean and flabby ancestors must have gone to the making of this man, whose capacity for crawling servility and obsequious deference gave him the right to claim spiritual descent from Uriah Heep. His big, round head was tangled at its base with bushy beard, and his forehead jutted out as if it had started on the road to nobility but had failed to get there. He wore a monocle screwed into his right eye, and he had a trick, when in doubt, of putting his hand to his mouth and holding his lip. His penury kept him continually on the hunt for money, and he plunged like a bewildered elephant from mess to mess, cadging at one moment from the Government and at the next from their enemies, and lying to each with ineptitude that was nearly innocence.

And further:

He was, perhaps, the most notorious and distrusted man in Dublin, always engaged in shady enterprises and walking perilously near the brink of blackmail, and yet, such is the singularity of human nature, undeniably an affectionate and devoted father to his four motherless children. There was no act of mean villainy to which Richard Pigott was not prepared to stoop; he was a blackmailer, a forger, a swindler, a thief, and a purveyor of indecent books and photographs; yet there can be few virtuous men in the world who love their children more deeply than he loved his.

In 1885, this contemptible but rather appealing man was more than usually pressed for funds. Accordingly, he put out feelers about writing a pamphlet to be called *Parnellism Unmasked*, which would establish Parnell's connection with political violence in Ireland. He was encouraged to continue his researches and, indeed, liberally subsidised by Edward Caulfield Houston, a young man who had been connected with the London *Times* and who was now secretary of the most prominent Unionist association in Ireland. Amassing credible evidence, however, proved a problem for Pigott, and presently it occurred to him that really satisfactory evidence could be manufactured in the form of forged letters. In July 1886, then, under a guise of cloak-and-dagger mysteriousness, Pigott summoned Houston to Paris. There were, he said, darkly, two men downstairs who had discovered various truly incriminating documents in an appropriately black bag, and who were willing to let them go for a price. There were no two men, and there was no black bag, but the gullible Houston handed £605 over to the gratified Pigott, who duly handed over the documents. Houston then approached the editor of *The Times* with his 'evidence'.

The Times was eager to discredit Parnell, so eager that several sound warnings about the reliability of the documents were ignored, and on 18 April 1887, in a series of articles entitled 'Parnellism and Crime', the paper published a facsimile of a handwritten letter signed and presumably by Parnell. The short letter clearly showed Parnell's general approval of the Phoenix Park murders and appeared to be no less than a bombshell.

On the morning of 18 April Parnell was with Katie at Eltham, and, although Katie gives the wrong date in her book, this is how she describes Parnell's reception of the news:

On that day I did not give Parnell the *Times* opened as usual for his glance over the political reports while he breakfasted. He asked for it, but I wanted him to finish his breakfast first, and replied: 'The *Times* is unusually stodgy; do eat your breakfast first.'

He said he *must* finish a bit of assaying he had left over-night, before going to London, and would not have time for papers afterwards, so I told him of the letters, and propped the *Times* against the teapot as usual.

He read the whole thing, meditatively buttering and eating his toast the while. I supplied him with marmalade, and turned over the folded paper for him so that he could read more easily.

He made no remark at all till he had finished breakfast, and carefully clipped the end off his cigar; then, with a smile, he tossed the paper at me, saying, '*Now* for that assaying I didn't finish! Wouldn't you hide your head with shame if your King were so stupid as that, my Queen.'

Katie was more alarmed than Parnell – as she was to be later in the divorce case. It was she who realised the need for action, he who shrugged the matter off as of little consequence. In fact, despite her urging that 'the thing was very serious', he actually went off for two hours or so to potter about among his crucibles. Indeed, she finally almost literally had to drag him away and force him to start for London:

> I said, 'Now, my King, you must attend to the *Times*. You must take an action against them.'
> 'No. Why should I?' struggling into his coat as I held it for him. 'I have never taken any notice of any newspapers, nor of anyone. Why should I now?'

When Parnell finally reached the House of Commons, he met Timothy Harrington, one of the Irish MPs, and together they looked over the *Times* facsimile. As R. Barry O'Brien reported the scene:

> 'He put his finger on the S of the signature,' Harrington recalled, 'and said quite calmly as if it were a matter of the utmost indifference, "I did not make an S like that since 1878." My God,' I thought, 'if this is the way he is going to deal with the letter in the House, there is not an Englishman who will not believe that he wrote it.'

Parnell did, in fact, rouse himself to denounce the letter to the House as a 'villainous and bare-faced forgery', but he did not sue *The Times* for libel, and gradually the affair died down. To his enemies his true character had been shown up for what it was; to his friends the matter was but another attempt at mud slinging; and in any event nothing could be proved.

It was then that Frank Hugh O'Donnell blew the smouldering embers back into livid flames. O'Donnell had been a testy and difficult member of the Irish Party, but he had retired from politics in 1885, and had been barely mentioned in *The Times* attack. However, he was something of a crank, and about a year after the original fuss he sued *The Times* for having libelled him. He was apparently impelled by a desire for notoriety and drama, and these also seem to have been the motives that led him a decade later to mount a venomous pamphleteering attack against the morality of W. B. Yeats's *The Countess Cathleen* on the occasion of its first production in Dublin.

What the O'Donnell lawsuit did was to give *The Times* the impetus to take up the whole matter with increased vigour and even to add fuel to the fire by new 'evidence' in the form of a new 'Parnell' letter. The letter was dated 9 January 1882, before the Phoenix Park murders when Parnell was in Kilmainham, and it read:

> Dear E.
> What are these fellows waiting for? This inaction is inexcusable; our best men are in prison and nothing is being done. Let there be an end to this hesitancy. Prompt action is called for. You undertook to make it hot for old Forster and Co. Let us have some evidence of your power to do so. My health is good, thanks.
>
> > Yours very truly,
> > Chas. S. Parnell

If accepted as authentic, the letter would be much more damning than the first. The first letter had merely shown Parnell approving of the Phoenix Park murders after they had been done; this letter showed him actually inciting them.

The House appointed a Special Commission to investigate the whole question of Nationalist activity and violence. And there was no doubt what this Conservatively dominated Commission would find. As Abels remarked,

> There was no illusion about how the cards were being stacked against the Irish. It was not the forgery that was to be investigated, but the Tories would now try the whole Nationalist movement on all the charges made by its enemies – in effect, as Burke said, a whole nation was to be indicted. The inquiry would trace all kinds of crime to the Land League and the Irish National League and then make all members, including members of Parliament, constructively guilty.

What is particularly interesting and, for the final act of this drama, particularly ominous is that the public issues rested solidly on the personal attack against Parnell.

In this case, the letters were the crux of the matter.

Katie says that:

> Soon my absorbed study of the forged letters caught Parnell's interest, he shook off his apathy and joined my study of his handwriting of many years, and those of the various possible (and impossible) imitators. Once he became interested he threw himself into it as whole-heartedly as he did into any other hobby. We spent hours in this study of calligraphy, and made some interesting discoveries.

What she does not say is that Parnell's chief suspect was no other than Willie. Paul Bew writes, 'He tried to persuade his Liberal backers to place a detective to spy on a public house which O'Shea used for assignations. When they refused, Parnell himself took to hanging around the spot. All this came to nothing: Pigott it was, and not O'Shea.'

The crucial clues occurred in the second letter, and these were the two misspellings, 'inexcuseable' and 'hesitency'.

On 21 and 22 February 1889, Pigott was called before the Commission to testify. The *Daily News* described him as 'a short, stoutish, round-shouldered man is Pigott, with a bald, shining head, bushy white whiskers and moustache, big, somewhat irresolute mouth, big, fleshy nose, and smallish eyes far apart'. *The Birmingham Daily Post* saw a 'coarsely composed and rather cheapened Father Christmas'. Hardly a prepossessing figure.

Nevertheless, Pigott was not really shaken until the second day when he was asked to write down a number of words. One of the words was 'hesitancy', and Pigott misspelled it 'hesitency'. With that gaffe, Pigott's culpability was suddenly blindingly apparent, and Parnell's counsel, Sir Charles Russell, took full advantage of his discomfiture. As F. S. L. Lyons wrote, 'What then followed was one of the classic examples of the art of cross-examination in Victorian legal history. With short, sharp questions Russell drove Pigott deeper and deeper into the mire of confusion and self-contradiction.' As the cross-examination continued, it developed, as Paul Bew adds, into 'scenes of ghastly farce':

> As even the sombre Victorian judges rolled about with laughter, the unfortunate forger disintegrated. His exit lines became more and more pathetic: 'Bad as I am, I am always true to those who trusted me. . . . I don't pretend to be virtuous. . . . Spelling is not my strong point.'

It was really the cleansing laughter that completely and instantly rehabilitated Parnell's reputation. But triumphant and funny as the scene was, it was comedy as written by a Sean O'Casey, and touched with pathos. As one woman observer wrote:

It was the most exciting time I ever spent. In the end we came away astonished that a fellow-creature could be such a liar as Pigott. It was very funny, too; but I could not help thinking of Becky Sharp's 'It's so easy to be virtuous on £5000 a year'; and to see that old man standing there, with everybody's hand against him, driven into a corner, after all his twists and turns, was somewhat pathetic.

When Pigott's examination was over, Parnell remarked to his solicitor, 'That man will not come into the box again. . . . If you do not keep your eye on him you will find that he will leave the country.' Prophetic words, for when the Commission met again on 26 February, there was no Pigott.

Parnell's triumph was complete. On his next appearance in the House, as Katie reported:

> every section of the House – Ministers, Opposition – all rose at his entry as one man, cheering themselves hoarse and shouting his name. I asked him afterwards if he had not felt very proud and happy then, but he only smiled, and answered, 'They would all be at my throat in a week if they could!' I thought of that speech a little later on.

Parnell's was a wise insight, but one weakened by the implicit self-assurance, the confidence of being above matters, of being unassailable. Unfortunately, there was to be one great difference between the Parnell who was assailed by Pigott's forgeries and the Parnell who was assailed by the charges of Willie O'Shea. In the latter case, he was guilty.

But in this case, what of the guilty Pigott?

He turned up in Madrid on 28 February and registered in a hotel under the rather romantic yet faintly ridiculous name of Ronald Ponsonby. His amazing ill-luck continued to dog him, for on the very same day he was spotted by, of all the incredible ironies, Willie O'Shea. However, the police were alerted to him also, and when he returned to his hotel room that evening they were waiting. As *The Times* reported:

> He turned deathly pale, and for a moment seemed to lose his nerve completely. But he soon pulled himself together. . . . At this moment the inspector entered the room and Pigott, muttering something about his luggage, stepped back a pace or two and opened the handbag which lay upon a chair. The inspector seemed to divine Pigott's object and sprang forward to seize him. It was too late. Pigott had a big revolver in his hand, placed the muzzle against his mouth, drew the trigger, and fell to the ground a horribly mutilated corpse.

Around his neck was a soiled scapular.

Pigott was only a minor character in the drama of Katie and Parnell, but a curiously memorable one. Sometimes the great dramatists will provocatively include just such a character. He may appear for but one brief scene, and yet he is unforgettable – the drunken porter in *Macbeth*, the unnamed soldier in *Lear* who is so appalled by the blinding of Gloucester that he fruitlessly springs upon the savage Cornwall and is killed. Pigott rather seems to combine something of both of those characters. Even though he was absurd, ludicrous and pathetic, and even though his name is forever associated with baseness, he was in this portion of the drama the most human figure, and he died because of it. Without Pigott, this portion of the drama remains simply an entertainment, a romantic courtroom melodrama. But he, like the drunken porter and the unnamed soldier, provided the fallible humanity; and fallible humanity, as the climactic act of this drama was so painfully to demonstrate, is what tragedy is about.

And how did people – even people who had ample reason to hate him – regard him? Parnell's lieutenant Justin McCarthy wrote to Katie's sister Anna, 'Poor dear Pigott – I had a genuine affection for him.' And Katie herself wrote of the suicide, 'It was a painful affair, and Parnell was sorry for the poor creature.'

Perhaps too much has been made here of Pigott's role, but all the great, sad stories seem to fall inexorably into the same tragic pattern, and Pigott's guilt as well as his end could be seen as prophetic of what was to happen to Katie and to Parnell.

It is a curious fact that the two most notorious sex scandals of the 1890s in England involved Irish protagonists. And it is equally curious that both well-known stories fell into the traditional tragic pattern of Western literature, and that both inevitably fostered a good handful of stage dramatisations.

The second famous and lurid scandal was, of course, that of the great Irish wit Oscar Wilde. It occurred just five years after the public furore over Parnell and Katie, but it had no political repercussions, and its core was homosexual rather than heterosexual love. Nonetheless, the two stories fell into such similar patterns and were impelled by such similar motivations and human psychological flaws that the story of Oscar Wilde can tell us much not only about the story of Parnell and Katie but also about the plight of any individuals in the same impossible situation. The story of Oscar, as well as the story of Parnell and Katie, is really the prototypical tragic situation. The specifics of this story may vary in inessential details determined by time and place, but the basic elements remain as constant in the centuries before the 1890s as in the decades since.

In both cases, there was an unlikely hero, and all the more heroic because he was so unlikely. It was as improbable for an obscure, little read and casually educated Irish landowner to become the dominant figure in Anglo-Irish politics as it was for the son of a Dublin aural surgeon and antiquarian to become the most glittering figure in literary London. Nevertheless, as Parnell in 1890 was the key figure in the dominant political issue of the day, so Wilde in 1895 was the most brilliant, the most successful and utterly the wittiest writer in London. His *The Picture of Dorian Gray* had been a scandalous success, and in 1895 he had not one but two sparkling comedies running in the West End. He was the Beau Brummel of literary taste and the prince of wits. His triumph seemed as complete as did Parnell's after the exposure of the Pigott forgeries. But it is not merely that their situations were the same; it was also, most unfortunately, that their psychology was the same, and that its most prominent characteristic was what the Greeks called hubris.

In Wilde's case, his literary and even social pre-eminence in 1895 gave him an imperturbable certainty that he was unassailable. That was the moment when his lover, Lord Alfred Douglas, chose to use Wilde as a means to humiliate Douglas's father, the insanely irascible Marquis of Queensberry. Queensberry, deploring Douglas's life in general and his association with Wilde in particular, had left his card at Wilde's club, and on it he had scribbled a note accusing Wilde of posing as a 'somdomite' – the Marquis was erratic not only in his character but also in his spelling. In any event, Douglas persuaded Wilde to sue Queensberry and, inflated with hubris, he did. Initially he regarded the proceedings with amused contempt and attempted to protect himself on the witness stand with only the thin rapier of his wit. But a rapier is a very ineffective defence against a machine gun, and those three notorious trials quite gunned Wilde down. The glittering, scintillating and genial Wilde was hauled ignominiously off to Reading Gaol, his career blasted, his character held in contumely, and even the shimmer of his wit now looking rather like the phosphorescence emanating from a dead fish.

After the Pigott affair, Parnell seemed in as unassailable a position as Wilde was to seem later. Then when in December 1889 Willie O'Shea cited Parnell as co-respondent in his divorce suit against Katharine, Parnell reacted with precisely the same hubris that Wilde was to affect. After all, had not the Pigott affair supremely vindicated him? What more was there to fear?

The dramatists have always insisted on the humanity of the hero by giving him a flaw that is his undoing, and more often than not the flaw is a blind pride. So it was with Wilde, and so it was with Parnell.

In the tragic pattern of Parnell's story, his total exoneration after the Pigott affair was his moment of highest triumph, his apotheosis. But what inexorably, brutally and quickly happened afterwards could have been plotted by Sophocles or Dostoyevsky.

In one of Wilde's comedies, a character tosses off the typically Wildean quip, 'Divorces are made in heaven.' At the time it seemed another frivolous witticism, to be taken no more seriously than the antics of the charming, unreal mannikins that cavort so delightfully through *The Importance of Being Earnest*. But Wilde was more than an inspired funnyman like W. S. Gilbert, or a purveyor of nonsense like Edward Lear, or of inspired fantasy like Lewis Carroll, and his quips were often wise insights. Katie and Parnell would surely have agreed with this one, even though the gods they fought did not. What they were to learn, however, was that even if made in heaven, divorces are granted in hell.

CHAPTER 12

THE DIVORCE CASE

On 18 December 1889 Parnell visited for the first and only time the Liberal leader Gladstone at his home at Hawarden. For four hours on that day and the next they discussed the Irish problem, and they parted from each other full of confidence and, apparently, mutual respect. Gladstone wrote in his diary, 'He is certainly one of the very best people to deal with that I have ever known.' In a speech on 19 December in Liverpool, Parnell heaped praise upon Gladstone and called upon the English people to support 'the great battle I trust we are on the eve of entering'.

The Hawarden meeting might be taken as the high point of Parnell's political power and achievement. Since December 1885 Gladstone had been committed to Home Rule for Ireland, and with the Home Rule Bill which had been defeated on its second reading in 1886 he had tried to establish a limited Irish legislature. It was only a matter of time until he introduced another Bill. So now the fullest co-operation of the Irish Party with the Liberals was a point firmly established, and Parnell seemed on the very verge of leading his followers into the Promised Land. Paul Bew writes, 'Parnell's ascendancy was at its height'. Lyons adds, 'that Parnell should be received as an honoured guest at Hawarden, and thus admitted to the inmost citadel of Liberalism, seemed to all observers the culminating point of his apotheosis, the attainment of the zenith towards which his star had climbed so steadily since Pigott's disgrace and death.'

He had now been in Parliament for fifteen years, and St John Ervine ably sums up what he had accomplished:

> In that time he had grown from a shy, stammering, nervous, and extraordinarily ignorant young man into one of the most powerful leaders in the history of English politics. The Irish party, which had been a disregarded and derided gang of amiable job-hunters when he joined it, was now an influential and highly-disciplined body of resolute and tireless patriots serving their country at some cost to themselves. This change in the status and character of the party was almost entirely the work of Parnell. . . . Finally, he had compelled the English Parliament to concern itself with Irish

affairs, and had put Home Rule into the programme of the Liberal party. Self-government for Ireland was no longer a matter for academic discussion on a Parliamentary off-day, but a practical proposal which might at any moment become a fact.

But a mere five days later, on Christmas Eve, Willie O'Shea instituted divorce proceedings against Katharine, naming Parnell as co-respondent. This action started an inexorable train of events that was to destroy everything which Parnell had spent a laborious fifteen years in building up, which was to split the Irish Party, and which was to set back the cause of Irish independence for a generation. It was also to destroy and to kill Parnell, and utterly to change the course of Katharine's life.

Curiously, the pattern was that of great tragic drama. The hero was raised to a seemingly triumphant height, a seemingly impregnable position, and then was quickly, brutally dashed down to his destruction. The great tragic dramas, however, are not merely the stories of particular individuais, but of individuals whose destinies are intimately intertwined with the fate of their society. As the sickness of Oedipus was also the sickness of Thebes, and the madness of Lear a symptom of the chaos of Britain, so was the downfall of Parnell the doom of Ireland's hopes.

The great tragic stories are not, of course, simply stories; they are stories imbued with point and meaning. The point and meaning arise from the incidents and give the incidents their poignance and power and continuing resonance through the ages. The great tragic stories, in other words, retain their vitality because they seem to contain clues central to man's overwhelming preoccupation, the question of what is to be his fate.

One meaningful conflict of issues – although surely not the only one – is certainly set in bold relief by this portion of the story of Katharine and Parnell and Willie. There were two sets of values involved – one a public and altruistic notion, the other a private and selfish motivation. And this clash was not a simple one with Katharine representing true love and Parnell representing disinterested public service on one side, and Willie representing jealousy, hatred and greed on the other. The whole business was much more tangled.

When Willie walked out of Parliament and resigned from the Irish Party in 1886, he cut his public ties with Parnell and his basic personal ties, if not his legal ones, with Katharine. Despite, however, his bitter rage against Parnell as, in his mind, the architect of both his public downfall and his private disgrace, he made no further move for about three and a half years.

There could be but one reason for a restraint which he found so galling – Aunt Ben's money.

When Parnell and Katie first began their affair in 1881, Aunt Ben was

88 years old, and nobody really expected that she would live very long. She lived, in fact, for eight more years, and did not die until 19 May 1889. During all this time, Katie remained, except for occasional short intervals, her almost daily companion. Aunt Ben supported Katie's nearby establishment, and she also contributed considerably to Willie, paying for his rooms in London and making many other periodic payments. But, most importantly, she had named Katharine as the sole heir to her fortune, and Willie was still Katharine's husband. All in all, it was hardly a satisfactory *status quo* for Willie, but it could be borne.

Of course, the state of affairs was no more satisfactory for Katie and Parnell. Aunt Ben had a rigid code of morality. She had of necessity, and for Katie's sake, to put up with the peccadilloes and vagaries of Willie and to contribute to his support. But it was highly unlikely that she would countenance even her favourite Katie, a married woman and a mother, living openly with another man. If Aunt Ben discovered the truth, Katie was certain that she would be disinherited and lose a fortune that Willie slightly over estimated at £200,000, a sum well over £1,000,000 in today's inflated terms.

There is no question of Katie's love for Aunt Ben. She had remained devoted to her for years. But the issue finally came down to wanting the money. And it was not merely the opportunistic and grasping Willie who wanted it; it was also Katie and Parnell. Consequently, they lived for years a life of subterfuge and deception. They were not able to keep their secret from the world, but it could be kept from a 90-year-old woman.

Until very recent years, the public expectation, if not always the private one of particular individuals, has been that heroes and heroines should be virtuous, whether they be characters in literature or public figures in politics. The perceptive have always known that the heroes and heroines of real life have been ordinary men and women. Not Galahads, not Virgin Marys, not like Dostoyevsky's Alyosha or Dickens's Esther Summerson, and certainly not like the impeccable figures of the stately Victorian biography or the idealised public statue, but simply men and women who act as men and women do. Consequently, it would be naive to condemn Katie and Parnell for acting like the overwhelming bulk of mankind always has. A modern historian may still have his heroes and heroines, but he recognises that in many instances their motivations are precisely the same as the villain's.

In popular literature and in political statements of public policy, the impelling motivations are still usually couched in terms of stark black and immaculate white. In real life, motives are more usually mixed, and Katie's desire for Aunt Ben's money was matched by her real love and devotion. On her aunt's death, she wrote in terms of undeniable sincerity:

She left a great void in my life, and the sensation of being always wanted and tied to one place that I had sometimes felt so keenly hard I would now have given much to feel again. With this old lady died, so far as my acquaintance went, the last of the old world – the old world of leisure and books and gentle courtesy of days when men might wear their gallantry without foolishness, and women knew the value of their sex.

Through all those years in which I waited on my aunt I never heard her use a clipped word, or use a sentence not grammatically perfect and beautifully rounded off, and although in the hurry of modern life I sometimes felt impatient when chided for some swallowed pronunciation or ignored g's, I look back upon the years of my life spent in that old-world atmosphere as a very precious memory.

With a fortune as large as Aunt Ben's at stake, it was not merely the nominal hero, heroine and villain who wanted it. Towards the end of her life Aunt Ben twice altered her will, leaving an ever larger share to Katie. This alarmed Katie's brothers and sisters who were initially to have been equal sharers in the money. The most acutely disturbed were her sisters, Anna Steele and Polly Chambers, and her brothers, Charles and Evelyn, the latter a Major-General and holder of the Victoria Cross. In late 1887 they began attempting to influence Aunt Ben against Katie. They did not go so far as to make direct hints about Katie's extramarital relations, but they did employ, as members of a family so viciously can, a barrage of subtly denigrating innuendoes about Katie's basic character. Their best strategy did not seem to be a frontal attack for, although Aunt Ben was aged, she was still a highly intelligent woman. Nevertheless, she immediately realised the import of the attacks against her favourite, her 'swan'. Perhaps her great wealth had helped make her an intractable and imperious woman, but now she was also an infuriated one; and in March 1888 she made a new will, leaving the brothers and sisters out of it entirely. There were a few small bequests, but otherwise the entire estate went to Katie.

Alarmed and angry, the brothers and sisters then instituted a most callous proceeding. They attempted to break the will by presenting a petition to the Masters in Lunacy, asserting that their aunt was insane. How they were able to secure sufficient medical documentation is not known, but Aunt Ben was very old and crotchety to the point of eccentricity. A plausible case could be made.

Joyce Marlow describes Katie's reaction as being:

appalled and horrified and her reaction was caused as much by fears for her aunt as by thoughts of the money. For if the Petition for an Inquiry were not fought, Aunt Ben could spend her remaining time on earth as a prisoner, and while the Woods (presumably) had in mind some private home rather than a grim Victorian lunatic asylum, to tear the old lady away from the gracious house and place her in some alien institution was not a pleasant idea, and even if they envisaged leaving her at the Lodge, she would have been placed under strict supervision.

Katie attacked the matter with the same energy and resolution she had shown in her attempts to get Willie returned to Parliament in 1886. But this time the matter was simpler, and she won.

Her tactics were the same. She went directly to the top – to Gladstone. She wrote to him, and the upshot was that his personal physician, Sir Andrew Clark, interviewed Aunt Ben. She called also on the now prominent novelist George Meredith, who had read to Aunt Ben for years, to testify to the old lady's sanity. When Clark's report was not quickly forthcoming, she not only appealed to Gladstone again but she also persuaded Parnell to write in support – the only time that proud man ever begged a personal favour from a politician. When Clark's report eventually came, it did say that Aunt Ben's sight was poor, that she repeated herself, and she tended to forget what had been said, but its basic thrust was that the old lady was 'attentive, capable of apprehension and reflection, to reply coherent and logical, free from illusions, delusions and hallucinations, full of old stories, able to quote largely from the French poets and sometimes seasoning her reminiscences with flashes of quaint humour'. When the Woods' petition came up, it was dismissed.

Willie's position remained uncomfortable, but was still not untenable. It was true that Aunt Ben's last will had given everything to Katie, and had given it quite outside the terms of the marriage settlement, so that Willie could not touch it. Still, if Willie would not directly benefit, he had yet one large ace in the hole – if he made no public fuss, things could go on as they had, and possibly they could go on even better. And there was another possibility: for a sufficient sum of money, he could allow Katie to sue him for divorce.

From the death of Aunt Ben in May 1889 until Willie's filing for divorce on Christmas Eve, his motives can only be a matter for speculation. Indeed, anything as constant or thought-out as a motivating strategy may probably not have existed, and Willie may simply have been swayed by changing and conflicting impulses. His explanatory letters to Joseph Chamberlain and Cardinal Manning really do not explain much, for Willie as usual presents a most one-sided case in which he depicts himself as, in Lyons's phrase, 'a paragon of disinterested virtue'. This is a view that would scarcely have convinced many people who knew Willie even slightly, although it is comically and undoubtedly the view that Willie sincerely held of himself. The only thing, then, that one may be certain of is that underlying Willie's muddled and confusing tactics lay two constants – his implacable hatred of Parnell and his own unwavering self-interest.

After Aunt Ben's death, the Wood family predictably returned to the attack and contested the will, claiming that Katharine had exerted an unfair influence over her aged aunt. The money, therefore, was going to be tied up in probate for a considerable time – three years as it turned out. One effect was that Katharine's own income was going to be considerably curtailed, as also was Willie's.

Nevertheless, it took him several months to act, and the reason may plausibly have been that he was undecided about what was the most profitable course. He had but one trump card in his hand which could influence the outcome of the game. That card was the threat of a divorce suit which would discredit Katie and which would have the pleasant side-effect of discrediting Parnell also. The problem was how to play the card so that it would take the trick.

It has been occasionally suggested that Parnell's political foe and Willie's political mentor, Joseph Chamberlain, may have encouraged Willie to instigate divorce proceedings. However, there is little supporting evidence other than motivation, and the extant letters between Willie and Chamberlain do not bear the theory out.

However Willie was still on friendly terms with the Wood family with whom he could share, although for different reasons, an animosity to Katharine. Indeed, it is Joyce Marlow's contention that the Wood family acted as the catalyst that finally impelled Willie to launch the divorce action. The Woods, of course, would have been delighted with a well-publicised divorce action which, whatever its outcome, would considerably have harmed Katharine's chances of the inheritance. However it was obvious even to Willie that if the money were divided among the whole family, his claim on a now smaller portion would be distinctly weakened.

The conflict must have been very frustrating for him. On the one hand, there was the almost irresistible pleasure of a divorce suit which would not only be a sweet revenge for all of the slights, humiliations and treacheries he had suffered at the hands of his nemesis Parnell, but which would also be a triumphant vindication of him who would now appear in the most sympathetic light. On the other hand, to file for divorce might be just the most effective way of cutting his own throat, or at least of cutting himself off from the realistic hope for any significant amount of cash.

And indeed it is not only the hero in tragedy who resolves his dilemma by making the wrong choice; villains also act foolishly. In Willie's case, it was inevitable that even so potent a motive as his overweening self-interest would cause him to lose out. It was finally a case of him biting off his nose to spite his face, and the leading impulse that finally brought about the divorce suit was not to be laid at the doors of either Chamberlain or the Woods – it came from Willie himself. For him, it was not merely the delights of revenge that were to prove irresistible, it was the lure of the drama itself.

Lest that seem too romantic an interpretation, let it be remembered that Willie was the consummate egotist. He had always seen himself in the brilliant glow of the limelight. It was insupportable to be cast in the upstage shadows as a mere spear carrier, and his actions in the election of 1886 were only his most dramatic previous attempt to force himself downstage centre. For ten years, self-interest had for the most part enforced a frustrating and galling silence and an impotent activity. In the meantime, his rival had reinforced his private conquest of Katie by even more dramatic public triumphs. The trump card of the divorce case, no matter what its effects, was going to be played. In classic tragedies, there is also this rather awe-inspiring inevitability of events. The particular actions may be utterly and obviously destructive, but the protagonists rush into them like lemmings to the sea.

Willie was a Roman Catholic, but although he occasionally took his children to Mass, he was not a practising and devout one like his mother or sister. He was one of that inexplicably large number of people upon whose lives religion has no apparent effect whatsoever, but who with a curious matter-of-factness consider themselves a bona fide member of a Church — at least in the important incidents of birth, marriage and death. Although hardly a frequent churchgoer, Willie was quite insistent that Claude Sophie, whom he probably regarded as his child, be baptised as a Catholic. In 1889 he took his marital problems to that eminent Victorian Cardinal Manning, and from mid-October to mid-December met and frequently corresponded with the prelate about the matter. He was, in effect, slowly persuading himself that the divorce was inevitable.

At the same time there was an alternative so attractive that it gave even him pause for thought. Willie was not particularly interested in a divorce per se. He was nearing 50, and whatever his casual liaisons may have been, there is no evidence of any woman to whom he was truly attracted. Indeed, after his youthful infatuation with Katie, which quickly wore off, there is no indication that he ever sincerely loved anybody. Parnell, however, wanted a divorce above all things, and Katie also wanted one although there were, in her mind, certain other matters to be considered, principally scandal and money. Had Parnell and Katie been willing to pay him a certain sum to allow Katie to divorce him for infidelity it might have been the perfect solution. A divorce would have been achieved, and there would have been no public scandal involving Parnell.

According to both Katie's and Willie's testimony that, as we shall see, was what very nearly happened. At any rate, the divorce action was launched, and Willie subsequently gave two different versions of why he had at last done it. One version was that Cardinal Manning had asked to see Willie's actual evidence of Katie's infidelity and, when Willie sent him incriminating letters, the Cardinal promptly passed them along to Parnell's barrister and solicitor, and this perfidy caused

Willie to act. A second story was that Willie and his son Gerard, then 19, visited 10 Walsingham Terrace in Brighton, where Katie and Parnell had moved after Aunt Ben's death, and there Gerard had discovered 'a lot of Parnell's things, some of which he chucked out the window'. Then, as Willie wrote to Chamberlain, 'on our return to London we went to the lawyers and settled that an action should be taken immediately.' At the same time he showed Chamberlain a letter Katharine had written to Gerard in June 1887, pledging better behaviour:

> My dear Gerardie,
>   I now write to confirm my telegram to you in which I was willing to meet the wishes you expressed in regard to Mr Parnell.
>   I am most anxious everything should be made as pleasant as possible for you and that nobody should come here who is in any way obnoxious to you, and I therefore readily agree that there shall be no further communication direct or indirect with him.
>
>   Ever my darling, Gerardie,
>   Your loving Mother

Surprisingly, the news of the divorce suit was not initially regarded as a bombshell. In fact, the English press kept very quiet about it. On 30 December Parnell himself was queried about the matter by the *Freeman's Journal*, and replied that O'Shea had known of the relationship and been threatening divorce for years, and had probably only now moved in the matter because he had been put up to it by *The Times*. Implicitly here was what amounted to a confession by Parnell, but curiously no one picked it up.

Even more curious is that in the eleven months between the filing of the action and its coming to court, there was little perturbation among the general public or the clergy, or even among Parnell's own followers. In February 1890 Parnell assured one of the most important Irish leaders, Michael Davitt, that he would come through 'without a stain on his reputation'. And so assured did Parnell appear that the other leaders of the party hardly approached him on the matter. There were probably several reasons. Part of Parnell's charismatic leadership had always lain in his aloofness and his imperturbability, and part of it in his obvious success, not merely in welding the Irish Party into a formidable unity but also in his recent total vindication in the Pigott forgeries case.

Nevertheless, to any perceptive onlooker, there should have been alarm or at least serious trepidation. The difference between the Pigott case and the divorce case was perfectly apparent to everyone. The first was a clumsy attempt to blacken a thoroughly innocent man, but in the second case it was common knowledge that Parnell had for years carried on an affair with Katharine O'Shea and that he was a thoroughly guilty man. Perhaps the general calm was the greatest tribute ever paid to Parnell's leadership. It was not greatly different from the trusting confidence with which the citizens of Thebes approached their king at the beginning of *Oedipus Rex*.

How did Katie and Parnell themselves react? Katie was all for dispatch and vigour and action; Parnell was for doing nothing. She not only wanted to defend the case; she wanted to launch countersuits. He was perfectly content not to defend the case and to let Willie win by default.

He probably had several reasons. One was that, although he was only 43, his health had been deteriorating for years. When he visited Hawarden in the middle of December, Gladstone's daughter had written, 'He looks more ill than any other I ever saw off a deathbed.' He still retained his inflexible control over the Irish Party, but his appearances in the House had become more and more infrequent, and the reason was partly his ill-health and lack of energy.

A second reason for inaction was one central to his entire public career. Parnell was one of the great Irish leaders, and in the popular mind leaders led. They have programmes; they are decisive. In reality, however, Parnell often led by doing nothing, by walking a tightrope between factions, by playing the parliamentarians of the Irish Party off against the vehement physical force element, by playing the Tories off against the Liberals, by accepting at one crucial moment the refuge of Kilmainham Gaol where he did not have to act, by refusing to sue *The Times* at another crucial moment. These actions were all conscious choices, and they had been successful, so why would the same tactics not work in this instance?

A third reason was that, above all, he wanted the divorce, and the easiest way to get it was not to defend the suit.

A fourth reason was that, until almost the very last moment, he might well have expected Willie to cave in and be bought off.

And perhaps a final reaon was hubris, that bounding confidence in his own invulnerability.

Katie's reaction was vigorous but extremely confused and even contradictory. Like Parnell, she wanted the divorce, but unlike him she wanted to fight back and to justify herself, even though fighting might well jeopardise her case. At the end of July she finally filed her defence, and also made some countercharges. She asserted that she was innocent of adultery, but at the same time she accused Willie of first conniving at and later condoning her adultery. In other words, the second charge did give her the human satisfaction of hitting back at Willie, but it also refuted her own first assertion that there had been no adultery at all.

Katie was full of anger and not merely at Willie. In another countercharge, she hit out at both Willie and her family by accusing Willie of an affair with her sister Anna in 1881. In 1881 Anna had intervened to smooth over the matter of the prospective duel between Willie and Parnell and, as Lyons relates, 'it was also the year when

O'Shea, flinging out of the house at Eltham in a rage, walked to Anna's house in London, arriving there at four o'clock in the morning, an hour not calculated to buttress her reputation for respectability.'

That Anna actually did have an affair with Willie is doubtful, She had, after all, fled from her husband on first learning what was expected sexually of a wife. And although she had friendships with many men, she did not marry. She was probably one of those people who are simply uninterested in sex. But whatever the truth of the matter about herself and Willie, it was certainly ancient history at this date, and it is chiefly interesting as a symptom of Katie's rage and her urge to hit back at both her husband and her family.

With her emotions so fevered, it was predictable that her actions would be confused. Katie knew that she wanted to strike out and hurt those who had harmed her, but occasionally wiser thoughts prevailed. After it was all over she told Henry Harrison that she had also assembled evidence proving no less than seventeen instances of Willie's infidelity. At the same time she explored quite the wisest course available to her, of making overtures to Willie to withdraw the case and to allow himself to be sued for divorce. Both she and Willie mentioned the sum of £20,000 as the payment, although he later in a communication to Chamberlain inflated the amount to £60,000.

Paying off Willie would probably have been the only strategy that would have brought the case off safely and without scandal. Parnell could have been entirely kept out of the matter, and the divorce would have been achieved. The only problem was that there was no £20,000 available. Katie had no income now that Aunt Ben's will was in probate, and Parnell's resources were even scarcer. Avondale was heavily mortgaged, and Parnell himself was thousands of pounds in debt, not through high living but from the failure of his experiments in mining and milling. A solution might have been to persuade Willie to wait for his money until the question of the inheritance was resolved – but neither he nor Katie was capable at the time of acting very rationally, and he was not to be persuaded.

Indeed, for Willie, hatred of Parnell dominated his every move, and even Katie's charge of adultery with Anna he attributed to Parnell's instigation. As he wrote to Chamberlain in August:

> During the intervening nine years she has not hinted such a thing either to myself or to any member of the family. You can imagine the indignation of her brothers and sisters. Low as she had sunk with him before, I confess I was astounded when I heard of the depths to which Parnell has now dragged her.

Meanwhile, Katie's own emotional confusion was apparent in her twice discharging her legal advisors, and indeed remaining for weeks without any legal counsel at all. As one of her discharged advisors,

George Lewis, remarked to his successor, 'I wish you joy of your client. I don't know how long you will keep her. She's a very charming lady but an impossible one.'

Everyone who contemplated the case thought that Willie was thoroughly reprehensible and had played an ignominious role throughout. However, Willie was not on trial, nor was Katie who could always, no matter what the outcome, sink back into the obscurity of private life. The trial was of public interest only because it involved Parnell, and, as the months passed, worries began to surface.

In January the diarist Reginald Brett recorded that Sir William Harcourt 'thinks Parnell is done for. Morley thinks he will be all right in Ireland but damaged in England. Stead thinks he will be all right in England, but damaged in Ireland. Davitt thinks he will be ruined in Ireland. Parnell thinks he will be all right all round.'

As the trial approached the Liberals, if not the credulous and cowed members of the Irish Party, began to worry. On 10 November, just five days before the trial, John Morley, whose brilliance Katie had so admired as a girl, made a point of having a lengthy chat with Parnell. Their talk ranged over many political matters, but Morley was really interested in reporting to his leader, Gladstone, what Parnell's own feelings were about the imminent divorce hearing. Parnell was particularly affable all evening, and finally at the end of the dinner Morley said:

> 'There's one point on which I have no right to speak to you – and if you don't like it, you can say no. But it is important we should know whether certain legal proceedings are likely to end in your disappearance from the lead for a time.' He smiled all over his face, playing with his fork.
>
> 'My disappearance? Oh no. No chance of it. Nothing in the least leading to disappearance, so far as I am concerned, will come out of the legal proceedings. The other side don't know what a broken-kneed horse they are riding.' 'I'm delighted to hear that,' I said, 'for I, for my part, regard you as vital to the whole business.' 'Well,' he said, 'the Irish people are very slow to give a man their confidence, and they are still more slow to withdraw it.' I inferred from his talk of the broken-kneed horse that he meant there would be no adverse decree.

What was the reason for Parnell's incredibly casual aplomb? He absolutely refused to defend the case or even to retain counsel, and he refused to let Katie defend herself, and so her counsel had only a watching brief. This meant that the entire handling of the case would be conducted by Sir Edward Clarke, Willie's counsel. There are several possibilities for Parnell's inaction. Willie had been manipulated so long and was himself so much at fault that Parnell could have felt confident that at the last moment Willie would cave in. Another possibility is a combination of hubris and ill-health. In recent months Parnell's guiding hand upon the political tiller had grown increasingly lax, and there had been implicit criticism of his leadership by the Irish bishops. Nominally his power was still at its zenith and, impelled by lassitude and success, he may simply have refused to admit that he was in any danger.

At any rate, he seems to have moved through the events of the last crucial days in something of a hypnotised stupor. On 14 November, the day before the case opened, he and Katie visited her counsel, Frank Lockwood, and Katie wrote, 'The last time I saw Sir Frank Lockwood, the day before the case came on, he begged me to get Parnell to let him fight it. I was suffering acutely from neuralgic headache at the time, but I did my best to get Parnell to defend the case, though to no purpose.' The best that Lockwood could obtain was their promise to telegraph him before eight the next morning, if they had changed their minds.

They journeyed by train back to Brighton, Katie riddled with worry and suffering her 'splitting headache'. She retired to bed early.

> After he had had his own dinner he came up and smoked by my bedside. I tried to persuade him to go up with me in the morning to the Court and make some fight in the case, but he said:
> 'No, Queenie. What's the use? We want the divorce, and, divorce or not, I shall always come where you are. I shall always come to my home every night whatever happens. Now I'm going to read you to sleep.'

Whatever she said, she could not shake his incredible fatalistic calm. 'I don't believe you are listening to what I say!' she charged.

'I am not, beloved. . . . We have been longing for this freedom all these years, and now you are afraid.'

It is unlikely that at such a crucial moment Katie would misremember what Parnell had said or that she would have misread his attitude, and so perhaps we must conclude that he had decided quite firmly what he most wanted. Perhaps it was simply that with Ireland weighed on the one side and Katie on the other, he had decided that, come what would, winning Katie was infinitely more important.

She brought up the issue herself:

> I broke down and cried, because I feared for him and for his work, and he soothed me as one would a child as he told me that his life-work was Ireland's always, but that his heart and his soul were mine to keep for ever – since first he looked into my eyes that summer morning ten years before.
> 'Queenie,' he went on, 'put away all fear and regret for my public life. I have given, and will give, Ireland what is in me to give. That I have vowed to her, but my private life shall never

belong to any country, but to one woman. There will be a howl, but it will be the howling of hypocrites; not altogether, for some of these Irish fools are genuine in their belief that forms and creeds can govern life and men; perhaps they are right so far as they experience life. But I am not as they, for they are among the world's children. I am a man, and I have told these children what they want, and they clamour for it. If they will let me, I will get it for them. But if they turn from me, my Queen, it matters not at all in the end. What the ultimate government of Ireland will be is settled, and it will be so, and what my share in the work has been and is to be, also. I do wish you would stop fretting about me. We know nothing of how or why, but only that we love one another, and that through all the ages is the one fact that cannot be forgotten nor put aside by us.'

He spoke, says Katie, slowly and 'with many silences between sentence and sentence', and, if she reported him correctly, he was not a man in a dazed torpor who was letting events swirl around him. He was one who had weighed up the consequences of what he was doing, who throughly understood the import of those consequences, and who was thoroughly prepared to accept whatever might befall.

If so, this makes him the highest example of the tragic hero.

But although Parnell was intellectually aware of the situation and stoically ready to accept the consequences of his choice, his stoicism, as we shall see, crumbled, and he later struggled most heroically, and impotently, against the consequences.

The next morning Katie slept late. When she awoke, she found Parnell sitting by her 'superintending the arrangement of "letters, tea and toast"'. When she anxiously asked the time, he quietly laughed and said, 'I've done you this time, Queenie; ... they must be enjoying themselves in Court by now!'

The hearing began at ten o'clock in the very room in which the Parnell Commission had sat and in which Pigott had been so discomfited. The outcome this time, however, was to be very different.

Willie's counsel, Sir Edward Clarke, announced that Willie was seeking a divorce for reason of his wife's adultery with Parnell, and that he also repudiated the charges Katie had made in her counterpetition. Frank Lockwood, for Katie, said that he would not call any witnesses or cross-examine. It was also established that Parnell was not represented.

After that, the canny Clarke had matters entirely his own way. He rehearsed the history of the case from, of course, Willie's viewpoint. Willie was then examined by junior counsel and introduced various letters in support. Then two independent witnesses, a maid and a cook who had once been employed by Katie, were examined. The evidence of the cook, one Caroline Pethers, was especially damaging. She told of Parnell appearing at the house and being introduced under various aliases; she mentioned that Parnell sometimes slept at the house; and, worst of all, on several occasions when the arrival of Willie interrupted a *tête-à-tête* between Parnell and Katie, Parnell slipped out of the house by means of a rope fire-escape, and then some minutes later presented himself at the front door asking to see Willie.

The spectacle of the aloof and dignified Parnell scuttling out of the window and climbing down a rope was vastly damaging. Its absurdity roused a delightedly malicious laughter and was just the sort of incident beloved by the gutter press. Joyce Marlow remarks, 'It was not only the newspaper columnists who enjoyed themselves; cartoonists had a field day, so did music-hall comedians and toy manufacturers, and models of the Brighton fire-escape, complete with miniature Parnell, were soon on sale.'

There is no way that silent dignity can combat giggling malice, but at the particular moment a good cross-examination might have scotched the story at birth and demolished a good deal of Caroline Pethers's testimony. The great irony of the matter is apparent in this story told by St John Ervine:

> One night, soon after the suit was heard, the late Sir Herbert Tree entertained Captain O'Shea to dinner. He said to him: 'I think you'll agree that ridicule can kill a man in England as surely as it can in France.' 'What do you mean?' demanded O'Shea. 'Well,' Tree replied, 'take your case. The fire-escape killed Parnell!' 'Yes,' said O'Shea, 'and the fun of it is *there was no fire-escape!*'

There was yet another day of the hearing, but the damage had really been done.

On Monday Katie's sister Anna, her brother Sir Evelyn and her son Gerard were in court. Clarke called more witnesses, servants, a groom, and house agents, and their testimony was collectively damaging, particularly in the establishing of a couple of other aliases that Parnell had used. Anna appeared briefly on the stand and denied committing adultery with Willie. The only thing that told for Katie and Parnell on Monday were the probing questions of two jurors into Willie's actual financial support for his family, into the infrequency of Willie's appearances at Eltham, and into Willie's curious and protracted delay in bringing the divorce case. However, what was needed was a professional cross-examination and the production of witnesses for the defence. There was neither, and on the basis of the evidence Mr Justice Butt in his instructions to the jurors had no alternative but to stress the strength of Willie's case. The jury immediately found for Willie on all counts.

Only then did, or could, Frank Lockwood on Katie's behalf ask that judgement be reserved in the matter of the two youngest dependent children. Claude Sophie, Katie and Parnell's dead first child, had been mentioned in the case already, but the two younger girls had been virtually ignored. Again, however, the judge had no recourse but to award custody to the innocent party, Willie. And so Willie, by playing the divorce card and taking the trick, now found that he had another winning card in his hand, the custody of Parnell's children.

The reaction of conventional Victorians was clear and immediate. Gladstone's daughter, Mary, who had been so impressed by Parnell shortly before on his visit to Hawarden, now wrote in her diary, 'He has lived this life of lies all these years. A heartrending revelation. "Blot out his name."' And the chief Victorian of them all, the Queen, wrote in her journal, 'not only a man of very bad character but . . . a liar and devoid of all sense of honour or any sort of principle'.

By not defending the case, Parnell had got what he most wanted, Katie's freedom. He was shortly to discover that he had to face some other consequences which he now found he could not accept.

To ponder what Parnell and Katie could have done to minimise the effects of the divorce action is probably beside the point. If they had fought the case, they would certainly have succeeded in blackening Willie's character, but in the process a good deal of dirty linen would have been publicly washed. And, even if they had won, Katie would still have been married.

The nature of the tragic dilemma is that either choice is disastrous.

CHAPTER 13

In The Wings

In Ibsen's play *John Gabriel Borkman*, there is a remarkable act in which the hero does not appear at all. He is, however, the focus of the onstage conversation, his footsteps are occasionally heard pacing nervously overhead, and his intangible presence permeates and dominates the entirety of the action.

In the next and climactic act of Katie and Parnell's story, it is the heroine who remains in the wings, publicly unseen. But she is the tacit and dominant factor in the consciousness of all the actors. And when finally her intangible presence can be suppressed no longer, it is she who tips the scales.

Parnell's strategy in his struggle to retain the leadership of the Irish Party was to keep the issue of Katie completely out of it. His broad tactics were to shift the argument entirely to public issues, and his specific tactics were to entangle the opposition in a web of parliamentary procedure. Never in his long public career had he shown such consummate mastery of the generalship of men. And he almost succeeded.

One almost unvarying technique of the tragic dramatist, from Sophocles to Shakespeare to Ibsen, has been an initial, slow, leisurely accretion of details, but as the plot approaches the climax the pace imperceptibly begins to quicken, and its last moments attain an intense, breakneck speed. The story of Katie and Parnell had its leisurely exposition and its inexorably developing conflict that took place over a period of ten years. But when that conflict reached its cumulative confrontation in the divorce court, events began to succeed one another with a bewildering and terrible rapidity. The trial was over on 17 November. In the next two weeks its consequences were to engulf all the players and the fate of a nation. And by 6 December it was all over.

Coincidentally the divorce suit was concluded only eight days before the re-opening of Parliament, the earliest opening in years. There was, in other words, no time for cooling down and no time for calm reflection – except perhaps for Parnell who simply disappeared until 25 November when he was due at Westminster. In the days immediately preceding, frantic and vain attempts were made to reach him. He was, of course, with Katie in Brighton. What went on between them in those days, what he said and thought, Katie does not tell us. She glosses over events light-heartedly:

> on Monday, the 17th, my Brighton solicitor brought me down a copy of the 'decree nisi'. We were very happy that evening, and Parnell declared he would have the 'decree' framed. We made many plans for the future that evening of where we should go when the six months had passed and the decree made absolute. I even ventured to suggest that he might marry someone else once I was set completely free, but my lover was not amused and scolded me for suggesting such disgusting ideas.
>
> Sir Frank Lockwood was terribly distressed about us and his inability to 'save Parnell for his country', but he was very kind to me, and did all he could to help me in certain legal matters.

The 'certain legal matters' were obviously the loss of custody of Parnell's two daughters. Katie does not mention how very distressed Parnell was about this. However, Frank Lockwood, Katie's counsel, describes him as being 'so wild and peculiar in his manner as to show signs of madness'. Apparently, around this time, Parnell visited Lockwood's offices in London and accused him of betrayal in regard to the two children. But, surprisingly, although Willie had been granted custody, he never claimed Clare and Katie (who were not mentioned in the memoirs and always bore the name O'Shea), and in 1892 surrendered them as part of the probate settlement. Of the other children, only Norah, who was nearly 17, stayed with Katie. Gerard, who was nearly 20 at the time, and Carmen, who was 15, had both gone to live with Willie.

But whatever Parnell felt privately, when he next appeared his usual public mask was firmly in place, and what the world saw was the usual aloof dignity, the unflustered calm and the quiet resolution. In this instance, the mask actually somewhat mirrored the face underneath, for Parnell had made good use of his week's seclusion to marshall his thoughts and to discipline his emotions. By 25 November he knew what he was going to do and how he was going to do it. Nevertheless, there were emotions, real and strong ones, beneath the mask and behind the face and the events of the next few days were sometimes to tax his discipline beyond even his iron control. Then the emotions would so violently contort the face that the impassivity of the mask itself was cracked.

While Parnell was coolly fashioning his strategy in Brighton, practically everyone else was plunged into confusion and contradiction. Of the Irish leaders, Michael Davitt was throughout one of the most consistent. Parnell had assured him, early and firmly, that the divorce would have negligible political consequences. When, however, the details of the trial were publicly aired, Davitt angrily felt that Parnell had deliberately misled him. What really seems to have happened was that Davitt, with his conventional but rigid austere morality, misunderstood Parnell's individual personal code. Parnell, in his own mind, had done no wrong, but to Davitt he was most flagrantly wrong. As Jules Abels pejoratively puts it, 'In characteristic *hubris*, Parnell had composed his concept of morality in place of the conventional one of society.' What is interestingly symptomatic, however, of Parnell's strength as leader, even after the divorce, is that Davitt, who was violently angry and who felt that both Ireland and he personally had been betrayed, made no more damaging public statement than that Parnell, for the good of the Irish cause, should *temporarily* retire as leader.

After an initial reaction of the Irish leaders to support Parnell staunchly and unanimously, and after an initial reaction of the English Liberals to wait and see, the reaction of the public began to be vociferously heard. Then it was that leaders of both parties seized upon the notion of a temporary retirement until matters had simmered down. No one in a position of political power or influence suggested that the retirement should be anything but temporary, for it was inconceivable that the national movement should ultimately proceed without Parnell. This was probably the only way out. It would certainly have averted the crisis, it could probably have been accomplished with some face saving to Parnell, and it offered the very plausible hope of a triumphant return in a few short months.

Yet Parnell did not accept it. He seems to have toyed with the idea; he even publicly accepted the idea upon certain rather far-fetched conditions. Yet basically and finally he did not accept it, and the question of why not is as central to an understanding of his character as it is ultimately perplexing.

There were compelling reasons, other than the political ones, to retire for a while. Above all, his health was wretched. In the last two years not only his health but also his private inclinations and probably his personal worries about the divorce had all contributed to his absenting himself frequently from Parliament and from Ireland, and from exercising any real leadership in the Irish Party. In one sense it would have been inordinately pleasant simply to retire from the public hurly-burly for a few months, to potter around Walsingham Terrace with his chemicals, to experiment with his ship models, to visit Avondale and supervise his obsessively fascinating mining operations, to go riding and shooting – above all, to enjoy a period of calm with Katie. In six months he would have been able legally to marry her, and perhaps in six months he would have been able to re-assume his leadership of the Irish Party, more strongly than ever.

And yet he did not.

It has been sometimes suggested that it was Katie who persuaded him to make a fight of it. This seems not to have been the case at all. After a hectic meeting of the Irish Party in Westminster on 26 November Parnell returned to Brighton, and Katie wrote:

> When my lover came to me that evening I would not let him speak till he had changed his cold boots and socks; then he came over to me, and took me into his arms, saying, 'I think we shall have to fight, Queenie. Can you bear it? I'm afraid it is going to be tough work.'

His mind was made up, and Katie was really powerless to change it.

> I said, 'Yes, if you can.' But I must confess that when I looked at the frail figure and white face that was so painfully delicate, whose only vitality seemed to lie in the deep, burning eyes, my heart misgave me, for I very much doubted if his health would stand any prolonged strain.
>
> I burst out passionately, 'What does it matter more now, they have all known for years?' and his rare, low laugh came out with genuine amusement as he replied, 'My sweetheart, they are afraid of shocking Mr Gladstone.'
>
> 'But Gladstone— ' I began, bewildered.
>
> 'Just so, but we are public reprobates now, it just makes the difference. He is a "devout Churchman", they tell me.'

Parnell's bitter irony about Gladstone may provide a clue, at least partially, to his motives. Despite his single, congenial meeting at Hawarden, Parnell's real feelings about Gladstone seem to have been ones of envy amounting to hatred. In the days to come, he was to complain about how Gladstone had monopolised the conversations at Hawarden, and he was to call Gladstone 'an unrivalled sophist', 'the grand old Serpent,' an English wolf, and 'a man with whom and to whom it is as impossible to give a direct answer to a plain and simple question as it is for me impossible to give an indirect answer to a plain and simple question'.

Parnell was generally not a hater. He spoke tolerantly of his foes. Even with Tim Healy, who was in the next two weeks to ascend to heights, or descend to depths, of quite personal vituperation, Parnell could rise above the fray. As Healy himself recalled, 'As we went towards the door, he drew me towards one of the pillars in the hall, saying, "Healy, let us shake hands for, it may be, the last time. . . ." I replied, "Thank you, Parnell." We shook hands and so parted for ever.'

In the Anglo-Irish politics of the day, Healy was only a Cassius to Parnell's Brutus. But the Caesar in the one dominating issue of Home Rule was Gladstone, not Parnell. Here, however, life and its literary paradigm part company. After killing Caesar, Shakespeare's Brutus was able to say, 'Not that I loved Caesar less, but that I loved Rome more.' In life, our Brutus was not able to kill his Caesar, nor was he able to love him. In fact, at one crucial point in the furious debates over the leadership of the Irish Party, Parnell's faithful supporter John Redmond ironically, if at the moment realistically, described Gladstone as 'the master of the party'. Healy's terrible rejoinder, as we shall see, was the comment that was at the time so devastating and is still the remark remembered: but for Parnell the bitter irony about Gladstone probably bit nearly as deeply.

Although Parnell loved his Rome, before the divorce he would probably have considered 'the world well lost' for the attainment of the beloved. But now that he had attained his beloved, he found he wanted the world too.

The world was the leadership of the party. In his attempt to gain both, he lost both, and brought catastrophe on both.

What specifically happened was this.

On 18 November John Redmond presided at a meeting of the Irish National League in Dublin, and the support for Parnell was total. Two days later at a meeting in Dublin in the Leinster Hall, that support was vigorously reaffirmed, with Justin McCarthy declaring that 'in all political matters Mr Parnell possesses the confidence of the Irish nation' and 'the determination of the Irish parliamentary party was to stand by their leader'. At the same meeting, Tim Healy ringingly declared:

> I say we would be foolish and criminal if we, the seasoned politicians who have seen and who have been able to watch the vagaries and tempests of political passages – if we, upon an occasion of this kind, at the very first blast of opposition, surrendered the great chief who has led us so far forward. If we, who have been for ten years under the leadership of this man, and who have been accused of harbouring all kinds of sinister ambitions and greedy desires to pull him down – if we join with this howling pack, would that be a noble spectacle before the nations?

In a few short days, both men were to reverse these positions.

With the sole demurrer from Davitt that Parnell should temporarily withdraw from politics, the Irish press was solidly behind Parnell. The Catholic hierarchy was not. Archbishop Croke of Cashel wrote in a letter to Archbishop Walsh of Dublin, 'I have flung him away from me for ever. His bust, which for some time has held a prominent place in my hall, I kicked out yesterday.' Nevertheless, the policy of the influential Archbishop Walsh of Dublin prevailed, and that policy was to do nothing public for the moment, but to wait and see.

In England the Tory press, led by *The Times*, was predictably vociferous in denunciation, and the Liberal press was generally against Parnell being hounded out of public life. However, the papers read by the nonconformists vehemently demanded Parnell's retirement, and it was an aroused and vocal nonconformist conscience that was to tilt the balance. Baptist and Methodist preachers wrote letters to the press and thundered denunciations from the pulpit. The most inflammatory was the Rev. Hugh Price Hughes, whom Ervine describes as 'another emotional Celt, but this time a Welsh one, who wrought himself into a state of hysteria, and had the hardihood to denounce Parnell as "the most infamous adulterer of this century"'. In the *Methodist Times*, Hughes further fulminated:

> We do not hesitate to say that if the Irish race deliberately select as their recognized representative an adulterer of Mr Parnell's type they are as incapable of self-government as their bitterest enemies have asserted. So obscene a race as in those circumstances they would prove themselves to be would obviously be unfit for anything except a military despotism.

Letters poured in, urging Gladstone to disassociate the Liberal Party from any connection with Parnell, and Gladstone began to worry.

A very similar instance must have weighed heavily on Gladstone's mind which had occurred a scant five years earlier, in which a leading Liberal politician had been ruined by another scandalous divorce case. The politician was Sir Charles Dilke whom Gladstone had actually at one time named as a leading candidate to succeed him in the party leadership. Dilke, then serving as Under-Secretary for Foreign Affairs, was named as co-respondent in a divorce suit brought by a Scottish lawyer named Crawford. The resulting two trials uncovered a wealth of titillating scandal and gamey sexual practices, and the upshot was that Dilke was quite disgraced and lost his parliamentary seat at the next election. The Katharine-Parnell affair was by comparison monogamously and dully bourgeois, no matter how its details were luridly exaggerated in the press. However, there were a number of depressingly close parallels, as Gladstone was well aware. The moral fervour was heated up in both cases by W. K. Stead whom Abels aptly describes as 'a supreme egotist and a crusader for purity obsessed with sex, very much an Elmer Gantry type'. The judge in both cases was Justice Butt, and in the first trial Dilke, like Parnell, did not take the stand, incurring thereby a widespread presumption of guilt. There was even some discussion of buying off the disaffected husband, and the well-known Liberal Henry Labouchere later wrote that Gladstone had actually asked him if Crawford could not somehow be induced to withdraw the suit.

'Crawford wants to be a judge,' said Labouchere, 'but of course that's impossible.'

'Why impossible?' mused the Grand Old Sophist.

It was impossible because Crawford refused to withdraw his suit, and the resulting consequences Dilke, unlike Parnell, understood immediately. As Abels recounts it:

> Dilke recorded in his diary, 'A sudden fall indeed. Such a charge even if disproved is fatal to supreme usefulness in politics.' To a friend who cited the case of the Duke of Wellington, who had answered the threat of a blackmailing madame with 'Publish and be damned,' Dilke replied, 'An aristocratic society then rather enjoyed a scandal. Today the middle classes rule and adultery to them is as bad as murder.'

This conclusion Gladstone was very well aware of, and from it inevitably emerged the further conclusion that, if Home Rule were to be saved, Parnell had, at least temporarily, to give up the leadership of the Irish Party.

It was necessary to move both quickly and delicately. Parliament was about to re-convene and, as always at the opening of a new session, the Irish Party would go through what was usually the mere formality of electing a leader for the term. It was vital, then, that Parnell be reached beforehand and apprised of Gladstone's opinion. This would have seemed a simple business, but what transpired was a series of misunderstandings and narrowly missed meetings that would have been appropriate in a Feydeau farce – if tragedy had not already, in such hoary devices as lost letters, missing documents and Desdemona's wandering handkerchief, accustomed us to the hopelessly improbable.

Parnell was sequestered in Brighton, and Gladstone could hardly have met him personally anyway. A trustworthy emissary had to be found, and Justin McCarthy was picked, a journalist, novelist and historian, one of the most prominent Irish leaders and a man whom Parnell was to refer to as 'a nice old gent for a tea-party'.

McCarthy called on Gladstone on 24 November, the day before the crucial vote, and later that night he described their conversation:

> He spoke with chivalrous consideration of Parnell's 'splendid and unrivalled services to Ireland', but told me very sadly that his remaining in the leadership now means the loss of the next elections and the putting off of home rule until the time when he [Gladstone] will no longer be able to bear a hand in the great struggle to which he has devoted the later years of his life. He spoke with intense feeling and earnestness. He said he would not write this to Parnell himself, because it might seem harsh and dictatorial and might hurt Irish feeling: but he authorized me to convey his views to Parnell when I see him. This will not be until tomorrow.... I have written to Parnell asking him to decide nothing as to himself until he sees me in the House, and have sent

the letter to the House on the off-chance of his going or sending there early tomorrow.... I am much perturbed ... all depends upon tomorrow.

Unfortunately the discussion with Gladstone was not a tea party, and McCarthy failed to grasp Gladstone's essential point. This was that Parnell's refusal to step down would, in Gladstone's words, 'not only place many hearty and effective friends of the Irish cause in a position of great embarrassment, but would render my retention of the leadership of the Liberal Party, based as it has been mainly upon the prosecution of the Irish cause, almost a nullity'. Had Parnell received and understood this message, even he could hardly have persisted in his course, for what Gladstone was prophesying was his own retirement and, in effect, the Liberals' abandonment of Home Rule.

Gladstone took a further precaution. These words and sentiments he embodied in a letter to John Morley, and Morley too was dispatched to find Parnell and show him the letter before the meeting of the Irish Party.

Things immediately began to go awry. At 11.45 the next morning Morley received a telegram from Parnell's secretary saying that Parnell could not be located. However, the first meeting of the Irish Party did not begin until 2.45, and McCarthy was waiting to intercept Parnell at the House of Commons Post Office where the leader was in the habit of first coming to pick up his mail.

What happened then is a little vague. Apparently Parnell did come in, although quite late, for his mail. He was buttonholed by McCarthy as he walked off to the committee room, opening his letters. But what McCarthy said, or what Parnell actually apprehended, is not in the least clear from McCarthy's typically vague later comments on the matter.

The probability is that Parnell received a hasty version of Gladstone's message, with the crucial part left out. Even so, however, Gladstone's general gist must have been clear enough even through the muddled medium of McCarthy's transmission, and that gist was clearly that Parnell should momentarily step down. The two certainties are that Parnell had little time to reflect on the matter, and that when he entered the committee room his resolve not to step down was unshaken. When he entered Committee Room 15, he looked, in the eyes of one observer, 'as if we had committed adultery with his wife'.

He was received with cheers and handshakes, he was proposed for renomination as party chairman, and he was elected unanimously. The hopeless McCarthy, awed as everybody else seems to have been by Parnell's imperturbable air of authority, said nothing.

But Parnell had to speak. There was the usual need for some acknowledgment of thanks for his re-election, and on this occasion a bit more was needed. A few years earlier when he had been presented with a tribute of a cheque for thousands of pounds, he was able to put it quietly in his pocket and without a word of thanks talk about something else. In this case, the something else that was in everybody's mind was Katharine, and even Parnell had to say something, however obliquely, about it. He said practically nothing. The official minutes simply record:

> He asked his friends and colleagues to keep their lips sealed as his were on this subject until the time came when he could speak freely on the topic. When that time came they would find their confidence in him was not misplaced. He would not further allude to the matter beyond once more asking them to keep their lips closed in reference to that topic.

What he was doing, in effect, was putting the divorce issue completely aside, and with the cowed and still loyal members of the Irish Parliamentary Party he was entirely successful – for the moment. There is a slightly fuller account of his speech which the Irish journalist Donal O'Sullivan wrote to his nephew, the ailing Tim Healy, who was still in Ireland:

> Then Parnell rose amidst cheers and cheers again. . . . He made a *long speech*, delivered coldly, calmly and bloodlessly. His strongest points were (1) That his lips were sealed – for some time. He asked his colleagues to seal theirs! (2) He *never* called O'Shea his friend! (3) He never drank a glass of wine at O'Shea's expense, nor accepted any hospitality from him. O'Shea never paid a sixpence for any compliment ever paid for him. (4) He asked his 'friends around' to continue their confidence in him till the 'fight he and his dead friend, Joseph Biggar commenced, was won'. (5) When they began it – only the two of them – they had to fight and did fight, not alone with the Tories but the Whigs, the Liberals and the Radicals. (6) Was he today with 85 trusted friends at his back to surrender? NO – the position of esteem and confidence which his countrymen placed him in he would not surrender for any section or party, and so he would remain to assist them and to guide them to their *final* victory.

He had done it again. He had utterly won, and entirely on his terms. He had relegated the issue of Katie not merely to a side issue, but to a taboo one; and he had changed the terms of conflict from personal issues to general political ones. It was an unqualified triumph – and it was to last for about an hour.

Shortly after the meeting was over, Morley ran across Parnell in the lobby, and immediately drew him aside. According to Morley, this is what happened:

'I am very sorry', he said, 'that I could not make an appointment, but the truth is I did not get your message until I came down to the House, and then it was too late.' I asked him to come round with me to Mr Gladstone's room. As we went along the corridor he informed me in a casual way that the party had again elected him chairman. When we reached the sunless little room, I told him I was sorry to hear the election was over, for I had a communication to make to him which might, as I hoped, still make a difference. I then read out to him Gladstone's letter. As he listened, I knew the look on his face quite well enough to see that he was obdurate.

Parnell said that he thought the whole matter a storm in a teacup, and that it would quickly pass. Morley answered that, if Parnell thought so, he little knew England, and 'that if he set British feeling at defiance and brazened it out, it would be ruin to Home Rule at the general election...'. This was a strong warning, clearly delivered, and, had Parnell heeded it, he could have resigned even at this late stage. Indeed, he was shortly to have the opportunity to resign, for after the meeting was over the Irish backbenchers heard for the first time of Gladstone's letter, and they were thrown into a state of perturbation and turmoil. But if Morley's persuasive description of Parnell is to be believed, the Irish leader was quite unshakeable in his resolve:

His manner throughout was perfectly cool and quiet, and his unresonant voice was unshaken. He was paler then usual, and now and then a wintry smile passed over his face. I saw that nothing would be gained by further parley, so I rose, and he somewhat slowly did the same. 'Of course', he said, as I held the door open for him to leave, 'Mr Gladstone will have to attack me. I shall expect that. He will have a right to do that.'

Gladstone arrived in his office shortly afterwards. He was taken aback by Morley's news and apparently so angered that he decided to send his letter immediately to the press. After all the manoeuvring, then, two decisive actions had now been taken, Gladstone's and Parnell's. Gladstone's action was irretrievable; Parnell could have reversed himself – but only if he had not been Parnell. If he would not do it before Gladstone made everything public, he was even less disposed to do it afterwards when public pressure was brought to bear.

There has always been something magnificent and absurd about the tragic hero's unswervable obstinacy. At its most magnificent, it might be summed up in the Duchess of Malfi's bloody but unbowed defiance, 'I am Duchess of Malfi still,' and at its most absurd it is beautifully embodied in Shaw's comic opera hero, Sergius Saranoff of *Arms and the*

Man, who is given to folding his arms impressively and intoning, 'I am never sorry!' or 'I never apologize!'

At any rate, Gladstone's action and Parnell's inflexible determination set in train an inexorable series of events that was only to end in Parnell's political defeat and ultimately in his premature death. St John Ervine, himself an able Irish dramatist, discussed the situation with an ironic dramatist's eye on the audience's response:

> If Mr McCarthy had told all or some of his colleagues of what he knew of Mr Gladstone's opinions; if Mr Gladstone had held back his letter from the press for another twenty-four hours; if Mr Parnell had had one friend in his own party in whom he could confide, not as leader to a follower, but as one human being to another; . . . if Biggar had not died on February 19, 1890, nine months before these events occurred. . . .

If . . . if . . . if . . . the most poignant word that tragedy evokes. However, given the unyielding character of the hero, 'if' is never really possible. Even if Joe Biggar had still been alive, his good sense would have had no more effect upon the determined Parnell that it had had in the Galway by-election, or, for that matter, than the sane and sensible Enobarbus had had upon the infatuated Mark Antony.

The die was cast, but, tantalisingly, there was still an avenue out if – if! The private news and then the actual publication of Parnell's letter stirred the alarmed backbenchers to action. Although Parnell was sitting, dourly depressed and unapproachable in the smoking room of the House of Commons, the general alarm was powerful enough to force him to meet that evening in the Westminster Palace Hotel with several of his colleagues, and even to elicit the admission then that, if Gladstone would include in the Home Rule Bill the new Irish Parliament's control over the Irish police and the land, he would retire. These were concessions unlikely to be admitted at this time, but the Irish backbenchers collected enough signatures to convene another meeting of the party the next day, 26 November.

Then the Wexford MP, John Barry, moved that 'a full meeting of the party be held on Friday to give Mr Parnell an opportunity of reconsidering his position' of remaining as party chairman. After predictable arguments on both sides, it was decided to reconvene on Monday 1 December, and also to wire to America for the advice of five prominent members who were there on a fundraising tour. After the meeting, Parnell returned to Brighton and said to Katie, 'I'm afraid it is going to be tough work.'

He then sat down to compose a public answer to Gladstone, a manifesto, and Katie wrote:

> While Parnell sat down at work at his manifesto I deliberated for hours as to whether I ought to let him go on. Should I urge him to

come abroad with me? – I knew he would come if I said I could not bear the public fight. I looked at him as he sat now absolutely absorbed in what he was writing, and now looking across at me when he had something ready to be pinned together. He did not speak, only the smoulder in his eyes grew deeper as he wrote.

Katie's dilemma was wrenching and, although she did not know it, this was the last decisive time in which she could act.

I loved him so much, and I did so long to take him away from all the ingratitude and trouble – to some sunny land where we could forget the world and be forgotten. But then I knew that he would not forget; that he would come at my bidding, but that his desertion of Ireland would lie at his heart; that if he was to be happy he must fight to the end. I knew him too well to dare take him away from the cause he had made his life-work; that even if it killed I must let him fight – fight to the end – it was himself – the great self that I loved, and that I would not spoil even through my love, though it might bring the end in death.

Despite Henry Harrison's charge that much of Katie's memoir was doctored, the passage just quoted has a resoundingly authentic voice of truth. It rings with sincerity.

Poor Katie, what could she do? Her memoir was written after the fact with a full knowledge of what had happened, but perhaps even at the time she had a hint of what was in store. She knew, of course, how ill Parnell was, but she also knew what he was, and therefore had no choice. As he sat composing, she wrote:

I looked up feeling that he was watching me, and met the burning fire-flame of his eyes steadily, through my tears, as he said, closing his hand over mine, 'I am feeling very ill, Queenie, but I think I shall win through. I shall never give in unless you make me, and I want you to promise me that you will never make me less than the man you have known.' I promised it.

Parnell's manifesto was addressed 'To the People of Ireland', and on the evening of 28 November he read it to several leading members of the Irish Party. When he was done, there was a silence, and then Justin McCarthy, the Party's vice-chairman, said he disapproved of every word. McCarthy's demurrer had no effect whatsoever, and the document duly appeared in the morning papers. Parnell was widely criticised in one wing of the party for printing the piece at the time, and the reason was chiefly that it made a rift between the Irish Party and the Liberals now seem like a chasm.

From his own point of view, however, the manifesto held to his predetermined strategy. It raised the whole argument between the Irish and the Liberals to several points of general political difference. It claimed that under the proposed Home Rule Bill Gladstone and the Liberals meant significantly to reduce the Irish representation in Westminster; it claimed that the land question would not be strongly pursued by the Liberals, and that the control over the Irish police as well as the appointment of Irish judges was to remain in the hands of the English. These points were all touchy matters, but they were also red herrings. The rift had been caused solely by the divorce case, and that Parnell had entirely sidestepped. Indeed, he managed to narrow matters to the one generalisation of the independence of the Irish Party. Under that banner, he thought, even his Irish opponents could rally, and that banner was quite broad enough to cover up the matter of Katie. He said, rather effectively:

> Sixteen years ago I conceived the idea of an Irish Parliamentary party independent of all English parties. Ten years ago I was elected the leader of an independent Irish Parliamentary party. During these years that party has remained independent, and because of its independence it has forced upon the English people the necessity of granting Home Rule to Ireland. I believe that party will obtain Home Rule only provided it remains independent of any English party. I do not believe that any action of the Irish people in supporting me will endanger the Home Rule cause or postpone the establishment of an Irish Parliament; but even if the danger with which we are threatened by the Liberal party of to-day were realised, I believe that the Irish people throughout the world would agree with me that the postponement would be preferable to a compromise of our national rights by the acceptance of a measure which would not realise the aspirations of our race.

Dignified words, but behind his last statement that no action of the Irish people in supporting him would endanger Home Rule lay the tacit presence of Katharine, and everyone knew it. Parnell's address was sober, dignified and occasionally strong. It sounded reasonable, but it was also a bit long-winded and, although it contained moderately moving passages, it lacked any real, raw emotional power.

On Monday 1 December the Irish Party again assembled in Committee Room 15. There were three days of discussion and, considering the heated feelings held by everyone in the room, the debate was for the most part dignified and fairly restrained. The issue was simply whether Parnell would retire as leader of the Irish Party, but the debate was conducted along the complicated lines that Parnell had laid out in the manifesto. That is, the issue remained, at least for a while, the purely political one that Parnell had stressed. Katie, for the moment, did not enter into the matter at all.

Parnell's tactics as chairman were obstructive, delaying and diversionary. He attempted to have the meeting changed to the – for him – safer atmosphere of Dublin. The charges of the Liberals' treachery which he had made in the manifesto were much hashed over, and his own encomiums about Gladstone and the liberals that he had made after Hawarden were questioned. Tim Healy, who had recovered from his illness, put the matter succinctly: 'Either Mr Parnell at Liverpool was false, or else his manifesto was false.' Finally it was decided to send a small group composed of Parnellites and anti-Parnellites to Gladstone to sound out the Liberals' response to the two main points the manifesto had raised about control of the police and settlement of the land issue. Parnell seemed to intimate that if he could be reassured that these two points would be included in the Home Rule Bill, he would step down from the chair. 'Don't sell me for nothing,' he said, 'If I am to leave you tonight, I should like to leave you in security. I should like – and it is not an unfair thing for me to ask – that I should come within sight of the promised land.'

Gladstone, however, finally would not treat of the matter until the Irish resolved the question of their own leadership. In the meantime, other forces were amassing themselves against Parnell. The condemnatory position of the Irish hierarchy appeared in the papers of 3 December. A statement from five of the six party members in America – John Dillon, William O'Brien, T. P. Gill, T. P. O'Connor and T. D. Sullivan – concluded, 'Mr Parnell has entered upon a rash and fatal path, upon which every consideration of Ireland's safety, as well as of our personal honour, forbids us absolutely to follow him.' The time for diversionary tactics was quickly running out, and the time for confrontation was at hand.

The leading anti-Parnellite spokesman in Committee Room 15 came to be Tim Healy. He was one of the most sagacious and fluent speakers and finally one of the most vitriolic, who was to deliver the climactic unkindest cut of all. It has been suggested that Healy's rancour and vehemence may have stemmed in part from his having been rebuffed and ignored by Parnell in the past, and there is some justice to the charge. St John Ervine is not far out when he cautions the reader to remember 'that this brilliant and sensitive man received extraordinary and unwarranted provocation which a man of his age, proud and passionate and swift in resentment, could not be expected to endure'. That feeling would certainly account for some of Healy's most heated extempore remarks. Nevertheless, it must also be noted that both publicly and privately Healy's remarks at the time show both a bruised loyalty and an implicit affection for his leader. At the end of Tuesday's session, Healy wrote to his wife, 'In all my life, I never spent so awful a time and I am harassed in body and soul.'

On Wednesday, as Lyons recounts it, the question was put to Parnell that:

> if the assurances were given [by the Liberals about the police and the land question] and found adequate by the majority, would Parnell then voluntarily retire? Healy, emotionally volatile as ever, interjected vehemently that if Parnell could satisfy the party on these two points, he would be the first to call him back as leader of the Irish race 'at the very earliest moment possible, consonant with the liberties of this country'.

On Thursday, however, Parnell appeared more adamant than ever.
Both the Parnellites and the anti-Parnellites were really acting for the good of the party and moved by their hopes of achieving Home Rule. In fact, the only man in the room who probably had another motive was Parnell. That motive he had largely succeeded in keeping out of the debate, but now, after many hours of talk and several days of intense manoeuvring, tempers began to fray, voices to grow heated, and the real resentment to emerge.
Healy wrote to his wife, 'It looks as if we have raised a Frankenstein which is now about to destroy everything. . . . He feels exactly as you might expect a god to feel – that he could not be wrong and that anyone who would not obey him and follow him must necessarily be damned.'
The exchanges between Parnell and Healy became heated. At one point Parnell said, 'And upon that answer I will stand or fall before the country.'
'Then,' cried Healy, 'you will fall, Mr Parnell, and now that both sides have made up their minds, what is the use of further debate?'
There was a furore of cheers and voices trying to be heard, and one of Parnell's followers, J. J. Clancy, cried out ironically, 'Crucify him!'
Parnell and Healy now, as the playwright Ervine put it:

> caught at each other's words like gladiators catching at each other's throats. There came a moment when the Celtic emotionalism of Mr Healy robbed him of all control of his tongue, and suddenly he uttered one blasting and unforgivable sentence. He quoted a passage from a speech by Mr Parnell, who had spoken of an alliance between the Liberals and the Nationalists, 'an alliance which I venture to believe will last', and like a prosecuting counsel he snapped out, 'What broke it off?'
>
> Three voices – Mr Parnell's, Colonel Nolan's, and Dr Fitzgerald's – answered: 'Gladstone's letter'.
>
> But Mr Healy had another answer. 'It perished in the stench of the divorce court. . . .'

Finally it had been said.

Everything broke apart on Saturday 6 December. Everyone's nerves were raw, and even Parnell himself found his iron control dissolved at moments by utter rage. At one point he snatched a paper from the hand of the mild Justin McCarthy and threw it to the floor. At that moment he seemed to launch himself at McCarthy, and John Redmond and Edmund Leamy dashed up to stop him.

Then the Parnellite John O'Connor said that if Parnell were deposed, the real leader of the party would then be Gladstone. The anti-Parnellite Arthur O'Connor pointed out that Gladstone was not a member of the party, and John Redmond replied ironically, 'He is the master of the party.'

Then it was that Healy administered the *coup de grâce*: 'Who', he cried out, 'is to be the mistress of the party?'

Parnell rose up infuriated, and Healy was quickly surrounded by his friends. Arthur O'Connor called out, 'I appeal to my friend the chairman.'

'Better', raged Parnell, 'appeal to your own friends. Better appeal to that cowardly little scoundrel there, who dares in an assembly of Irishmen to insult a woman.'

After that, there was little more to say, and McCarthy, the vice-chairman, finally said it: 'I see no further use in carrying on a discussion which must be barren of all but reproach, ill-temper, controversy and indignity, and I will suggest that all who think with me at this grave crisis would withdraw with me from this room.' He walked out followed by forty-four members, a solid majority.

On this last day, Parnell was moved to rage twice, once by a seeming attack against his own leadership, and once by a very personal attack against Katie. These were the two impulses that had governed his actions, his leadership and his love; and left alone with his depleted band of loyal followers, Parnell said to them, 'Gentlemen, we have won today. Although our ranks are reduced in numbers, I hold this chair still.'

This was the affirmative kind of statement that, one might cynically note, politicians always make in defeat, and the indomitable kind of statement that, one might admiringly note, tragic heroes sometimes make – in their blindness.

CHAPTER 14

THE LAST BATTLE

Sometimes in saga or in tragedy, the hero must fight his last battle, a battle in which his doom has been prophesied and foreordained.

Parnell's last battle was going to be fought out in Ireland. There were three major skirmishes in it, and he lost each one. The anti-Parnellites had acted immediately to form their own organisation with the novelist Justin McCarthy as chairman. And they resolved to put up a candidate in an imminent by-election in North Kilkenny, which would be the first real test of strength.

As early as the evening of 9 December Parnell set out for Ireland. Euston Station was packed with his supporters who carried him to his carriage. Tim Healy and his brother Maurice were taking the same train, and if it had not quickly pulled out there might have been a riot. When the boat-train disembarked its passengers at Kingstown, Parnell was cheered and Healy hissed and booed. The same thing happened when the train from Kingstown arrived in Westland Row. Parnell was staying in Rutland Square, and the horses were unhitched from his carriage and he was triumphantly drawn through the streets, crowds cheering as he passed.

That evening there was another triumphant procession to the Mansion House in Dawson Street to pick up the Lord Mayor, and then with bands and torchlights the procession made its way back to an overflowing and tumultuous crowd at the Rotunda. The young poet Katharine Tynan wrote:

It was nearly 8.30 when we heard the bands coming; then the windows were lit up by the lurid glare of thousands of torches in the street outside. There was a distant roaring like the sea. The great gathering within waited silently with expectation. Then the cheering began, and we craned our necks and looked on eagerly, and there was the tall, slender, distinguished figure of the Irish leader making his way across the platform. I don't think any words could do justice to his reception. The house rose at him; everywhere around there was a sea of passionate faces, loving, admiring, almost worshipping that silent, pale man. The cheering broke out again and again; there was no quelling it. Mr Parnell bowed from side to side, sweeping the assemblage with his eagle glance. The people were fairly mad with excitement.

I said to Dr Kenny, who was standing by me, 'He is the only quiet man here.' 'Outwardly,' said the keen medical man, emphatically. Looking again, one saw the dilated nostrils, the flashing eye, the passionate face; the leader was simply drinking in thirstily this immense love, which must have been more heartening than one can say after that bitter time in the English capital. Mr Parnell looked frail enough in body – perhaps the black frockcoat, buttoned so tightly across the chest, gave him that look of attenuation; but he also looked full of indomitable spirit. . . .

When Mr Parnell came to speak, the passion within him found vent. It was a wonderful speech; not one word of it for oratorical effect, but every word charged with a pregnant message to the people who were listening to him, and the millions who should read him. It was a long speech, lasting nearly an hour; but listened to with intense interest, punctuated by fierce cries against men whom this crisis has made odious, now and then marked in a pause by a deep-drawn moan of delight. It was a great speech – simple, direct, suave – with no device and no artificiality.

He said in part, 'I have not misled you. I have never said that this constitutional movement must succeed. I have never promised you absolute success, but I have promised you this, that if you trust me, I will do all that mortal man can do to perform it.' And, he went on to say that, should the constitutional movement fail, 'England will be face to face with that imperishable force which tonight gives me vitality and power. . . . And if Ireland leaves this path upon which I have led her . . . I will not for my part say that I will not accompany her further.' In other words, should the parliamentary way be succeeded by violence, he would probably still be in the vanguard.

In fact the Dublin visit was to be capped with violence. Earlier in the day Parnell had visited the *United Ireland* offices and dismissed the editor, Matthew Bodkin, who had gone over to the anti-Parnellite side. During the Rotunda meeting some anti-Parnellites had retaken the office. When he learned of this Parnell drove there and drew up his horse so quickly in front of the building that the animal fell flat in the street. Parnell leapt through the waiting crowd and seemed to hurl himself over the area railings to effect an entrance. Dissuaded by his supporters, he seized a crowbar, battered the door in, and then, as one onlooker reported:

One of the windows on the second storey was removed and Parnell suddenly appeared in the aperture. He had conquered. The enthusiasm which greeted him cannot be described. His face was ghastly pale, save only that on either cheek a hectic crimson spot was glowing. His hat was off now, his hair dishevelled, the dust of conflict begrimed his well-brushed coat. The people were spellbound, almost terrified, as they gazed on him. For myself, I felt a thrill of dread, as if I looked at a tiger in the frenzy of its rage. Then he spoke and the tone of his voice was even more terrible than his look. He was brief, rapid, decisive, and the closing words of his speech still ring in my ear: 'I rely on Dublin. Dublin is true. What Dublin says today Ireland will say tomorrow.'

The Parnell of the Rotunda meeting and of the battle for the *United Ireland* offices seemed a far cry from the aloof, remote, sometimes passive figure of the past ten years. It is true that when relating the incident to Katie, he sounded like the easy and low-keyed Parnell of old: 'all, or nearly all, I could get out of Parnell himself on the subject was a soft laugh and, "It was splendid fun. I wish I could burgle my own premises every day!"'

But had the struggle of Committee Room 15 changed him? In Dublin, there seemed to appear a different Parnell. There had been charges in recent months that he was actually mad, and it was remembered that there was eccentricity, even insanity, in his family. Even Davitt wrote, 'Well may it be asked: "Is Mr Parnell mad?" That there are evidences of insanity in his actions no one can doubt.' And it is not merely the Irish Party leaders or the Liberals who looked on with the nonplussed awe of the bystander outside the *United Ireland* offices. Summing up Parnell's state of mind during the following months of stress and tension, even the judicious historian F. S. L. Lyons wrote:

> The deliberate breach of faith with Gladstone, the breaking off of the Liberal alliance, the aspersions hurled at his former colleagues, the violence of his behaviour in Dublin, the invective poured upon his opponents at Kilkenny – all these suggested hidden depths which made men shudder and fear for his reason.

In the heroic stories, it is not unusual to find that at some late point the hero – a Roland, a Launcelot, a Cuchullain – descends to madness, to a kind of uncharacteristic frenzy. And in the tragedies the hero – a Macbeth, a Richard III – is sometimes no more vehement than in the moments just before his death. Yet while it is true that Parnell in his last months sometimes spoke and acted with an alarming and strange violence, it would be well to note what one of his most astute opponents, John Dillon, wrote in his diary: 'Men say here that Parnell is mad, but it seems to me that his astuteness is absolutely infinite....'

Perhaps, then, what impelled him was an astuteness which would allow for frenzy, which would utilise it and channel it, which would make effective dramatic public use of it while at the same time giving him the therapeutic private benefit of blowing off steam and relieving some of his own frustration for having been, really for the first time, thwarted. Further, Parnell had always been a sound strategist and consummate tactician, but the strategy and tactics appropriate for bringing the Home Rule issue to a head in the Westminster Parliament would no longer, after the events of the divorce court and Committee Room 15, work. It was no longer a time for bargaining and compromising, but a time for fighting. Fighting, then, was to be his strategy, and his tactics were to be no-holds-barred – a startling stance for a calm, cool, level-headed parliamentarian, but a dramatically effective one.

With Katie he was still quiet, mild, bantering and self-possessed. In fact, he was Parnell as he had always been – except in one respect. In his best days with Katie, he had been indolent and languid about his public life, indeed relegating it to a back seat. She had actually to drag him away from his hobbies, to shove him into his frock-coat and to push him out of the house to catch the train to London. Now he went vehemently, savagely, about his business, and was seldom at home. Yet it was probably not Parnell who had basically changed but the situation, which now required different strategies.

The vehemence of his actions, however, might well have been exacerbated by personal reasons. As the struggle in Ireland intensified, the issue was not merely Parnell and his leadership. Another issue was Katie. There were rumours afloat, not in the least substantiated by her own later account, that she was the manipulative Cleopatra or Lady Macbeth in the background. Tim Healy led the pack. In his campaigning in North Kilkenny, as Ervine said, he 'raged about the constituency, spitting venom wherever he went on the the the name of "Kitty" O'Shea. He swore that he would drive Parnell into his grave or the lunatic asylum. There was no outrage on language which Mr Healy did not commit in the North Kilkenny election.'

It may not have been Healy who coined the name of 'Kitty', but soon this was how she was referred to in the press and on the lips of everyone who did not know her. Neither Katie nor Katharine but 'Kitty', with its subtly frivolous and feline overtones. There were also more damaging names that she was called. In London Vanity Fair, taking a line from H. Rider Haggard's novel She, called her 'the Political Princess – O'Shea Who Must Be Obeyed'. The unscrupulous journalist W. K. Stead, whose high moral principles did not exclude mudslinging, called her 'the were-wolf of Irish Politics'. Even the faithful John Horgan, at whose wedding Parnell had been best man, was later to refer to her as 'an ignoble woman'. And, of course, it was inevitable that the sneering denigration of 'the Uncrowned Queen of Ireland' would soon be widely bandied about.

Parnell always tried to protect Katie by keeping her out of the public glare. Now while he fought publicly, she was a virtual prisoner at Walsingham Terrace, anxiously waiting for news. During these days she was particularly bitter towards Gladstone, charging him with ditching Parnell and Home Rule at the last moment. She writes:

> For ten years Gladstone had known of the relations between Parnell and myself, and had taken full advantage of the facility this intimacy offered him in keeping in touch with the Irish leader. For ten years. But that was a private knowledge. Now it was a public knowledge, and an English statesman must always appear on the side of the angels.
>
> So Mr Gladstone found his religion could at last be useful to his country. Parnell felt no resentment towards Gladstone. He merely said to me, with his grave smile: 'That old spider has nearly all my flies in his web,' and to my indignation against Gladstone, he replied: 'You don't make allowances for statecraft. He has the Non-conformist conscience to consider, and you know as well as I do that he always loathed me. But these fools, who throw me over at his bidding, make me a little sad.'

For the Irish Party members, Katie says she felt nothing but pity 'that they were not worthy of the man and the opportunity ... and ... that their craven hearts could not be loyal to [Ireland's] greatest son'.

The attacks upon Katie continued and were, of course, an effective means of getting at Parnell. The more mud slung at her, the more would attach to him. If the national leader were to be seen as being led by the nose by a woman, particularly a designing, unfaithful and contemptible one, then his own stature would be significantly diminished, and he would be made to appear weak, henpecked and ludicrous.

Small wonder, then, that as the personal attacks intensified, Parnell's own retorts became increasingly vitriolic. 'I will not waste my time on such miserable scum,' he cried. And, as Abels summarised:

> He castigated Davitt as a 'Jackdaw', Dillon a a 'sick raven' and 'as vain as a peacock with about as much brains', Sexton as 'uncertain and maudlin', and Justin McCarthy as 'a nice old gentleman for a tea party and if you visit his hotel, you would find him with his feet in a mustard bath and with a jug of whiskey punch beside him.' He accused Healy of being a 'scoundrel who betrayed prisoners to the Crown when there was no more money to put in his filthy pockets'.

In this fight to the finish, the gloves were off.

In his book *Parnell to Pearse*, John Horgan vividly describes Parnell at this time:

> On the 11th December Parnell came south to Cork. He was received by the people with all the old affection and enthusiasm.

Cork, at least, had not wavered in its allegiance. He stayed at my father's house that night and I shall never forget his appearance as I saw him standing before the fire in the dining-room just after he arrived. He looked like a hunted figure, his hair dishevelled, his beard unkempt, his eyes wild and restless. My father made some vehement remark about those who had deserted him, and the hatred in Parnell's face was terrible to look upon.

The election day in North Kilkenny was on 22 December, and the battle was intense and vicious. Dozens of MPs descended on the district to speak for the Parnellite or the anti-Parnellite candidate. The voice of the clergy, now that the bishops had come out against Parnell, was widely and stridently raised. Healy was everywhere. Parnell, he cried, 'will go through Ireland with a new banner constructed out of the petticoat of Mrs O'Shea. The green flag of Ireland with its sunburst is to be set aside. The sunburst and the harp are to be toned down and are to be replaced by the sign of the fire-escape.' A procession even invaded one of Parnell's meetings waving a tattered petticoat on a pole and asking if Kitty's petticoat was to be the flag of Ireland. On 16 December, fighting broke out at one meeting, and Davitt was hit by a stick. Later in the day someone threw a bag of what was purportedly lime into Parnell's face. His opponents charged that it was only flour, and that underneath his bandaged eye he was unmarked. Katie said, 'It was not flour, but lime, and had not Parnell shut his eyes in time he would undoubtedly have been blinded. As it was his eyes were not injured, and but for a tiny scar on the outer edge of his right eye he was not hurt.'

The result of all of this anger and violence was that Parnell's candidate was beaten by almost two to one, 2,527 votes to 1,362. It was hoped that after this resounding defeat Parnell might give up the battle, but his reception back in Dublin was tumultuous when he rode through the streets with his bandaged eye. As he passed the old Parliament building in College Green he simply pointed to it meaningfully, and the crowd exploded with cheers.

Parnell returned to Brighton, and Katie wrote, 'My husband said to me after the Kilkenny election, "It would really have hurt, my Queen, if those devils had got hold of your real name, *my* Queenie, or even the 'Katie' or 'Dick' that your relations and Willie called you." '

There was to be little rest or respite for Parnell. The Irish leader, William O'Brien, had returned from America and was in Boulogne. He could not appear in England or Ireland without being arrested, and so Parnell was persuaded to travel to France at the end of December and in the middle of January and again at the beginning of February for complicated and finally futile talks about healing the rift. He was also frequently in Ireland, making speeches at such places as Ennis and Limerick. He was now frequently seen in the House, and one person who observed him there said he looked 'miserably haggard and worn' and, 'I never saw him look or heard him so tired.'

His feelings must have been considerably depressed, as they were in one extraordinary scene with Katie on Brighton pier. In her account, it is difficult to pinpoint precisely when the scene occurred, but Joyce Marlow argues plausibly that it had to have happened after the divorce. It was a wild and stormy day, and Katie writes:

> Then we stood looking out at the great waves – so near, and shaking the whole pier-head in their surge. Parnell remarked that the old place could not last long, and as I turned to get a fresh hold on him, for I could not stand against the wind, and the motion of the sea sickened me, the blazing fires in his eyes leapt to mine, and, crushing me roughly to himself, he picked me up and held me clear over the sea, saying, 'Oh, my wife, my wife, I believe I'll jump in with you, and we shall be free for ever.'
>
> Had I shown any fear I think he would have done it, but I only held him tight and said: 'As you will, my only love, but the children?' He turned then, and carried me to the upper deck, hiding my eyes from the horrible roll and sucking of the sea beneath our feet.

After the Boulogne negotiations had broken down, the contest continued with redoubled fury. The next scene was Sligo where there was to be a by-election in March. Each week Parnell journeyed from Brighton to Ireland, constantly making speeches and looking more and more wan and haggard. The sides had become even more entrenched, the speeches were coarser and more abusive, and physical fights broke out between the warring factions. And when the vote was counted, Parnell's candidate had lost again, this time by 3,262 votes to 2,493. Nevertheless, it was a fairly close thing, and Healy wrote worriedly to Archbishop Walsh, 'The wonder is that we won, which we owe entirely to Sligo town. The whole affair has given our men an awful shake, and has enormously encouraged Parnell.'

After the Sligo election came the new charge that Parnell had misappropriated party funds. Healy published an article in the new anti-Parnellite *National Press* called 'Stop Thief'. He fulminated, 'We will force him to face [this charge], or amidst the contempt of his own supporters "lash the rascal naked through the world." '

In this increasing crescendo of invective there was one bright spot. On 25 June Katie and Parnell were married. That morning Katie wrote, 'I was awakened at daybreak by my lover's tapping at my door and calling to me: "Get up, get up, it is time to be married!" '

The early rising was not entirely the lover's eagerness; there were subterfuges to be gone through. They had wanted to be married in a church, but none of the Anglican divines in the vicinity was willing to perform the service for such a notorious couple. Parnell had therefore driven the day before to nearby Steyning to arrange for a marriage in the Registry Office at 8.30 in the morning. However, the press had got wind of the story, and its violently inquisitive representatives had to be circumvented. Parnell told his groom that the carriage would be required at eleven, and the hapless youth leaked this information, as he was meant to, to the reporters. However, the two witnesses to the ceremony, Katie's maid and the children's nurse, were put on an early train to Steyning, and the surprised and dishevelled groom was told to bring the phaeton with Parnell's horse Dictator in the shafts round for him and Katie. She later wrote:

> Parnell hardly spoke at all during this drive. Only, soon after the start at six o'clock, he said, 'Listen,' and smiling, 'They are after us; let Dictator go!' as we heard the clattering of horses far behind. I let Dictator go, and he – the fastest (driving) horse I have ever seen – skimmed over the nine miles in so gallant a mood that it seemed to us but a few minutes' journey.

They even succeeded in beating the maids' train to Steyning and, as they were waiting for them to appear, Parnell blew a kiss at Katie and jokingly said, 'It isn't every woman who makes so good a marriage as you are making, Queenie, is it? and to such a handsome fellow, too!'

After the simple ceremony, on the return drive with the hood of the phaeton up, they passed the reporters galloping into Steyning. There were still others, however, waiting at Walsingham Terrace, and one particularly obnoxious American correspondent actually made her way over the balcony from the adjoining house into Katie's bedroom. Parnell did give a short interview to some reporters, but not to the American woman. This did not defeat her, and she cabled an interview to her paper anyway. When the paper sent Katie a copy, she remarked:

> I must admit that even if not exactly accurate, it was distinctly 'bright'. It was an illustrated 'interview', and Parnell and I appeared seated together on a stout little sofa, he clad in a fur coat, and I in a dangerously décolleté garment, diaphanous in the extreme, and apparently attached to me by large diamonds. My sedate Phyllis had become a stage 'grisette' of most frivolous demeanour, and my poor bedroom – in fact, the most solid and ugly emanation of Early Victorian virtue I have ever had bequeathed to me – appeared to an interested American State as the 'very utmost' in fluffy viciousness that could be evolved in the united capitals of the demi-mondaine.

'I don't think', remarked Parnell, staring sadly at the interview, 'that American lady can be a very nice person.'

The wedding day was sunny, and when the reporters had finally dispersed, Parnell and Katie walked across the fields to Aldrington where there was a brick works. They watched the bricks being made, and when the men went off for dinner Parnell, with all his old enthusiasm for mechanical tinkering, said, 'Come on, Queenie, we'll make some bricks, too. I've learnt all about it in watching them! And so they made two bricks and put them in the kiln with the others.

Then they walked down to the sea, and Katie wrote:

we had the shore to ourselves and talked of the future, when Ireland had settled down, and my King – king, indeed, in forcing reason upon that unreasonable land and wresting the justice of Home Rule from England – could abdicate; when we could go to find a better climate, so that his health might become all I wished. We talked of the summer visits we would make to Avondale, and of the glorious days when he need never go away from me. Of the time when his hobbies could be pursued to the end, instead of broken off for political work. And we talked of Ireland, for Parnell loved her, and what he loved I would not hate or thrust out from his thoughts, even on this day that God had made.

None of the classic tragedies is quite complete without its omens and portents and superstitions presaging disaster. And even as Parnell and Katie stood by the seashore a thunderstorm came up, and they had to flee for shelter under the breakwater. Parnell said, 'The storms and thunderings will never hurt us now, Queenie, my wife, for there is nothing in the wide world that can be greater than our love; there is nothing in all the world but you and I.'

And, wrote Katie, 'I was comforted because I did not remember death.'

The news of the wedding brought hundreds of letters and telegrams, many congratulatory and some full of abuse. There were also presents, and the one they liked best was a little alabaster clock in the form of a ship's wheel from Parnell's sister, Emily Dickinson. But there were also some awful presents, and Katie's eldest daughter, Norah, tried to keep one registered parcel from her, for it contained a mouse and 'not at all the kind of mouse that anyone could have wanted for days past'.

The honeymoon was short-lived, for just two days after the wedding Parnell had to leave for Ireland to fight another by-election. This was in Carlow and was brought about by the death of the 89-year-old O'Gorman Mahon, 'the hoary old ruffian', as Ervine called him, who had as late as the debates in Committee Room 15 issued a challenge to Parnell to fight a duel.

The fight in Carlow was made difficult by a statement from the Irish hierarchy on Parnell's wedding day 'that Mr Parnell, by his public misconduct, has utterly disqualified himself to be ... leader'. There was some stone throwing, and there was beating of kettles to disrupt Parnell's meeting, for his candidate was named kettle. And there was, despite the marriage, a continued vilification of Katie, that 'convicted prostitute' and 'bad, base, immoral woman'. The result was a resounding defeat for Parnell, with his candidate going down by 3,755 votes to 1,539.

Despite his frantic activity, the tide was flowing against Parnell. He still had overwhelmingly the support of Dublin and some of the cities, but the Catholic countryside was almost solidly against him. And to make matters worse he lost the support of the widely read *Freeman's Journal*. To combat the defection he threw himself energetically into the establisment of a new paper to be called *The Irish Daily Independent*. At the same time, with an eye to the coming general election, he travelled around the country, giving speech after speech. He told Barry O'Brien that he would pull the country back together in five years:

'Well, Gladstone will be dead by then,' I said. 'The whole question to me is you and Mr Gladstone. If you both go, Home rule will go with you for this generation.'

'But I will not go,' he answered angrily. 'I am a young man and I will not go.' And there was a fierce flash in his eyes which was not pleasant to look at.

There is no question that Parnell in these last few months was driven by a steely determination to re-establish his leadership and to vanquish his foes, and it was an obsessive determination that was now even more important than Katie.

His total inflexibility on the matter is grimly illustrated by another incident that Barry O'Brien related. The last time that O'Brien saw Parnell was on the platform at Euston Station as Parnell was leaving for Ireland. Parnell asked him how many seats would he win in the general election, and O'Brien answered, 'I should think that you will come back with about five followers, and I should not be surprised if you came back absolutely alone.'

'Well, if I do come back absolutely alone,' said Parnell, 'one thing is certain, I shall then represent a party whose independence will not be sapped.'

It was not Parnell's independent will that would ever be sapped; it was the strength of his sick and tiring body.

Patricia Lavelle in her biography of her father, James O'Mara, tells of Stephen O'Mara, a staunch Parnellite M.P., her grandfather and my own great grandfather, seeing Parnell at another station around this time:

Years afterwards (Grandfather) told me how he had met Parnell once after the debacle. It was at a junction on the railway somewhere in Ireland. Parnell was getting out of a train and no one was there to meet him, no one knew him, no one noticed him, he who but a year before, had been the idol of thousands. Grandfather went over and greeted him and said a few words but his train came in and he had to leave Parnell there, standing alone and unnoticed.

Katie was an astute political observer and, within the limits available to her, even an astute political manipulator. How clearly she read the Irish scene in the summer and autumn of 1891 it is impossible to tell from her memoirs. It is clear, however, that she realised the physical toll that Parnell's exertions in Ireland were exacting on his ailing body. But she was as powerless to divert him from his course as anyone.

It was a curious but protypical situation. The dominating impulse in most of Parnell's life from 1880 was not the achievement of Home Rule but the winning of Katie. Now he had won her, and with her the kind of life that he most valued – tranquil, domestic and with plenty of leisure to enjoy the tinkering pursuits that most absorbed him. He could have retired, possibly recouped his health, and probably returned in something like triumph to lead the Irish Party, instead, he chose to engage in a struggle that, if it had no other consequences, was perfectly obviously going to postpone Home Rule for years and going to destroy every semblance of the political unity he had so painfully built up. It was a determination that was as perverse and as mad as it was heroic and inevitable.

His own speeches were still as defiant. On 13 September in Listowel in County Kerry he said, 'If I were dead and gone tomorrow the men who are fighting against English influence in Irish public life would fight on still. They would still be independent nationalists. They would still believe in the future of Ireland as a nation.' Yet everyone noticed how wan and worn he was. Accompanied by his sister Emily, he spoke one Sunday in Cabinteely near Dublin, and the jostling crowd broke one of the windows of his carriage. Emily wrote, 'I could see by his face that the breaking of the glass disturbed him. We always thought it unlucky to break glass.'

It was a rainy day, and he spoke with his hat off and got drenched. When he returned to Brighton Katie saw that 'he was looking so worn out and ill that I was thoroughly alarmed about his health'. When she persuaded him to sleep, 'he had that absolute stillness which one only finds in very healthy children or in the absolutely exhausted sleep of adults.' She tried to get him to see a doctor in London, but he did not want to waste the little time he had at home.

'I am not ill,' he said, 'only a little tired. Queenie, my wife, you do not *really* think I am ill, do you?'

She did, and told him 'that nothing, not even Ireland, was worth it', and she begged him to stop, 'to hide away with me till a long rest, away from the turmoil and contention, had saved him . . .'.

He lay watching me as I spoke, and after a long pause, he answered, 'I am in your hands, Queenie, and you shall do with me what you will; but you promised.'

'You mean I promised that I would never make you less than –'
'Less than your King,' he interrupted, 'and if I give in now I shall be less than that. I would rather die than give in now – give in to the howling of the English mob. But of you say it I will do it, and you will never hear of it again from me, my love, my own wife.' And as I gazed down into the deep, smouldering eyes . . . I knew I could not say it.

When she saw him off on 25 September he was in good spirits and raised the white rose in his buttonhole to his lips in parting. In Ireland he was committed to speak in the remote village of Creggs in County Galway. He was obviously in some pain from his rheumatism, and his friend Dr J.E. Kenny tried to dissuade him from going. Of course he could not be dissuaded, but set off with his left arm in a sling to ease the pain. The Sunday evening meeting in Creggs proved to be as wet as the week before's in Cabinteely, and again Parnell spoke bare-headed in the rain. It was to be his last speech, and he said: 'We shall continue this fight . . . I know that you look to Ireland's future as a nation if we can gain it. We may not be able to gain it, but if not it will be left for those who come after us to win; but we will do our best.' Katie had packed a change of clothing for him, but for a while his bag was misplaced and he had to remain in damp clothes.

Back in Dublin, he stayed with Doctor Kenny until Wednesday, working on details of his new newspaper. On Wednesday, despite Kenny's advice that he should not attempt to travel, he took the boat for England, promising, 'I shall come back on Saturday week.'

On Thursday morning in London, he took a Turkish bath to relieve his pains, and then journeyed down to Brighton. Katie wrote, 'I helped him into the house, and he sank into his own chair before the blazing fire which I had made, in spite of the warm weather, and said: 'Oh, my Wifie, it is good to be back. You may keep me a bit now!" And later he sat before the fire with Katie and with Groucher and Pincher, their setter and terrier. He smoked a bit of a cigar, he dozed a bit, and finally he decided to go to bed. He was too weak to walk alone. She helped him up the stairs, undressed him, and massaged his shoulders and arms with oil. Nevertheless, it was a disturbed and restless night, and Katie wrote:

He talked a good deal, chiefly of the Irish peasantry, of their privations and sufferings, the deadly poverty and the prevalence of the very pain (rheumatism) from which he was suffering, in their case aggravated by the damp, insanitary cabins in which they lived. And he murmured under his breath: 'There are no means at hand for calculating the people who suffered in silence during those awful years of famine . . . . I wish I could do something for them – the Irish peasantry – they are worth helping. I have always wished it, but there is so much between – and they "suffer in silence", Wifie.'

On Saturday he was a bit better but refused to see a doctor. On Sunday he was a little worse, and Katie sent for a local doctor. Although Parnell said he felt improved, he did not sleep again on Sunday night, and it was another of his superstitions that if he did not sleep for two consecutive nights he would die. On Monday he was in great pain and tried to get out of bed but was too weak. She lay down beside him, and he 'spoke of the "sunny land" where we would go as soon as he was better.'

'We will be so happy, Queenie; there are so many things happier than politics.' But that was a truth which had come to him too late.

Again on Monday night he did not sleep, and on Tuesday he was feverish. The local doctor called a couple of times and said there would probably not be much change for the next day or two. Late that evening he was dozing, but suddenly opened his eyes and said:

'Kiss me, sweet Wifie, and I will try to sleep a little.'

I lay down by his side, and kissed the burning lips he pressed to mine for the last time. The fire of them, fierce beyond any I had ever felt, even in his most loving moods, startled me, and as I slipped my hand from under his head he gave a little sigh and became unconscious. The doctor came at once, but no remedies prevailed against this sudden failure of the heart's action, and my husband died without regaining consciousness, before his last kiss was cold on my lips.

CHAPTER 15

DENOUEMENT

After Parnell died he passed, like all heroes, into legend. On 9 October, the *Freeman's Journal* manufactured these last dying words: 'Let my love be given to my colleagues and to the Irish people' – not, it may be noted, to Katie, for legends are spiritual things and naturally without feet of clay.

There was no death mask made because when he died Parnell's temperature was abnormally high, and the body began quickly to deteriorate and had to be placed in a lead casket. The fact that there was no death mask, of course, helped the growth of the legend. There was no death mask, therefore the king did not die.

When Parnell's body was interred in Glasnevin cemetery in Dublin on the evening of 11 October, the thousands of people in attendance were startled by, as Abels wrote, 'a strange phenomenon . . . in the sky – a meteor or falling star'. Standish O'Grady, who was sometimes called the Father of the Irish Literary Renaissance, wrote to W. B. Yeats, 'I state a fact. It was witnessed by thousands. While his followers were committing Charles Parnell's remains to the earth, the sky was bright with strange lights and flames.' Katharine Tynan was also there and wrote:

> That night our chief we laid
>   Clay in the ice-cold sod
> O'er the pale sky sped
>   A strange star home to God.
>
> Ran the East sky cold
>   The bright star glistened and went
> 'Twas green and living gold
>   That lit the firmament.

A fitting and legendary ending, with supernatural signs and portents.

However, another kind of legacy quickly grew up, that saw Parnell as a Messiah figure whose mission was yet unaccomplished. There was immediately a rumour that Parnell was not really in the sealed coffin and that it was filled with rocks. No less a level-headed figure than John

Dillon believed that he saw and even heard Parnell years later at a performance of Wagner's *Götterdämmerung* in Munich. St John Ervine remembered being told as a small boy in Belfast that the Boer leader, General De Wet, was really Parnell. Lennox Robinson, the playwright, wrote a much-admired piece called *The Lost Leader* which was produced at the Abbey Theatre in February 1918, and in which an old man in the West of Ireland, who may or may not have been Parnell, emerges to save the country from its current political problems.

The Messiah image was a strong one, and on the base of the Parnell monument at the north end of O'Connell Street in Dublin are today written these words: 'No man has a right to fix the boundary to the march of a nation; no man has a right to say to his country – thus far shalt thou go and no further.' An appropriately heroic and messianic statement clothed in striking words; however, one of the problems of the mythmaking process is that it simplifies. The words are Parnell's true enough, but what the man really thought was hardly so far-reachingly simplistic.

Literature, too, abetted the mythmaking, heroicising process and simplified the memory of the man. Sometimes he was written about in simple public poetry, of the kind that had in years past been hawked by ballad sellers or collected in the vastly popular and much reprinted anthology *The Voice of the Nation*. One typical such piece by Katharine Tynan read in part:

> *Say now to Emmet and Wolfe Tone, moreover –*
> *Who hold their hands to you –*
> *That never your Ireland had a better lover*
> *Than you your Ireland slew.*

> *Say yet that not their names are holier keeping*
> *Than yours, O dear and brave,*
> *For whom to-day your Ireland's wild with weeping,*
> *Her face wet on your grave.*

James Joyce's Joe Hynes in the story 'Ivy Day in the Committee Room' wrote another such piece, which reads in part:

> *He is dead. Our Uncrowned King is dead.*
> *O, Erin, mourn with grief and woe*
> *For he lies dead whom the fell gang*
> *Of modern hypocrites laid low.*

> *He lies slain by the coward hounds*
> *He raised to glory from the mire;*
> *And Erin's hopes and Erin's dreams*
> *Perish upon her monarch's pyre. . . .*

They had their way: they laid him low.
But Erin, list, his spirit may
Rise, like the Phoenix from the flames,
When breaks the dawning of the day,

The day that brings us Freedom's reign.
And on that day may Erin well
Pleadge in the cup she lifts to Joy
One grief – the memory of Parnell.

There were to be more poems, by Yeats, by Lionel Johnson, by Thomas Kettle. There were to be plays by W.R. Fearon, Elsie T. Schauffler, Paul Vincent Carroll, G.P. Gallivan. But perhaps the simplifying, heroicising mythmaking could go no further than the *Parnell* film of the 1930s in which Myrna Loy played Katharine and Clark Gable, the King of Hollywood, played the hero with a thick and glossy head of hair but without a beard and without even the famous rakish moustache, so beloved of cinemagoers. Mythmaking could hardly go further.

Today, the myth has gathered a bit of dust. Avondale is now a popular museum with many relics of Parnell, although one of the rooms is mistakenly painted the much-hated green. Parnell's life is studied in the Irish schools, and the fat and scholarly tomes are sometimes written about him by the historians. But as a figure he has really passed into history, and has become as remote as O'Connell, Emmet and Wolfe Tone. The time has receded when his memory was such a throbbing issue that Joyce's Mr Casey could sob loudly and bitterly, 'Poor Parnell! My dead king!' A generation after the Parnell split came the split that brought about the Irish Civil War, but the principal victims of that trauma did not, save Michael Collins, have the quality that inflamed men's imaginations. Collin's opponent, de Valera, who inherited Parnell's title of the Chief, perhaps lived too long and was too dry a figure to evoke the strongest emotions. But already Collins and even the only fairly recently dead de Valera seem remote from the Irish issues of the present, and the politicians who embody the present issues hardly appear the stuff of mythmaking. Perhaps, then, the moral is that heroism has small effect on the present, that it really exists in the past, that perhaps it was all a fiction after all.

And yet the human psyche obviously has the need for such fictions. While writing this book, I have heard of three different people – in England, Ireland and America – who claim to be illegitimate descendants of Parnell. Presumably, just as we need heroes in literature to compensate for the drabness of life, we need heroes for ancestors.

Indeed Patricia Lavelle has another interesting quote from our own ancestor, Stephen O'Mara, when asked by de Valera at the time of the

Irish independence, 'What did you really think of Parnell?'

> 'I'll tell you what I thought of him,' Grandfather replied. 'If I were crossing over Sarsfield Bridge and Parnell said to me: "Jump into the river", I would jump.'

And this was a quarter of a century later.

What happened to the other principal characters in the story?

After the Anglo-Irish treaty was signed in 1922, Tim Healy was appointed Governor-General of the Free State and took up residence in Phoenix Park. It was not a particularly popular appointment from any view along the political spectrum, but he served until 1928, and died in 1931.

In the last decade of the nineteenth century, Michael Davitt served in Parliament, but he resigned from politics in 1899 and devoted himself to journalism. He published several books and died in 1906.

John Dillon stepped down as leader of the Irish Parliamentary Party in 1900 in favour of John Redmond. When Redmond died in 1918 Dillon reassumed the leadership, but the last remnants of the party were swamped in that year's general election, and Dillon himself was defeated by de Valera in the race in East Mayo. He died in 1927.

Parnell's nemesis, Gladstone, 'the grand old serpent', formed his fourth ministry in 1892 and introduced his second Home Rule Bill which passed the Commons but was thrown out by the House of Lords. In 1893 the old statesman retired from public life. G.M. Trevelyan summed him up like this:

> He had taught Englishmen to think nobly, and foreigners to think nobly of England. He had kept our parliamentary institutions in the forefront of all men's thoughts. He had done, perhaps, more than any one man to adapt the machinery of State to modern and democratic conditions. His achievements lay thickly scattered over many pages of our history, and if his failures were great too, the last and greatest of them has added immensely to his fame.

The last and greatest of them was, of course, the second Home Rule Bill which was now pretty much a dead issue. The Irish Party after Parnell was ineffective, and the Liberals themselves were overwhelmingly defeated in the general election of 1895. Gladstone himself, full of age and honours, died in 1898, but Parnell at least would have regarded the many encomiums which that occasion called forth with a sardonic wryness.

Of his own family, Parnell was perhaps closest to his quiet and retiring brother John. However, during most of Parnell's years in politics John was farming in the American south. In 1891 he arrived back in Avondale, but his various schemes could not keep the estate solvent. In 1898 he was City Marshal of Dublin, a sinecure which paid a small salary. In 1895 he had been elected as MP for Meath, but had made no real mark in Parliament. As R.F. Foster wrote, 'His very inoffensiveness must have made him a marked man at this most squalid and back-biting era of Irish politics.' He was finally more or less forced out of politics, and in 1900 he had to sell Avondale. On 16 July 1904, the legendary, stately and plump Buck Mulligan saw him playing chess in a Dublin cafe. In 1907 he married, in 1916 he published a kind and diffident memoir of his brother, and in 1925 he died, the last of the Parnell children.

Parnell's mother, Delia, lived on in America for several years after his death, the same rackety, scatty, garrulous woman she had always been. She did return to live at Avondale in September 1896, an old lady in her eighties, and she died there on 27 March 1898 when, after a dinner party, she was breakfasting alone in her room and her dress caught fire and hideously burned her. Her funeral was a huge public event, but as Foster remarks:

> in the long list of notables at Mrs Parnell's funeral, there is no mention of any of her neighbours among the Wicklow gentry. In her death as in life, what defined her was her son's reputation: not the Irish county circle she had married into over fifty years before and to which she had never been able to adapt.

Her daughter Anna, who had figured so importantly in the Ladies' Land League, was seldom in Ireland afterwards, but she did keep in touch with events and supported the formation of Maud Gonne's organisation Inghinidhe na hEireann. She was always superbly intractable and as Foster wrote:

> A typical flash of Anna's spirit comes out in a letter she wrote to the *Irish Times* after Parnell's death, objecting to the choice of Glasnevin as a burial place: she said that the statement that her brother's body 'belonged to the Irish people' was only true if their having killed him gave them title to it.

She also wrote a self-effacing account of her experiences called *The Tale of a Great Sham*, which was not published in book form until 1986 by an Irish feminist press. In this she attacked the Home Rule movement, observing perceptively, 'We have no evidence that Mr Gladstone meant to pass Home Rule but much ground for suspecting that he knew he could not pass it.' The book scathingly denounces parliamentarianism, and concludes dourly, 'Ireland may perhaps be a free country again in a short time, in the hands of a new people from somewhere else, who would have the qualities its present inhabitants lack – all those indispensable for either getting or keeping freedom.'

On 20 September 1911 she drowned while bathing in the sea at Ilfracombe where she was living under an assumed name. At the inquest her landlady reported that she had warned her against bathing that day, and Anna had retorted 'Rubbish', and as usual gone her own way.

Of the other Parnell children, perhaps only Emily need be mentioned. Her tippling husband, Arthur Dickinson, had died in 1884, but she lived on at Avondale and then in Dublin, as eccentric, as prominent and as self-dramatising as her mother had been. In 1905 she published a memoir of her brother called *A Patriot's Mistake*, which is as romantic about herself as it is unreliable about Parnell. Later a runaway marriage took her to Monte Carlo from where her brother John had to rescue her, and finally, in May 1918, she checked into the South Dublin Union Poorhouse under an assumed name and died in a few days. Despite her improvidence she had, according to John, a sufficient income, but she had been more than a little mad for several years, and she died, Foster wrote, 'as unreasonably as she had lived'.

Of Katie's brothers and sisters, Evelyn lived on until 1919 and then was given a plaque commemorating his memory in St Paul's Cathedral. Charles Page Wood and Polly Chambers received some of Aunt Ben's money, and Anna, in Joyce Marlow's excellent summation:

> lived òn at Rivenhall Place for many years until the upkeep was beyond her means[,] it fell into the same ruined state from which Sir John had rescued it, and she too moved to Brighton. In her last years (she died before Katie), Anna became an eccentric recluse, surrounded by animals, monkeys in particular, with a favourite which consumed vast quantities of anchovy-paste sandwiches.

Of Katie's children, Norah was the closest and looked after her till her death. It must have been very difficult, especially as she believed Parnell to have been her mother's ruin and had always felt 'inimical tolerance' for him. After Katharine's death T.P. O'Connor helped Norah to find a job as a governess and then helped her obtain training as a nurse in Queen Charlotte's Hospital where she changed her name to Norah Wood. However in 1923, not long after qualifying, she died of lupus and is buried with her mother.

Gerard, who seemed to have inherited many of Willie's more unfortunate characteristics, turned up in 1913 objecting to an article by William O'Brien in the *Cork Free Press* which claimed that if all were known Parnell 'would have been shown to be rather a victim than a destroyer of a happy home'. Subsequently Gerard was said by Henry Harrison to have meddled considerably in Katie's 1914 memoir of Parnell. Certainly Gerard hated Parnell and was always on his father's side in the affair. He had been used by his parents as a conduit and, just before the divorce, it was he who had thrown Parnell's things out of the window in Brighton. It could not have been easy to have been a child torn between two warring parents, yet Gerard does not seem to have had much to recommend him. However, although he did not later scruple at presenting his mother in an unfavourable light in the memoirs, he is thought to have kept in touch with her, particularly after his father's death.

Apart from being the guardian of his father's reputation, Gerard is not known to have held down any other job. Joyce Marlow writes: 'He married his cousin, Christabel Barrett-Lennard, according to one family source because he seduced her, got her pregnant and Sir Thomas Barrett-Lennard forced him to do so, but the marriage was not a happy one and the only child was, alas, retarded.' He is known to have fought in the First World War, although he must have been then in his forties. And in 1936 he protested at the London staging of the Elsie T. Schauffler play *Parnell*, because his father was portrayed as conniving in the affair. His comments at the time quite echo Willie's supercilious snobbery: 'Captain O'Shea would have asked his maid to "bring" and not "fetch" the whisky. He had not the misfortune to be educated in the USA but at Oscott and Trinity College, Dublin. He did not call himself O'Shay, neither did he pronounce the words "sea" and "tea", "say" and "tay".' However, the play eventually went on with the young James Mason playing Willie. About this time, in true Willie fashion, Gerard sacrificed his principles and disappeared to Hollywood to be a handsomely paid adviser on the Clark Gable film. He was never heard from again.

Carmen married Dr Arthur Herbert Buck, the physician who had signed Willie's death certificate. She had three children but was divorced in 1914 and remarried the co-respondent, Edward Linguard Lucas, who subsequently inherited his father's baronetcy. There is a family rumour that she was unhappy and became an alcoholic. Nothing else is known of her, however, except that she did not attend her mother's funeral and died in the same year.

Of Parnell's two surviving children, Clare, who most resembled him, married Dr Bertram Maunsell. She is thought to have been happily married but sadly died in 1909, giving birth to a son. Dr Maunsell, Norah, Gerard and his wife comprised the four official mourners at Katie's funeral. Dr Maunsell's son, Assheton Clare Bowyer-Lane Maunsell – who was said to have inherited Parnell's looks – died of enteric fever while serving as a British army officer in India in 1934.

The life of Parnell's younger daughter, Katie, is obscure but it is thought that she married an army officer, Captain Louis D'Oyley Horsford Moule, and went abroad with him; they had one stillborn child. She too turned up at the time of the Parnell play in the 1930s, and was said to be living in poor circumstances in Camden Town. In a newspaper article at that time she claimed to have remembered many events of her childhood, including Parnell's death. Her last years were spent in an asylum and she died in 1947.

It is curious how little is to be discovered about those close to Parnell after his death. It is rather as if his life were a light which, when extinguished, left everything surrounding it in obscurity – and that applies even to Willie and Katie.

When Parnell died Willie was living in Brighton with Gerard and Carmen who were frequent visitors at Walsingham Terrace. Also frequently there was the young Henry Harrison who became Katie's invaluable advisor. However, Willie apparently so resented Harrison – there were even insinuations that he was Katie's, if not Norah's, lover – that Harrison issued him a challenge to a duel, which was rejected.

Although Parnell had made a will leaving Avondale to Katie and his children, by a final ironic twist this had been invalidated by his marriage; it seems he did realise he had to make a new will. And his brother John, who inherited the estate, could not be persuaded by Harrison to honour Parnell's wishes. However, after Parnell's death, Harrison did manage to arrange a loan which tidied the hard-pressed Katie over until the matter of Aunt Ben's will finally came to court in March 1892. After all the squalid bickering the Woods emerged with half the money, but Katie was granted custody of Parnell's two children. Of the rest of the money, about £65,000 came to her. Willie received an immediate £7,500 and about £800 a year, and Gerard received an immediate £9,000.

After 1892 Willie virtually disappeared from public life. Of his later activities there is really only a letter to Chamberlain to tell us anything. In it he is seen trying unsuccessfully to raise money for yet another scheme – this time the building of an African railway. He died at Hove on 22 April 1905, at the age of 65.

After the matter of Aunt Ben's will had been resolved, Harrison set Katie's affairs in what he thought was final order. He signed a lease for a house for her in Surrey, a house which she had actually picked with Parnell before his death. Harrison also arranged a further loan to keep her going until the money should actually come through, and having acted the part of the good guardian angel, he then passed out of her life.

Katie was then 46 and, although she was emotionally highly strung, she was mentally healthy. However, this was not to last. After the resolution of the will in March 1892, she too disappeared into obscurity and mental illness. For a dozen years her life had been lived on a plane of high dramatic intensity, in intricate private subterfuge and complex public manoeuvring. I have perhaps too strongly stressed the tragic parallels and analogies to her story and Parnell's, but in one sense the story is almost too fully plotted for a tragedy. It was a melodramatic plot of ever-rising climaxes – an aborted duel, the struggle of Kilmainham, the Galway by-election, the Pigott forgeries, the divorce case, the debate of Committee Room 15, the subsequent

Irish by-elections, the final disposition of Aunt Ben's fortune. There was no dearth of incident in this plot and no slackening of tension. But now, after all the hectic and incessant manoeuvring, the plot was complete. The denouement had come, the last strands of the story were nicely tied up, and above all the hero was dead.

Katie could not really pick up all the pieces of her life and start anew. The pieces had been shattered into too many minute fragments, and some of them were lost. It would have taken an extraordinary woman to start anew. Katie was, of course, extraordinary, but she was also a Victorian woman. She had the courage if not quite to defy, at least to attempt to circumvent the rigid morality of the day. Like Parnell, she was able to erect and to remain true to a code of behaviour which she thought more just even though it was quite at variance with that of society. Her actions were remarkably courageous, for their conse-quences – indeed their almost predictable consequences – resulted in extended psychological tensions and suffering. Her unfaltering persistence and the notoriety it received were not without an ultimate effect, however, and it is no exaggeration to call them part of the birth pangs of the modern world and its changed view of the relations of men and women.

Nevertheless, it was inevitable that living for a dozen years on the emotional heights, as if life were a perpetual grand opera, would have its effect upon her. From the time of the divorce to the time of the probate judgement, we can perceive in her rising emotionalism, an increasingly uncontrollable hysteria. The efficiency with which she had gone about trying to secure Willie a seat in Parliament in 1885 was by the time of the divorce reduced to a confusion of angry, contradictory impulses. And that confusion was succeeded by the uncharacteristic passivity with which she allowed the dying Parnell to make his last fight in Ireland. Sadly she had become a vine rather than a bough. Parnell once told Dillon, 'I have never heard that anybody could ever persuade a woman to do, or not to do, anything which she had made up her mind to do, no matter what the consequences to herself or others might be . . .' Had Katie known he thought this, her actions might well have been different. Certainly the person she was five years earlier might have been able to dissuade him from the folly of that last fight.

However it is too easy to say what she should have done. It is a biographer's task to report facts, not to pass judgment or to speculate on what might have been. Parnell was a supreme egotist and a stronger person than Katie was. He had gained her, but she was not enough. He wanted the leadership of the Irish Parliamentary Party too, and consequently ruined both their lives. Another destructive factor was the hope of Aunt Ben's money. The money was very important and involved them both in years of deception which in the end brought nothing but tragedy. But we are dealing here with people and not with the heroes of romance. The love of money may indeed be the root of all evil, but it is certainly a dominating emotion for most of humanity.

After Parnell's death and the settlement of the will, Katie's exhausted passivity erupted into hysteria and breakdown. The reason was partly the inevitable effect of years of crisis and partly the effect of simply being a Victorian woman and at the same time a rebel. She did not betray her marriage for a giddy promiscuity or the kind of liberation a modern feminist might admire. She was always 'Wifie'. She left one monogamous relationship to enter another which had more meaning but was no less iron-bound. As the Victorian wife was completely dependent upon her Victorian husband, this Victorian ex-wife created a new life completely dependent upon her new mate. And when he died no centre remained.

T.P. O'Connor wrote that she soon had her first nervous breakdown and spent two years in a home, and 'of how she would get up in the middle of the night, in a state of wild alarm, and call on them to go downstairs to the hall, where, as she thought, Parnell and O'Shea were fighting and attempting to kill each other'. When she was out of the homes, she and the faithful Norah moved from one leased house to another. She is known to have lived all along the south coast, moving inland for a while to Maidenhead and then back to the Brighton area. As Norah wrote to Henry Harrison:

> She had never stopped mourning Parnell and I, knowing the misery of her heart and soul, have spent my life in keeping her from the follies of so many ways of 'forgetting for a little while' when I could; and when I couldn't in nursing her back to health and sanity. Her periods of delusion have always been Parnell, Parnell, Parnell.

What these 'follies' were is uncertain. Did Norah mean that Katie was simply deluded, or did she become an alcoholic? Henry Harrison said as much to Conor Cruise O'Brien. Or, as Joyce Marlow writes, 'perhaps Norah, as a good Catholic, was merely referring to the spiritualism which became one of her mother's interests and solaces.' Whatever they were, Katie's troubles were compounded in 1906 when she lost most of her fortune through an absconding solicitor. Parnell's solicitor, Sir George Lewis, did come to her aid and managed to save something, despite Katie's insistence on paying for the fraudulent solicitor's defence. However, the remaining money was invested in the Grand Trunk Railway of Canada, and it stopped paying dividends before the First World War. In 1914, being pressed for money, she published her memoirs; and even though it is possible that they were edited and slanted by Gerard to put Willie in the best light, they contain many of Parnell's letters to her and something at least of her own true feelings. The memoirs were published in two volumes and created such a stir on publication that they were reprinted twice that year. The author's name appeared on the book as Mrs Katharine O'Shea with Mrs Charles Stewart Parnell in parenthesis underneath, so obviously Katie wanted to cash in on the notoriety of being 'Kitty O'Shea', yet could not use the hated sobriquet. Many readers and reviewers were shocked to learn about the birth of Claude Sophie. The other two children were not mentioned at all, so hardly anyone knew of their existence. And there were mixed reactions to the publication of Parnell's love letters. In addition Katie's relationship with Gladstone and her role in the Home Rule struggle was disputed. However, her letters to him, now in the British Museum, show a clear grasp of the complex situation.

The publication of the memoirs brought Katie some much-needed money, so her last years were spent without want. Although her physical health began to wane, her mental health was said to have improved considerably from then on. She was still restless, however, and, according to Joyce Marlow, a Brighton hotel employee remembers Katie as a stout, eccentric old woman who, during a long stay, got up at two in the morning to go walking on the seafront. Her last move was to Littlehampton to a small terraced house, very different from the splendours of Rivenhall.

On 1 February 1921, Norah wrote to Henry Harrison to tell him that Katie was dying:

> She was seventy-six last Sunday, and has been ill for some months. Now, the doctors say, it is only a question of how long she can keep up her fight against death. The heart attacks grow more frequent and she struggles back with more difficulty and pain each time. She has happy delusions that Parnell comes to her at night, when things are worse, and draws her 'out of the black waves'.

Perhaps these were the same waves into which he had once contemplated plunging with her in his arms.

Four days later, on 5 February, she died.

In Ireland her death received but cursory notice. For one thing, times had changed, and Ireland was in the last throes of the Black-and-Tan war and had other, more pressing and violent issues to deal with than the dead passions of a past and now incredibly remote generation.

For another thing, she was not the hero – merely the wifie. As one Irish paper, the *Freeman's Journal*, reported:

> The death of Mrs Parnell, in her seventy-fifth year, at Brighton, recalls one of the most tragic and poignant chapters in Irish history – the fall of the the great leader who made the Irish Party feared and respected in the English Parliament, and whose work led to the emancipation of an oppressed and impoverished

peasantry. Little was heard of the deceased lady after Parnell's death until she once more came into the limelight by a publication in 1914 of two unsavoury volumes which purported to give the whole history of her relations with the Irish leader, who had then been mouldering in Glasnevin for a generation, and over whose grave an appalling internecine struggle was fought for many years, until the National forces were re-united under Mr Redmond's leadership. She then relapsed once more into obscurity and was soon forgotten in the great world events which have since taken place. For a considerable time Mrs Parnell was in failing health, and her death was not unexpected by the few friends who were associated with her in her declining years.

Katie was forgotten and fated to be separated from her husband even in death. While his remains lie under a massive granite rock in Dublin's Glasnevin Cemetery, she was buried in an obscure Littlehampton graveyard. For years that grave was neglected, but recently, through the efforts of Winifred Murphy, an Irish woman living in Britain who raised funds through the Irish community there, it has been restored. Today the inscription on the large granite cross erected by Norah can be clearly read: 'In loving memory of Katharine, widow of Charles Stewart Parnell. Born 30th Jany. 1846. Died 5th Feby. 1921. Fide et Amore.'

A little of the legend has rubbed off on her though. In a footnote to his Parnell biography, F.S.L. Lyons records receiving two letters from Miss A. Dinan of Terenure in 1977:

In these she mentions that her father (over ninety-five when she wrote to me) remembered as a young man meeting Mrs Parnell (as she would then have been) in a solicitor's office in Cork or Limerick about 1904 in connection with the sale of a ground-rent. Although his memory of the event seems very firm and specific-she was very polite but had poor teeth! – Mrs Parnell's presence there at that time and on such a trivial errand still seems to me to be somewhat improbable. Lacking further proof, I prefer to leave open the question of whether, and if so precisely when, she ever visited Ireland.

A second instance which Lyons refers to is recounted in Harold Nicolson's not always reliable Helen's Tower, a biography of his uncle, Lord Dufferin:

I recollect also, when I was very small, being taken to some fete or horse-show in the neighbourhood of Dublin. I drove there with my grandmother in a landau and I remember how silent the carriage became as it left the main road and swung squeaking into the meadow where the fete was held. 'Look!' said my grandmother, in sudden excitement. 'Look at that lady over there in the tilbury.' There was in fact a woman in a high dog-cart with a little groom holding a restless horse. 'Look,' repeated my grandmother, 'and remember that you have seen Mrs O'Shea.' I looked again. She seemed an ordinary lady in a man's straw hat and with the tight bust of the time. 'Who is she, Grannie?' I asked. 'Never mind,' she answered, 'remember only that you have seen Mrs O'Shea.' That name, that hour-glass silhouette, the smell of trampled grass, the amused look in my grandmother's eyes still live in my recollection. I had seen the cause of Ireland's greatest tragedy.

Did these events happen? They have all the specificity of fact – or legend.

BIBLIOGRAPHY

Books

Abels, Jules (1966) *The Parnell Tragedy*, Bodley Head, London.

Bew, Paul (1980) *C.S. Parnell*, Gill & Macmillan, Dublin

Blunt, Wilfred Scawen (1919, 1920) *My Diaries 1884–1914*, Secker, London.

Bradhurst, Mrs Minnia Evangeline (1929), *A Century of Letters: Letters from Literary Friends to Lady Wood and Mrs A. C. Steele*, privately printed.

Chapman, Raymond (1968), *The Victorian Debate*, Weidenfeld & Nicolson, London.

Dickinson, Emily (1905), *A Patriot's Mistake: Being Personal Recollections of the Parnell Family*, Hodges Figgis, Dublin and Simpkin Marshall, London.

Disraeli, Benjamin (1845), *Sybil, or the Two Nations*, Henry Colborn, London.

Ervine, J.G. St John (1925), *Parnell*, Little Brown, Boston.

Foster, R.F. (1979), *Charles Stewart Parnell: The Man and His Family*, Harvester Press, Hassocks, Sussex.

Harrison, Henry (1931), *Parnell Vindicated: The Lifting of the Veil*, Constable, London.

Healy, T.M. (1928), *Letters and Leaders of My Day*, Thornton Butterworth, London.

Horgan, John (1948), *Parnell to Pearse*, Browne & Nolan, Dublin.

Houghton, Walter, E. (1957), *The Victorian Frame of Mind*, Yale University Press, New Haven, Connecticut and London.

Joyce, James (1956), *Dubliners*, Penguin, Harmondsworth, Middlesex.

Lavelle, Patricia (1961), *James O'Mara, A Staunch Sinn Feiner*, Clonmore Reynolds Ltd, Dublin; Burns and Oates Ltd, London.

Lyons, F.S.L. (1968), *John Dillon*, Routledge & Kegan Paul, London.

Lyons, F.S.L. (1971), *Ireland since the Famine: 1850 to the Present*, Weidenfield & Nicholson, London.

Lyons, F.S.L. (1977), *Charles Stewart Parnell*, Collins, London.

Magnus, Phillip (1954), *Gladstone*, John Murray, London.

Marlowe, Joyce (1975), *The Uncrowned Queen of Ireland*, E.P. Dutton, New York.

Moore, George (1888), *Confessions of a Young Man*, Sonnenschein, London.
Morley, John (1903), *The Life of William Ewart Gladstone*, Macmillan, London.
Morley, John (1921), *Recollections*, Macmillan, London.
Nicholson, Harold (1937), *Helen's Tower*, Constable, London.
O'Brien, Conor Cruise (1957), *Parnell and His Party 1880–1891*, Clarendon Press, Oxford.
O'Brien, R. Barry (1898), *The Life of Charles Stewart Parnell 1846–1891*, Smith Elder, London.
O'Brien, William (1905), *Recollections*, Macmillan, London.
O'Brien, William (1926), *The Parnell of Real Life*, T. Fisher Unwin, London.
O'Connor, T.P. (1889), *The Parnell Movement*, T. Fisher Unwin, London.
O'Connor, T.P. (1891), *Charles Stewart Parnell: A Memory*, Ward & Lock, London.
O'Connor, T.P. (1929), *Memoirs of an Old Parliamentarian*, Ernest Benn, London.
O'Shea, Katharine (1914), *Charles Stewart Parnell: His Love Story and Political Life*, 2 vols, Cassell, London.
Parnell, Anna (1986), *The Tale of A Great Sham*, Arlen House, Dublin.
Parnell, J. Howard (1916), *Charles Stewart Parnell: A Memoir*, Constable, London.
Steele, Anna Caroline (1867), *Gardenhurst: A Novel*, 3 vols, Chapman and Hall, London.
Steele, Anna Caroline (1867), *Lesbia*, G. Bell, London.
Trevelyan, George Macaulay (1964), *British History in the Nineteenth Century and After: 1782–1919*, Longmans, London.
Trollope, Anthony (1936), *The Warden*, Modern Library, New York.
Tynan, Katharine (1913), *Twenty-five Years*, Smith Elder, London.
Tynan, Katharine (1924), *Memories*, E. Nash & Grayson, London.
Ward, Margaret (1983), *Unmanageable Revolutionaries*, Brandon, London.
Wood, Anthony (1960), *Nineteenth Century Britain: 1815–1914*, Longmans, London.
Wood, Emma Caroline (1868), *Sorrow on the Sea: A Novel*, 3 vols, Tinsley Bros, London.
Wood, Mrs Henry (1861), *East Lynne*, Richard Bentley, London.

Manuscript material
Gladstone Papers, British Library, main catalogue: Add. mss. 44160, 44250, 44256, 44269, 44314, 44315, 44316, 44503, 44506, 44766, 44787.

Newspapers and periodicals
Evening Mail, Dublin.
Freeman's Journal, Dublin.
Irish Independent, Dublin.
Irish Times, Dublin.
Nation, Dublin.
The Times, London.
United Ireland, Dublin.

INDEX

Also available . . .

CONSTANCE MARKIEVICZ
Irish Revolutionary

ANNE HAVERTY

'Anne Haverty writes with a cool and intelligent eye. She balances the personal life of Constance with the political and social situation with great skill.'   *Books Ireland*

'Haverty knows how to write . . . She knows Ireland and its history and has studied her subject well.'   *Sydney Morning Herald*

Constance Markievicz was a woman who entered the male dominated world of conspiracy and revolution; an aristocrat who became a committed socialist, a member of the Anglo-Irish ascendancy who was a fervent Irish nationalist. She was also the first woman ever to be elected to the British Parliament and to become a Minister of State in any European government. Her extraordinary story moves from the hunt balls of the Irish aristocracy through bohemian Paris and literary Dublin to a world of insurgent nationalism, of street battles and the 1916 Easter Uprising, of barricades and prison terms. This biography of Constance Markievicz includes much new material, throwing figures close to her, such as Yeats and James Connolly, into vivid relief and reveals her to be one of the first women to have struggled with the issues of nationalism and feminism still hotly debated by women today.

MAUD GONNE
A Life

MARGARET WARD

'From her we get a picture of a complex woman, one who relished the adulation of a crowd, yet was deeply devoted to those close to her.'
Irish Times

'Maud took her power for granted and used it without being conscious of any let or hindrance. How she came to use it, selflessly and devotedly in the cause of Irish Independence is the theme of Margaret Ward's valuable book.'   Mary Stott, *Liverpool Daily Post*

'Absorbing'   *Times Literary Supplement*

In this compelling biography Margaret Ward gives us a sympathetic yet balanced portrait of Maud Gonne as a significant figure in Irish politics and as a truly remarkable woman. She successfully dispels the popular myth that Maud was little more than a flamboyant beauty and the inspiration of WB Yeats' great love poetry. Despite her privileged position as the daughter of a British army officer she took up the cause of Irish freedom as her life's work and as a woman of independent means she was able to escape many of the stifling conventions of Victorian Britain. Dismissive of her own beauty, yet constantly pursued because of it, in Ireland she was a symbol of romantic nationalism while in France she led a secret life with her lover, Millevoye, and her children. In her later years she campaigned tirelessly with the women relatives of those in jail and endured prison and hunger strike on behalf of those she regarded as political prisoners languishing in Irish jails.

Margaret Ward sheds a new light on this extraordinary figure and reveals her to be one of Ireland's most courageous and charismatic women of modern times.

BEATRICE WEBB
Woman of Conflict

CAROLE SEYMOUR-JONES

'An excellent new biography ... which makes Beatrice's life memorable for the contradictions it embodies.' *Financial Times*

'Timely and welcome ... a well researched biography with an incisive feminist perspective.' Harriet Harman, *Times Educational Supplement*

'Remarkably good and interesting. The style is clear and unobtrusive ... (and the author) makes penetrating use of the diaries.'
Roy Jenkins, *Observer*

History has not been kind to Beatrice Webb: caricatured as a puritanical Fabian reformer who, with her husband Sidney, wrote 'unreadable books' and approved of Stalin's Russia, the real Beatrice has gone unsung and unloved.

Born in 1858 into a wealthy and privileged family, she was a brilliant and beautiful young woman who renounced society life to fight for the 'people of the abyss', venturing in disguise into the slums of the East End, and challenging Lloyd George in a campaign to abolish the workhouse.

Passionate but iron-willed, she gave up the one man she loved – Joseph Chamberlain, dazzling leader of the Radicals in the 1880s – and married Sidney Webb, a Cockney hairdresser's son, in a determined act of class rebellion. The world never knew Beatrice's private distress, seeing only a confident, beautiful and fiercely dedicated woman; but all her life, tormented by the choices that lay before her, she was torn between following the desires of the body and the demands of her spirit. Her repressed sexuality gave rise to agonies of anorexia, whilst her intellectual anguish 'tortured' as Leonard Woolf said – 'in the old-fashioned religious way'. This thorough and incisive biography illuminates as never before the private woman and hidden struggles behind a magnificently modern Victorian rebel.

GERTRUDE AND ALICE

DIANA SOUHAMI

Gertrude Stein and Alice B Toklas first met on 8 September 1907 in Paris. From that day on they were together until Gertrude's death on 27 July 1946. They never slept under different roofs, or travelled without each other, or entertained separately. They were central to the cultural life of Paris for four decades. Everyone who was anyone went to their salons at the rue de Fleurus. They became a legendary couple, photographed by Stieglitz, Man Ray and Cecil Beaton, painted by Picasso and written about in the memoirs of Hemingway, Beaton, Paul Bowles and Sylvia Beach.

Gertrude and Alice is the story of their life together, of the paths that led them to each other and of Alice's years of widowhood after Gertrude died. From letters, memoirs and published writings, Diana Souhami reconstructs one of the most solid marriages of the century. In this unique biography, Gertrude and Alice come alive: 'so emphatically and uncompromisingly themselves, that the world could do nothing less than accept them as they were'.

'Souhami hits a true note in her ebullient introduction and sustains it throughout. Her narrative is terse and exact and her book, the story of two serious ladies, is very funny indeed.'

Lucy Hughes-Hallett, *Sunday Times*

'Souhami is deeply sympathetic to Gertrude and Alice; she is also witty and unsentimental.'   *Sydney Morning Herald*

'Wonderfully entertaining . . . not many biographies can make you laugh out loud. A real treat.'   *Time Out*

NAOMI MITCHISON
A Biography

JILL BENTON

'a study of one woman's struggle to find and keep her voice – a struggle which is both particular to Naomi and general . . . the book's great strength and value is that it addresses those larger questions, insists on taking Naomi Mitchison seriously as a writer and argues convincingly that everyone should, too.'   *The Listener*

'this is a revealing account of a dynamic woman and her influential milieu. It is in no sense a hagiography and Benton's judgements are often unsparingly incisive.'   *Independent*

This is the first biography of the remarkable English and Scottish writer Naomi Mitchison. The author of over 80 books, many of them women's quest novels, and a notable feminist and socialist, she was at the centre of London's intellectual and political life in the 1920s and 1930s.

Here is the story of a life that spans the twentieth century. It describes her Edwardian childhood in the prominent Haldane household in Oxford; her relationship with her husband Dick, a Member of Parliament, with whom she raised five children while creating and practising a philosophy of open marriage; her friendships with people such as Aldous Huxley, Wyndham Lewis and W. H. Auden; how she brought her own brand of socialism to the Scottish village where she still lives; how she came to be the adopted 'mother' of an African tribal chief. Naomi Mitchison gave Jill Benton access to her private papers to write about a life that is restless, experimental and never dull.

CONSTANCE MARKIEVICZ	0 86358 161 7	£7.99	☐
MAUD GONNE	0 04 440881 1	£7.99	☐
GERTRUDE AND ALICE	0 04 440848 X	£9.99	☐
BEATRICE WEBB	0 04 440872 2	£9.99	☐
NAOMI MITCHISON	0 04 440862 5	£7.99	☐
CHARLOTTE DESPARD	0 86358 213 3	£7.99	☐
EVA GORE-BOOTH AND ESTHER ROPER	0 86358 159 5	£6.99	☐

All these books are available from your local bookseller or can be ordered direct from the publishers.

To order direct just tick the titles you want and fill in the form below:

Name: _____

Address: _____

_____

_____ Postcode: _____

Send to: Thorsons Mail Order, Dept 3, HarperCollins*Publishers*, Westerhill Road, Bishopbriggs, Glasgow G64 2QT.
Please enclose a cheque or postal order or your authority to debit your Visa/Access account —

Credit card no: _____

Expiry date: _____

Signature: _____

— to the value of the cover price plus:
UK & BFPO: Add £1.00 for the first book and 25p for each additional book ordered.
Overseas orders including Eire: Please add £2.95 service charge. Books will be sent by surface mail but quotes for airmail despatches will be given on request.

24 HOUR TELEPHONE ORDERING SERVICE FOR ACCESS/VISA CARDHOLDERS — TEL: 041 772 2281.